JESUS CARITAS PUBLICATIONS

12116 Woodholm Court

Fort Mill, SC 29708

November 2021

First published by

Antoine Chatelard, Charles de Foucauld-Le chemin vers Tamanrasset

Editions Karthala – Paris 2002

Published in English   First English Publication

Printed for the Little Brothers of Jesus

By Claretion Publications

Bangalore - 560 055, India

ST CHARLES DE FOUCAULD

Journey to Tamanrasset

Antoine Chatelard

Little Brother of Jesus

Translated into English

by

Little Sister Cathy Wright

Little Sisters of Jesus

Introduction
to the new edition

Antoine Chatelard was an amazing Little Brother of Jesus, having for so many years in the actual places where Charles de Foucauld lived for so many years. Most of his writings on Charles de Foucauld remains untranslated from the French. Thanks to Little Sister Cathy Wright, the present translation of Chatelard's *Journey to Tamanrasset* is a pleasure to read and a wonderful gift to English speaking public. This book is such a needed important addition to the English language library of books on Charles de Foucauld, which are very few.

The insights and chronological history that Antoine gives is a significant shift in so many biographies of Foucauld. Suppose this is your first book on Charles de Foucauld you have chosen well. There are other excellent biographies of Charles de Foucauld. Still, the spiritual insights offered here are a detailed look at the evolution of the mission and true contemplative life of St Charles. It was in his contemplative heart, madly in love with Jesus at Nazareth, that St Charles could hear the risk and vocation to what he was called to be. It is here I hope that you find *your pearl of great price,* something of yourself, and the unique and vital role you play in the Nazareth of your little world.

Please don't just read this book but take as a book of meditations. Take this as a book of maps of sorts, reflecting on your own evolving life within God and calling you to a more profound and more intimate love for Jesus. Charles de Foucauld wants you to know Jesus Christ, Our Lord is the best picture and revelation of God that we can ever receive as human beings. This book and Charles de Foucauld are not about himself; none of us are about ourselves but opening our lives to see and think with a new reality of God, in your Nazareth. Together as individuals in the community, we can cry the Gospel with our lives.

> Rev Leonard J Tighe,
> Feast of All the Saints, November 1, 2021

Taken for the public domain

"He was a born monk, or rather, a hermit. Those were his deepest instincts. It just took him a little while to find his way. Those deep hermit instincts were already visibly present in the explorer." **E.-F. Gautier**

"He is one of those men of whom it is difficult to write something without resorting to animosity or admiration — that is, without passion. He is an enormous figure and very human: he is a bit beyond us. At different turns, he disconcerts us, humbles us, comforts us and irritates us. We like to know that he is human, even very human. And then we suffer to see how human he is at times, while he is so holy in other circumstances. Did he make a synthesis of these contradictions, and is it possible for us to do the same?... It is not a question of trying to violate... the secrets of his story... but of trying to recognize the true greatness that was his and which made him and makes him a guide for us."

Dom Jean Leclerc
Quoted in reference to St. Bernard in *Nova et Vetera*,
June 1967, p. 159 Charles de Foucauld Journey to Tamanrasset

Table of Contents

Introduction 1

Biographical Landmarks 4

A Happy Childhood 7

A wild young man 9

The pleasure of adventure 15

The time of conversion 25

The time for vocation 32

The day of the greatest sacrifice 40

Seven Years as A Trappist Monk 52

The Act of Abandonment 64

To Imitate Jesus of Nazareth 70

Extract from the "Counsels" for the brothers and sisters of the Sacred Heart 76

The Temptations of Nazareth 77

    The first Temptation: to beg funds for the Poor Clares 77

    The second temptation: return to the Trappists 78

From a letter to Father Huvelin – Pentecost 1899 85

    The Third Temptation: The Jerusalem Dangers 85

    The fourth temptation: a better place elsewhere 92

    The Fifth Temptation: The triumph of "willfulness" under the appearance of "devotion" and "piety." 95

A Change of Direction **107**
    A new idea 111
    The hermits become brothers 113
    Where to go? 116

From distance to the nearness **124**

Beni Abbès and the time for fraternity **134**

The universality of the fraternity **138**
    Becoming a brother 141
    All without exception 142
    Those closest or those furthest away? 145
    Brother or Universal 146
    To be a brother 148
    Brother and Friend 149
    Brother in all the little details 150
    Prayer and universal salvation 151

The first call to the Hoggar **154**

Obedience and Initiative **171**
    "Providence speaks clearly" 175

The Second call of the Hoggar **179**
    And the first steps outside of the cloister 179

Meditations from February 4th and 5th, 1905 at Beni Abbès 198

The Third Call to the Hoggar January 24 to May 3, 1905 202

On the Way to the Hoggar May 3rd - August 11, 1905 214

Settled in Tamanrasset 223

Life in Tamanrasset **227**

    1st Period 228

    2nd Period 232

    3rd Period 233

    4th Period 235

    5th Period 237

Strength in Weakness **240**

    Sickness 240

    Loneliness: solitude of the heart 242

    Isolation 244

    Anguish over the salvation of others 245

    A Useless Life 245

    Without the Eucharist 246

    I abandon myself to you 247

    Too rich 248

    Too powerful, too knowledgeable 249

    The situation is reversed 250

    A parable of the reign of God 252

A new kind of monk with a special mission **257**

The attractiveness of an exceptional personality **276**

A message for everyone **285**

About the letter written to Henri Duveyrier **290**

    Letter to Henri Duveyrier, Feb. 21, 1892 291

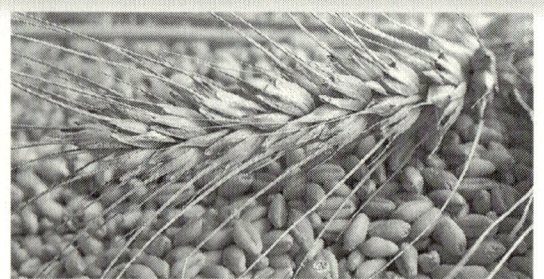

PRAYER OF ABANDONMENT

Father,
I abandon myself into your hands;
do with me what you will.
Whatever you may do, I thank you:
I am ready for all, I accept all.
Let only your will be done in me, and
in all your creatures.
I wish no more than this, O Lord.
Into your hands I commend my soul;
I offer it to you
with all the love of my heart,
for I love you, Lord,
and so need to give myself,
to surrender myself into your hands,
without reserve,
and with boundless confidence,
for you are my Father.

- Blessed Charles of Jesus

Introduction

This book grew out of a session in Lyon, France, for the lay communities of Charles de Foucauld from July 26, 1998, to August 2, 1998. The text, which had been taped, transcribed, and edited, had kept its oral style and appeared under *Regard Neuf sur Charles de Foucauld*. The supplies quickly ran out, and continuing interest has led to a new re-working and editing of the text.

What is still to be said about this man that has not been saying before? Why another book about someone who has already been the subject of so many biographies?

I have tried to approach the life and writings of Charles de Foucauld by limiting myself to specific events and circumstances of his life in detail. I have tried to respect the context and chronology of those events to discover the true motivation behind them. I had to resist the temptation to answer the needs of those who desired a chronological overview of his journey. Instead, my research led me over paths where few had traveled before and sometimes into forests where there was always a risk of getting lost. But it also led me to discover hidden marvels.

While it may seem exciting today in this approach to Charles de Foucauld, there was already interest back in 1921 following the publication of René Bazin's biography. A journalist of the time wrote,

> *"I would like to know how grace worked its way in this soul. I have been shown the beginning and the end of the journey but no one has said anything about what happened along the way... It would be so interesting! That is why the story of Father de Foucauld must be retold. The ins and outs of his soul must be thoroughly turned over in the hopes of discovering an admirable harvest."*[1]

Dr. Dautheville, a contemporary who spent six months in Tamanrasset in close contact with Charles de Foucauld, wrote in the same vein:

> *"I saw in him someone much more human and much more interested by the events of this world than what Mr. Bazin presented in his book. There he comes across as a saint ready for beatification."* [2]

A half-century later it seems somewhat indiscreet and irreverent to want to dig into the "ins and outs of this soul" who, though not beatified, seems already haloed and idealized as someone to imitate. It could seem inappropriate to dig into not only his writings but also the details of his life and to take a close look at his behavior and the idiosyncrasies of such a great man, his ways and temperament. Doing so might seem to be jumping on the bandwagon of those who try to denigrate the iconoclasts of certain times. But it is necessary to delineate the pious images that hagiography has presented us and to remove the plaster that hides the natural person, without giving the impression of destroying the statue itself.

---

[1] Robert Kemp, *La Liberté*, Oct 31, 1921. Quoted by Jean-François Six in the second edition of René Bazin's *Charles de Foucauld, Explorateur au Maroc, ermite au Sahara*, Paris, Plon, 1959, p.7.

[2] Georges Gorrée, *Les Amitiés sahariennes du Père de Foucauld*, Paris, Arthaud, 1946, vol I, p.272.

This research has instead led us to discover at every step along the way a new dimension of both his humanity and his holiness. The results of this long study of Charles de Foucauld led us to the same conclusion that Dr. Hérisson reached after a much shorter encounter with him. He wrote this to René Bazin, "Contrary to what they say about famous people, Fr. de Foucauld disproportionately grew in stature when one saw him close up, everyday."[3]

In this book, I have tried to limit myself to specific moments of Charles de Foucauld's life without hiding the evolution and changes of direction. These changes always followed the same pattern of, first, an "inner movement" or a "profound impulse," which then grew into an "intense desire," which then became a "duty." These are the words that he used when seeking advice and counsel and which we find even more often in the notes that Fr. Huvelin wrote back to him on these occasions. They invite us to discover the motivations behind the apparent changes throughout his life. They are a unifying factor throughout his many different experiences to Tamanrasset. That "power that moves him" remains mysterious. It is not just the inner dynamic of an extraordinary man. That is why it does not cease to raise questions for those who take an interest in this man, a man who fascinates some while confusing others.

---

[3] Charles de Foucauld, *La Dernière Place*, Paris, Nouvelle Cité, 1974, p.101.

Biographical Landmarks

The following two pages contain a table that divides Charles de Foucauld's 58 years into two nearly equal parts.

Each page is further divided in two: the first page separates the period in which he had completely lost his faith (thirteen years); the second separates the last into 2 periods of fifteen years that we will compare, analyzing significant moments in his evolution.

These four periods revolve around events that are marked by abandonment of religious practice, conversion to God in October of 1886 and his priestly ordination in 1901.

1858	Strasbourg	Birth September 15th Birth	
1859	Wissembourg	of his sister, Marie Death	6 years old
1860	Strasbourg	of his parents	12 years old
1861	Switzerland	War	14 years old
1862	Nancy	1st Communion, April 28th	
1863			
1864			
1865			
1866			
1867			
1868			
1869			
1870			
1871			
1872			
1873			

1887 1888 1889 1890 1891 1892 1893 1894 1895 1896 1897 1898 1899 1900 1901	NancyParis Paris-NancySt. Cyr St. Cyr Saumur Pony-à- Mousson-Bône Sétif-Evian- Mascara Algiers Marocco Algiers Algiers-Algerian Sahara Paris	School at St. Genevieve (Rue des Postes) Expelled from school, MarchPreparation for St. Cyr Death of his Grandfather, February 3rd Dismissed from the militaryExploratory trip through Morocco (June 1883-May 1884) Marriage Plans Conversion end of October	20 years old 25 years old 28 years old
1887 1888 1889 1890 1891 1892 1893 1894 1895 1896 1897 1898 1899 1900 1901	Paris Holy Land Notre Dame des NeigesAkbès Akbès – Algiers – RomeNazareth Nazareth – N. D. desNeiges N.D. de Neiges – Algeria	Pilgrimage Entered the Trappists Left the Trappists Hermit in Nazareth Preparation forOrdination Return to Algeria	32 years old 43 years old

1902	Beni Abbès		50 years old
1903	Trip to the South	August, Settles in	58 years old
1904	Beni Abbès –	Tamanrasset	
1905	Hoggar –	Trip to Algiers via Beni	
1906	Tamanrasset	Abbès	
1907	Tamanrasset-	Trip throughout the South	
1908	Algiers	Illness	
1909	In Salah-Adrar-	1st trip to France (5 months)	
1910	Tamanrasset	2nd trip to France (5	
1911	Tamanrasset	months)	
1912	Tamanrasset –	3rd trip to France (7	
1913	Assekrem	months)	
1914	Tamanrasset	War Construction of	
1915	Tamanrasset	"castle"	
1916		Moved to "castle" –Death Dec 1st	

A Happy Childhood

Charles de Foucauld described the first fifteen years of his life as taking place in the bosom of a faith-filled, practicing Catholic family. In general, most people have described his childhood as unhappy. But that is not at all what he remembers about it. For him, it was a time of happiness. However, he was hardly six years old when both of his parents died within a few months of each other. His mother died first, followed by the death of his father. He practically did not know his father as he lived away from the family due to illness. If he barely mentioned his father, he kept a vivid memory of his mother, whom he considered a saint. He especially recalled his grandfather, colonel Morlet who raised Charles and his younger sister Marie after their parents' deaths. We can read what he has to say when his grandfather's death if we are not convinced. Without this affectionate upbringing that many have described as too relaxed, would Charles have become the free-spirited man who was admired by a whole generation?

His childhood was also affected by the war of 1870. As for many French, especially those who lived in Alsace or Lorraine, it was a time of exile. The family had to flee Strasburg and take refuge in western France and, later, in Switzerland. He was twelve years old. Letters that he wrote to a cousin during this period give us his child's eye view of this time of war and destruction. It is necessary to mention this, even though it is not of primary importance in our study, because his life would also end in a time of war.

Among his happy memories is the 19th birthday party for his very dear cousin, Marie Moitessier. Eleven years old at the time, he already considered her as his confidante and as a second mother. He and his sister spent summer vacations in Normandy with the Moitessier family, with Marie and her sister Catherine. The correspondence between Charles and Marie began at this time.

We should also recall his first communion at this time, as it is something that he mentioned. His cousin, Marie, came from Paris to participate in the celebration and gave him a book by Bossuet, *Les élévations sur les Mystères*. It was a small book of meditations on the Gospels that was typically given for first communions. This book had a certain influence on the rest of his life.

Later he said that he lost his faith at the age of 15 and attributed this to his choice of reading materials as well as to a lack of philosophical formation. It is interesting to note that the marriage of Marie Moitessier to Olivier de Bondy took place at this time.

The person that was closer to him that anyone else married and, in some sense, left him. He never made any reference to what many have considered his broken heart.

A WILD YOUNG MAN

The second period of his youth, the time of his lack of faith, covers a thirteen-year period. Charles de Foucauld characterized it as a "descent into death." He abandoned all religious practices and references. He "unlearned how to pray," and his life became meaningless. What was he looking for? Later he said that he had been sliding into a way that led to death, drowning him in evil. "My life began to be a death," he wrote.[3] Only his grandfather's love for him kept him from giving in to the most extreme excesses. He was sent to a Jesuit school in Paris to prepare for higher studies (in English, we do say College for studies after what we call high school). He was expelled for unruly conduct and for not doing his assignments.

He experienced a natural breaking point during this period of his life. Charles was barely 20 years old when, on February 3, 1878, his grandfather died. He was in his second year at St. Cyr Military Academy. Even fourteen years later, he remembered this as a tremendously painful event. It would remain a painful memory his entire life, even more so than the deaths of his parents. From that time on, life lost its sweetness, happiness, and the joy of being family. His letters to a childhood friend, Gabriel Tourdes, with whom he corresponded until his death, tell us a lot about his youth. On February 5, 1878, the day after his grandfather's death, Charles wrote,

"I don't have to think when I write to you. We can tell each other everything. It is so good! Among other things, when I write to you, it reminds me of a whole period of my life that is now past. I have such happy memories of that peaceful time with my family. We shared such good times, discovering literature and the quiet goodness that I enjoyed while close to my grandfather. All of this comes back to me as I write to you, and it is infinitely precious to me. I can see myself as we began to discover how to think as we entered manhood. In the springtime, we took walks together at the plant nursery, and we would share and read books there. We were so happy, at peace, and carefree. We trusted the future. (I think this is good) You are still happy. You still take walks at the nursery when the weather is nice. But it's not like it used to be. We no longer go there alone to walk along the little-used paths where it's quiet. You go with groups of friends and women to enjoy the music, lively atmosphere, and crowds along the pathways. You have also begun a new period of your life. I have to tell you that you have lost something in the process. But you are happy at least. When you have tired of the fun, you will return to the bosom of your family as before, glad to be with them and with your books. It is not the same for me.

All at once I have lost my family, my peace of mind and that carefree spirit that was so sweet. I will never have it again. I will never again be happy like I was at Nancy in the good old days that we so often spent together. My only consolation is that I have understood the happiness at that time, and I enjoyed it. Try to do the same." 4

A letter that preceded his grandfather's death, although undated, gives an insight into the feelings of this twenty-year-old:

"Oh, if I were only ten years older! I don't know what I'll be doing in ten years, but I will probably have retired from military service. I will begin my life as a bachelor, living alone in a small country house. It is so good to be free and at

---

[4] Charles de Foucauld, Lettres à un ami de lycée, Correspondance inédite avec Gabriel Tourdes (1874-1915), Paris, Nouvelle Cité, 1982, pp 72-73.

peace. But it is hard to be alone. And it seems to me that I will necessarily be condemned to such an existence. At the same time, you will be peaceful and happy with your family: I am not that way and probably never will be. But who knows? Maybe I will still have some happy moments, but they will never be happier than those that I will spend with you."5

The last sentence expresses the tone of many of his letters to Gabriel Tourdes. It also reveals a certain possessiveness and the absolute quality of his friendship. He wanted to have him all to himself during their vacations and planned what they would do each day ahead of time. We can already recognize the bent towards the organization that we find throughout his life. He wanted it all, right away and all the time.

These letters are a good indicator of the depth of his "state of boredom." Whatever he did was aimed at chasing away this boredom, distracting and amusing him. On one level, we can characterize this period with two words: "food" and "books." The books were not only about the content, although he would always read a great deal. They were also about the quality of the bindings. He inherited thousands of books from his grandfather, which he had had to classify. We see how attached he was, not only to books but to anything that he could possess. If we stop for a moment and look at what he purchased, we can already understand his relationship with money. He had to buy what no one else yet owned, the clothes that no one else had access to. There are bills from shoe stores and tailor shops, etc., and they are very significant.

"All goodness, kindness, and care for what others thought had disappeared from my soul. What was left were self-centeredness, sensuality, pride, and the

---

5 Op. cit., pp 70-71.

vices that accompany these. My ardent love of family was still lively, although less so. It was a beacon, the last light amid profound darkness. It, too, lost much of its brilliance, although it did not completely go out. And then it was night, and there was nothing left. I could no longer see either God or others. There was only me... And I was self-centered, in darkness and filth. The worldliest of my companions had lost all esteem for me. I was disgusted and revolted against them. I was more like a pig than a man. I was rolling in this muck!"6

Charles entered the School of Cavalry of Saumur at the end of his military formation at St. Cyr. Even though he did very little work, he managed to graduate with his commission, albeit at the bottom of his class. If we read his letters to Gabriel Tourdes, we would be led to believe that learning horsemanship filled his days. But other sources tell us that he was a relatively poor horseman, probably because he was so overweight. (When he arrived at St. Cyr, they couldn't find a large uniform to fit him.) To keep loneliness and boredom at bay he organized parties and lived in high style, disposing of and abusing the inheritance he had received from his grandfather.

Upon graduation, he was assigned to the 4th Hussard division, garrisoned at Pont-à-Mousson. There he led a life of pleasure, having found a few companions worthy to share his company.

But this life of pleasure only further provoked the feelings of emptiness:

"...a sadness I never felt before or since. It returned each evening as soon as I found myself alone in my apartment... It held me numb and depressed during the parties. I had organized them, but when they took place, I was speechless,

---

[6] Charles de Foucauld, La dernière place, Paris, Nouvelle Cité, 1974, pp 93-94.7 Op. cit.,.101.

bored, and disgusted... I have never felt such sadness, uneasiness or worry as I did then."[7]

Is this the emptiness that can hollow out a space and prepare the way for something else? Would a genuine love have been able to open up and fill the loneliness of his heart? A woman, about whom we know nothing, played a role for several months. We know her only as Mimi and their dalliances earned him disciplinary action. They thought that this situation would resolve itself, as his regiment was due to leave for Algeria. But his superior officers became suspicious when they saw the amount of baggage that Lieutenant de Foucauld was taking along. They sent orders ahead to impose further disciplinary action should he bring that woman with him. And so, shortly after his arrival at Bône, Algeria, he was placed under arrest. The imposed punishment became more severe as the process made its way through the chain of command resulting in prison time from November 1880 until January 1881. Upon his release his squadron was sent to Sétif which was located further in the interior of the country. It was there, on February 6, 1881, that he received the order to leave Mimi. He protested that their relationship in no way impeded his military service and that it was a matter of his personal life. As a result, he received notification on March 25th that he was discharged for "disobeying orders in addition to notorious misconduct."

---

[7] Op. cit., p. 101.

Whatever You may do,
Let only Your will be done
and in all Your creatures.

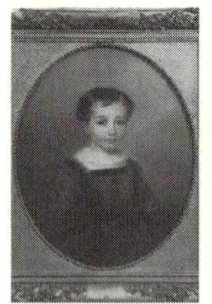

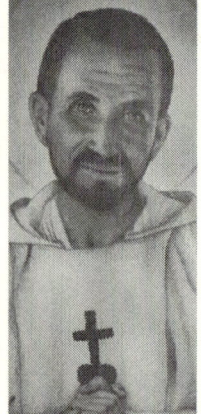

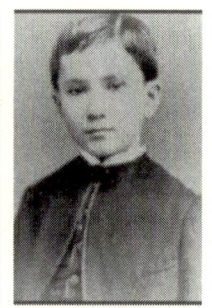

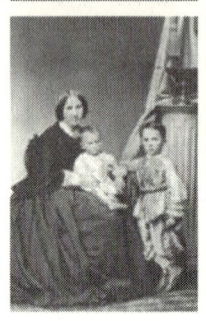

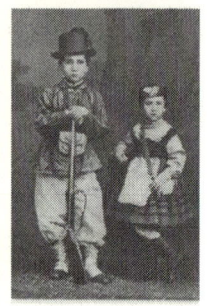

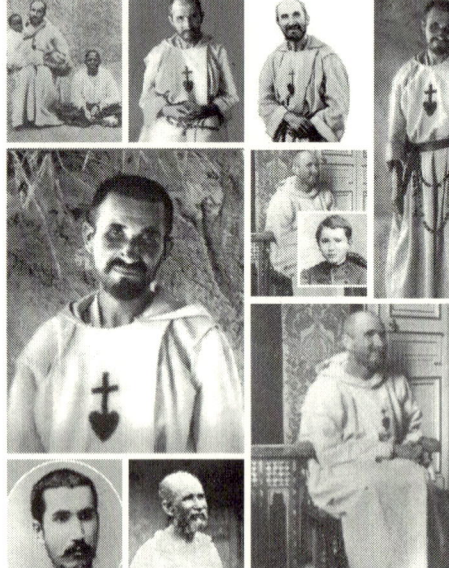

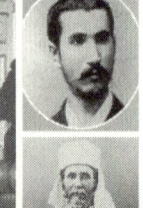

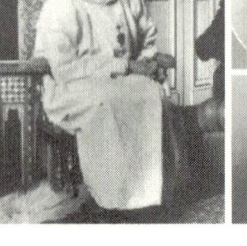

The pleasure of adventure

I think that "Adventure" communicates the sense well Charles de Foucauld left for Évian, France with Mimi. They had hardly been there a week or two when he received a letter from Sétif that would change his life. In a letter dated October 2, 1881, to Gabriel Tourdes, he described it this way.

> *"I should have kept you up to date with my wanderings. As you know, I left the 4th Hussard Division in April (because of a woman). I brought the discharge on myself. Sétif is an awful garrison, and the work was boring. And so I happily returned to France and where I decided to settle into this enjoyable life-style as long as possible. I settled near Évian. You know what a wonderful place it is. I had hardly had time to taste the pleasure of it when I received a letter from Sétif telling me that part of my regiment was leaving for Tunisia. Such an expedition is too rare a pleasure to pass up without trying to take part."*[8]

He immediately asked to be reinstated, even without his previous rank, no matter what they asked him to do, and promised never to see Mimi again. We could say that he was ready for all, accepting all, as long as they sent him where the action was because he didn't want to live his life in a garrison. To enjoy such a rare pleasure was the reaction of the gourmet in him. His reading material these months was Aristophanes.

---

[8] Charles de Foucauld, Lettres à un ami de lycée, Correspondence inédit avec Gabriel

His motives may have been more complex than what he expressed but are we able to find another explanation than the one that he provides us with? His various biographers have not been able to keep themselves from imagining nobler or deeper motivations. They have come up with any number of suggestions: laziness and boredom, dissatisfaction with his love life, regret, nostalgia for a better life, a surge of chivalry, a sense of patriotic duty, colonialist passion, his military mindset and a sense of solidarity with his comrades in arms, a sense of honor… what else? No one mentioned pleasure. And on this note he ended what he simply called "the situation with a woman."

Due to the sanctions against him Charles was not allowed to re-enlist with his old regiment. Instead, he was sent to the 4th Chasseurs of Africa. (It is often erroneously said that he went to the 4th Hussards which had changed their name.) He landed in Oran, Algeria and met up with the troops in Mascara who were waging a campaign against the rebels of Cheikh Bou Amama. He is a totally different man than the one who had been at St Cyr, Saumur, Pont-à-Mousson or Sétif. But it is difficult to know exactly who he was now. We mostly have from recollections from those who had known him that were written down at a much later time or from Laperrine who had heard stories about him.

Fitz-James had met him both just before and just after this expedition south of Oran and wrote only many years later:

> *"He acted notably from the start and immediately liked by his new Regiment. Foucauld showed he was able to endure fatigue and hardships just as well as he had given himself over to pleasure. He was always in a good mood, happily put up with hunger and especially thirst and was very good to his men. He was always thinking of making it easier for them and shared everything he had with*

*them. Having to ration water, he gave his share to others. He always gave an example of initiative, courage, intelligence and energy."*9

Laperrine supplied us with these better-known comments:

"Amid the dangers and hardships of these colonial expeditions, this educated playboy showed himself to be a soldier and a leader. He happily put up with the most difficult situations, giving of himself and devotedly caring for his men. The only thing left of the de Foucauld of Saumur and Pont-à-Mousson was the tiny edition of Aristophanes that he always carried with him.

He remained a little bit snobbish in that when he was not able to obtain his favorite brand of cigars, he simply quit smoking… The Arabs had a profound effect on him."[10]

The little that can be said about this short period of his life underlines that the motivating factor of his decision at Evian was pleasure. It led him to change directions and undertake a warrior expedition. Was it the pearl of great price for which he was ready to leave everything that had begun to be a source of pleasure for him?

If we continue to read his October 2, 1881 letter to Gabriel Tourdes we discover the source of his new-found happiness:

"They did send me back to Africa but not to the Regiment I had desired. I would have at least wanted to be sent to the province of Constantine. Well, I haven't lost much by coming here instead. In the three and a half months that

---

[9] Paul Lesourd, *La vraie figure du Père de Foucauld*, Paris, Flammarion, 1933, p. 62.

[10] Revue de Cavalerie, octobre 1913, *CCF*, no. 8, p.143, "Les étapes de la conversion d'un Hussard, le Père de Foucauld."

> *I have been with the 4th Chasseurs of Africa I have not spent 2 nights in a house… I am part of a military column that tours the high plateaus south of Saïda. It is so funny. I like the patrol life as much as I dislike life in the garrison. And that is saying a lot. I hope that this tour of duty will last a long time. When it does end I will try to be transferred someplace where the action is. If I am unable to do that I don't know what I will do. Nothing could make me ready to live in a garrison again."11*

The campaign ended rather quickly, and he couldn't stand the idea of living in the garrison at Mascara. Around January 20, 1882 he asked to be sent elsewhere and finally resigned from the army. His military experience in Algeria lasted less than 18 months. He explained his reasons for leaving for Gabriel Tourdes in a letter dated February 18, 1882.

> *"I hate living in the garrison. I find it so tiresome in peacetime, which is most of the time, and I had decided a long time ago that I would quit the military for good. Since I felt this way, I preferred to leave immediately rather than drag around for a few more years, aimless and bored with it all. I would rather enjoy my youth by traveling. At least then I would be learning something and not wasting my time."12*

> *We can underline the word "immediately."*

Some new motivations also appeared: the desire to travel as well as not to lose his time. Ten years later, he described this period of his life in a letter to his friend Henri Duveyrier dated February 21, 1892:

---

[11] Charles de Foucauld, Lettre à un ami de lycée, Correspondance inédite avec Gabriel Tourdes (1874-1915), Paris, Nouvelle Cité, 1982, pp. 116-117.

[12] Op. cit., p.118.

> *"I spent seven or eight months living in a tent in the Sahara south of Oran. It gave me a real taste for the traveling that had always attracted me. I handed in my resignation in 1882 to give free rein to my desire for adventure."*

He had now substituted the words taste, desire and attraction for what he used to call pleasure and enjoyment. He would use this same vocabulary the rest of his life in speaking of his vocation. If he had been asked why he left the army at that moment he could have used the exact words that he used to speak of later leaving the Trappists:

> *"I left for the same reason that I entered, not from inconsistency but rather consistency in seeking an ideal that I hoped to find there. I did not find it there."*13

Further letters to Gabriel Tourdes tell us about his travel plans throughout North Africa, Saudi Arabia, and possibly Jerusalem, where he hoped to meet Dr.

Balthazar, a doctor whom he had met south of Oran, Algeria. In his letter of February 18, 1882 to Gabriel Tourdes, he wrote:

> *"Now let me ask you for a favor that I need you to do for me. You can appreciate that it would be a shame to undertake such wonderful trips stupidly and as nothing more than a tourist. I want to be serious about it. Find out about all of the books that I will need I don't know anyone else who is serious enough to do this for me and who would be willing to do it out of friendship. So I am simply asking you directly."*14

---

[13] Charles de Foucauld, *Crier l'Evangile*, Paris, Nouvelle Cité, 1982, p.145.

[14] Charles de Foucauld, Lettres à un ami de lycée, Correspondance inédite avec Gabriel Tourdes (1874-1915), Paris, Nouvelle Cité, 1982, p.119.

Not wishing to travel "stupidly," but usefully and intelligently, he sent a list of the books he wanted his friend to obtain for him.

Then, suddenly, it is no longer a question of traveling East but rather West to the Magreb (Arabic word for Morocco) region of North Africa. For the Arab world this is considered the far West, the opposite direction from the Middle East. This was the first change of direction. Why did he want to go to Morocco? Was it because it seemed to him to be the only one that had not been explored? We can see in this his desire to do what others had not done before or had not been able to do.

In June 1882 he was in Algiers. He left some very concrete traces of his passage there. At the National Library, there is the list of books that he borrowed, returned and later borrowed again as he called on the help of some of the most competent people of his time in preparing this exploration. Among these were MacCarthy, Maunoir and

Duveyrier, the noted explorer who would become a close friend. Duveyrier had just published his book about the Tuareg people after completing the first expedition among them.

What was his work schedule? In a letter to Gabriel Tourdes dated November 27, 1882, after excusing himself for not having written in a long time he wrote:

> *"You know me. You know, too, that although I don't write often, I also don't forget about my friends, especially you who are not friends but friends. At present I feel less like writing than ever. The reason is that the one habit that I kept from my former position is drawing up a work schedule. The old soldier that you are, you know all about those. Once I had arrived here I made one up for myself and I have filled it up. According to it I begin work at 7 in the morning and finish around midnight, with two half-hour breaks for meals.*

Every moment is filled with some class or other, Arabic, History, Geography, and so on.

As for correspondence, I left it for after working hours, meaning after midnight, but by that time, I am so sleepy; That is why I have fallen so behind in my correspondence."15

We can be surprised to know that when he lived in Tamanrasset he spent 10 hours and 45 minutes a day on linguistic studies. But when we know that when he was 24 years old he spent 16 hours a day studying, we are less surprised!

We will not insist on the importance of Charles de Foucauld's Moroccan expedition. Would that adventure be enough to fill the emptiness that was making itself felt within him? He found some sort of fulfillment in the risks that he undertook. He could have become intoxicated by the dangers as well as by his success. It brought out the best in him; his inner strength, his courage, and his tenacity as well as his ingenuity, his tact, and his drive to accomplish his goal. The de Foucauld family motto was, "Never retreat." His sister worried about him and begged him to come home. He wrote to her in January 1884, "When one sets off to do a thing, one must never return without having done it."[9] In the same vein, he wrote to a cousin, "At no price do I want to return without seeing what I set off to see or going where I said I would go."

---

[15] 15 *Op.cit.*, p.125.

When he did return, Duveyrier presented him to the French Geographical Society who accorded him a gold medal for his work. We can recall a few notable quotes from the awards ceremony:

> *"He accomplished this without government help of any kind, at his own expense, sacrificing his future in the military. An even greater sacrifice, if that is possible, is that he traveled disguised as a Jew during a population that considers Jew's inferior, although useful. He bravely shouldered this role, with absolute disregard for his own wellbeing, without tent or bed, and with little baggage. He traveled this way throughout eleven months among a people who two or three times discovered his masquerade and threatened him with the merited punishment, that is, death. One does not know what to admire more: the beautiful and useful results of his work or the devotion, courage and ascetic self-forgetfulness with which this young officer accomplished it, sacrificing more than his comfort, having taken and lived out much more than a vow of poverty and misery."*[16]

These words carry something of a prophetic weight on the lips of someone who did not believe in God and who, when he wrote them, knew nothing of the future that lay before Charles de Foucauld.

But this expedition would not satisfy the growing feeling of emptiness that Charles de Foucauld was experiencing. He had regained a particular place of prestige, one that he had lost, especially in the eyes of his family. And it was not just any place, but first place. His gold medal won him international esteem as one of the great explorers of his day and a career opened before him. Did he understand his first article, "Journey through Morocco," to be the story of his own inner journey? Next came the publication of *Reconnaissance au Maroc*. Did he begin to "recognize"

---

[16] René Bazin, *Charles de Foucauld, explorateur au Maroc, ermite au Sahara*, Paris, Plon, 1921, p.72.

something else that seemed just beyond his grasp? His expeditions had taken place in southern Morocco, in the zaouïa of Tisint. Undoubtedly the loneliness of that trip, the difficulties, and repeated death threats played some part in it all. But it was especially his contact with people of faith that was the determining factor. Did not his contact with people whom he said "live in the continual presence of God", people who became his friends, open up another whole dimension of life? (I think this is good)

> *"...the sight of this faith and these souls living in the continual presence of God helped me to recognize something greater and truer than worldly preoccupations."17*

Charles at age 28, the time of his conversion

---

[17] LHC, 08.07.1901.

THE TIME OF CONVERSION

Having returned from Morocco, Charles de Foucauld was busy writing his *Reconnaissance au Maroc* [18] in the course of which he made several trips between France and Algeria. He regularly visited Commander Titre in Algiers and worked on his maps, and met the Commander's daughter, Marie-Marguerite. Romance blossomed and there was even talk of becoming engaged. But his family was vehemently opposed to the marriage. His brother-in-law, Raymond de Blic, then his Aunt Inez Moitessier tried to dissuade him. Finally, his cousin, Marie de Bondy, managed to convince him, and he would later say that she had "saved" him from this marriage.

After this painful break-up, at the end of July 1885, Charles de Foucauld became ill. After some rest, he traveled alone to southern Algeria to verify and compare the observations he had made in Morocco. His lengthy three and a half months took him from Tiaret, to Aflou and on to Ghardaïa. There he connected with a military column headed to the oasis of El Golea about 1000 kms. from Algiers. They were to set up a station for homing pigeons to facilitate communication with this area that did not yet have a permanent French post. Before leaving El Golea he wrote to his friend, Henri Duveyrier, the first Frenchman to

---

[18] Charles de Foucauld, *Reconnaissance au Maroc*, Paris, Challamel, 1888. Réédition de la 1re partie de l'ouvrage, Plan de la Tour (Var), Éditions d'Aujourd'hui, collection "Les Introuvables", 1985.

travel that far. They setout for Ouargla from where the military column went to Ghadhaïa while Charles de Foucauld traveled East to Tunis, passing through Touggourt, El Oued, and southern Tunisia. His desert meandering ended with the year 1885.[19]

He returned to France at the beginning of 1886 and after a visit with his sister near Grasse in the Midi region of the country, he settled in Paris at 50 rue de Miromesnil, not far from where his Aunt and cousins lived at rue d'Anjou. He lived there as if he were still in the Sahara, sleeping on the floor and wearing a gandoura, while working on his maps, proofreading the text for his book and planning further travels.

His letter to Duveyrier dated February 21, 1892 underlines the importance of the events of 1886 for his inner journey. He continually mulled it over.[20]

> *"I returned to Paris in 1886 in this state of mind. My sister was no longer in Paris, having married and moved to Bourgogne. But I was welcomed at my aunt's home as if I had never left or caused so much worry to those who loved me. Within these walls that became my home, although I was actually living in another house, I found people who modeled every virtue combined with great intelligence and deep religious conviction. I became captivated by such virtue and chose my reading material in the function of it, reading the ancient moralists, far from any religious thinking. The virtue attracted me... but I found less nourishment and insight than I expected from these ancient philosophers*[21]*..."*

---

[19] The sketches that he made during this trip can be found in *Esquisses Sahariennes* published by the Centre d'études sur l'histoire du Sahara, Paris, Jean Maisonneuve, 1985.

[20] The complete text of this letter can be found in the annex. It contains the first written account of his conversion.

[21] His reading consisted entirely of ancient philosophers without any of the modern writers.

And then, quite by accident, I came across a few pages of Bossuet [22] and found in them so much more depth than I had in any of the ancients... As I continued to read this book, little by little, I began to realize that the faith of such a keen mind – the same faith that I saw each day in the bright minds of my own family– was perhaps not as incompatible with common sense as I had thought. It was the end of 1886. I felt an overwhelming desire for silence and recollection. At the core of my being I wondered if the truth were known to men... I made that strange prayer to a God in whom I did not even yet believe to reveal himself to me if he existed... It seemed to me that, in the state of doubt and confusion in which I found myself, the wisest course of action for me would be to study the Catholic faith of which I knew so little. I went to see a priest, Fr. Huvelin, whom I had met at my aunt's house. He was kind enough to answer all of my questions and patient enough to receive me as often as I wished. I became convinced of the truth of the Catholic faith and Fr. Huvelin became for me a birth father. I began leading a Christian life.

Several months after this turnabout, I thought about entering a religious order, but Fr. Huvelin and my family encouraged me to marry... I let sometime pass...."

In his *Meditations on the Gospels*[23], written in Nazareth and Jerusalem between September 1897 and February 1899, we find the following commentary about the return of the prodigal son:

"My God, you are so good! This is what you did for me! I was young and I went far from you, left your house etc., and went to a foreign land, the land of the profane, of unbelief, indifference and earthly passions. I stayed there a long time, thirteen years, squandering my youth in sin and folly. Your first grace, not the first in my life because your graces to me had been countless throughout

---

[22] It was *Elévations sur les mystères* that Marie de Bondy had given him for his first communion.

[23] Charles de Foucauld, *L'Imitation du Bien-Aimé*, Montrouge, Nouvelle Cité, 1997, p. 78.

every hour of my life, but the first in which I saw the first glimmer of my conversion, was to let me know famine, material and spiritual famine. You had the goodness to let me suffer from material difficulties, to suffer from the thorns of such a crazed lifestyle. You let me suffer from material famine24. You let me suffer from spiritual famine through a deep desire for a better moral state, a thirst for virtue and a need for moral well-being. And then, when I turned so timidly towards you and prayed that strange prayer, 'If you exist, let me know you', Oh God of goodness, who has never ceased to work within me and around me at every moment since my birth, who has brought me to this moment, with what tenderness you ran to embrace me and with what swiftness you once more gave me the robe of innocence."

In a letter dated August 14, 1901 to Henry de Castries he wrote:

"For 12 years I lived believing nothing and denying nothing, having given up all hope of ever finding the truth and not even believing in God. Nothing could be proved to me."

He went on:

"While I was in Paris... An inner grace was urging me on. I started going to church even though I still had no faith. It was the only place where I felt some peace and I spent many hours there repeating that strange prayer, 'My God if you exist, let me know you.'"

We find this exact phrase in at least six or seven different letters. It underscores the importance of this prayer in his life. He even wrote to his cousin, Louis de Foucauld, who was just a bit older than himself and equally unbelieving, "You can do it, too." (November 28, 1894). And it

---

[24] Seeing how he was squandering his fortune, his family had his money placed into a trust fund by thecourts.

must have had some effect on him since he rediscovered his faith when he was about to be married. Could this prayer have become something of a method for him? We find the same suggestion in a letter to his friend Gabriel Tourdes who had just lost his sister[25]. "Pray this short prayer that I made to him."

In a meditation on Psalm 31 he again recalled the time of his conversion, insisting as in the following quotes, on the crucial role of certain persons.

> " *'Blessed are those whose sin is forgiven.'* At this time, eleven years ago you converted me. Eleven years ago, without looking for it, you brought my sinful soul back to the fold; And with what sweetness you bestowed that grace upon me; It wasn't that there was no pain at this time, as pain is necessary for the purification of the soul, but how you let me feel the sweetness of your hand! ... You placed me in such hands. You entrusted me to such souls! How gentle and dear were those whom you used to do your work! You were so good! Divinely good!"[26]

In a meditation from November 8, 1897, we find the same thoughts:

> *"Such graces! It was all your doing, my God: this need for silence, the recollection, the spiritual reading, the desire to go inside your churches even though I didn't believe in you, the confusion in my soul, the anguish, the seeking after the truth, and that prayer, 'My God, if you exist, let me know you!" It was all you are doing, your work alone... A lovely soul helped you through silence, gentleness, goodness and perfection... It showed itself and was so good and spread a fragrance that drew me but it did nothing of itself! You, my Jesus,*

---

[25] Charles de Foucauld, *Lettre à un ami de lycée, Correspondance inédite avec Gabriel Tourdes (1874-1915)*, Paris, Nouvelle Cité, 1982, letter of February 6, 1892, p. 149.

[26] Charles de Foucauld, *Qui peut résister à Dieu*, Paris, Nouvelle Cité, 1980, p.210.

my Savior, you did it all, both within and without! ... You drew me to yourself through the beauty of a soul in whom virtue was so beautiful that it ravished my heart forever... You drew me to the truth through the beauty of that same soul: You gave me four graces. The first was to inspire this thought in me, 'since this soul is so intelligent, the religion which she so fervently believes must not be the folly that I thought it was.' The second was to inspire another thought within me, 'Since this religion is not folly, maybe the truth that cannot be found upon this earth or within any philosophical system is to be found there.' The third made me say, 'Then study this religion. Find a professor of the Catholic faith, an educated priest and go to the bottom of it and see if it is worth having faith in it.' The fourth was the incomparable grace that had me ask Fr. Huvelin to teach me... In making me enter his confessional on one of the last days of October27, between the 27th and the 30th I think, you gave me every good thing, my God. What a blessed day, what day of blessing...!"28

Charles de Foucauld frequently alluded to October 1886 and the events that filled its days. A whole series of circumstances brought him to seek out Fr. Huvelin: "unexpected solitude, illnesses among those he loved," he said. Marie de Bondy was sick at this time. He also learned that because of his state of health, Huvelin was discontinuing the conferences that he usually gave. This motivated him to ask Fr. Huvelin for private catechism lessons. There was also another notable event that is very revealing of Charles' temperament.

During the summer of 1886, the Duke of Aumale was sent into exile along with all of the royal family members. He had been the commander of the 4th regiment of Chasseurs of Africa. Charles de Foucauld felt it was his duty to represent his regiment in Paris at the

---

[27] One of the only dates that he did not precisely record. He will always refer to it as one of the last days of October, 1886.

[28] Charles de Foucauld, *La dernière place*, Paris, Nouvelle Cité, 1974, pp.105-106.

moment of this departure into exile and requested official authorization from the colonel in charge of that regiment. His request was seen as anti-republican provocation and was sent on to the Minister of the Army who handed down his judgment on September 18. Charles was suspended from military service for a one-year period and expelled from the ranks. Charles de Foucauld had arrived just one week earlier in Tunis to fulfill his military service as a reserve officer. This sanction meant that he found himself alone and aimless.[29]

Is that what this "unexpected solitude" was all about that made him return to France in October 1886? He found Marie de Bondy sick and, in the midst of a certain number of emotional upheavals, he addressed himself to Fr. Huvelin for "religious instruction. He had me kneel down and make my confession and sent me to receive communion forthwith."[30] In asking him to make an act of humility through confession. Huvelin asked him to do something that provoked a complete about face.

Over the following months he often went to speak with Fr. Huvelin at length. It did not happen all at once but from that moment on, Fr. Huvelin became his spiritual father and remained so until his death in 1910. Marie de Bondy became a real mother to him, one who had birthed him in the faith after having been already like a second mother to him.

---

[29] Cf. Pierre Sourisseau "Quelles circonstances étonnantes?" BACF, Paris, October 1986, no. 84, pp.17-22.

[30] Charles de Foucauld, La dernière place, Paris, Nouvelle Cité, 1974, p. 106.

THE TIME FOR VOCATION

In his letter to Duveyrier we read that just a few months after what he called his "big change" he was already thinking about entering a religious order. That would have been at the beginning of 1887. But Fr. Huvelin was encouraging him to marry, as was his family. His family was unaware of the "enormous change" that had taken place in him. They simply thought he had started going back to church. Even Marie de Bondy only realized later what an important role she had played in his conversion. But we must take what he wrote to Henri de Castries on August 14, 1901 very seriously:

> *"As soon as I believed there was a God, I understood that I could do nothing else than to live for him alone. My religious vocation dates from the moment I believed. God is so great! There is such a difference between God and all that is not God!...."*

His "all or nothing" tendency shows itself clearly here: everything and right away. He can't do anything else. He went on to say in this letter, "I wanted to be a religious and to live for God alone, to do whatever was most perfect to do, no matter what."

Among the young women who attended Fr. Huvelin's conferences were the two daughters of his friend, Mr. de Richemont. One of them had taken private vows while living in the world and was not interested in marriage. The second, however, was not only free to marry but was just the type that would have suited the Viscount Charles de Foucauld. But he wanted nothing to do with marriage.

His book, *Reconnaissance au Maroc*, was published at the beginning of 1888. Having finished this he was free to consider other things and prepare other expeditions. Fr. Huvelin insisted that he make a pilgrimage to the Holy Land so that, geographer that he was, he could walk where Jesus had walked. Charles de Foucauld was not at all interested in this plan. He was in too much of a hurry, but he finally agreed to go. So at the end of 1888 he sailed for the Holy Land and made the pilgrimage in his usual style, alone. He wrote:

> *"After spending Christmas, 1888, in Bethlehem, having assisted at Midnight Mass, receiving communion in the Grotto, and spending two or three days there, I returned to Jerusalem. I had felt such unspeakable sweetness in that Grotto where I could almost hear the voices of Jesus, Mary and Joseph and where I felt so close to them. And then, alas, after one short hour's walk I was before the dome of the Church of the Holy Sepulcher, Calvary and the Mount of Olives.*
>
> *Whether I wanted it or not, my thoughts shifted, and I found myself at the foot of the cross."*[31]

At the beginning of January 1889, he arrived in Nazareth. There he discovered the humble and obscure life of the *divine worker*. It was a kind of shock and also a call that had a determining effect upon him. It especially held an answer to the question that he had been asking himself since the day of his conversion, "What must I do?"

---

[31] Charles de Foucauld, *"Cette chère dernière place" Lettres à mes frères de la Trappe*, Paris, Cerf, 1991, letter of december 21, 1896 to Fr. Jerome, p 147.

Confessional at St Augustine's Paris, where Bl Charles made his confession of conversion.

In Nazareth Charles de Foucauld glimpsed this God who had walked among us. He met him at the fountain, with Mary. He saw him as he watched the craftsmen at their work. And he saw him according to his present state of mind, of one who wants to make radical lifestyle change. In the streets of Nazareth, he received a revelation of what he should do: God took on our humanity and lived among us. Therefore, to walk in the footsteps of Jesus, he must take that same road. He understood the life of Jesus of Nazareth not so much in an authentic historical sense but in the sense that it could serve as a model for him as he sought to change the direction of his life. Charles had been reintegrated into the heart of his family. He had received fame and recognition as one of the greatest explorers of all time. He had received the gold medal from the French Geographical Society. If he were going to make a change, he would not be content with living like everyone else. He was going to have to move to the opposite end of the spectrum from what his life had been.

For him "conversion" meant to allow oneself to be transformed by something that came from outside of himself. It meant to lead a life that was different from what his life had been. The aristocrat who was so self-conscious of his rank and attached such importance to the refinements of appearances, could not be content with something simple and ordinary. For the famous explorer, a lifestyle change meant living not just without fame or recognition but as someone, unknown, forgotten, looked down on and mistreated. He loved his work: to discover lands and peoples and to share that knowledge with others.... What could be more thrilling? He had edited his manuscript with tremendous attention to detail, a surprising scientific rigor and consummate perfection. From now on, he wanted to give himself to work that held no interest for anyone, was monotonous and worthless.

If he had grown up in a working-class or family farm, he would not have considered the life of Jesus of Nazareth as undesirable, degrading or abject. That is clear. But his extremist temperament pushed him to create a model to imitate, a Jesus in whose Passion he had seen what true abasement was all about. He could only see Jesus as one who was mistreated, scourged, tortured and condemned to a shameful death. At that moment he could not see the beauty of manual work, the quality of the harmonious relationships that Jesus, in his perfect humanity, had with his neighbors nor the surprising intimacy of his family life. In his way of thinking, Jesus could only be the poorest man who ever lived in Nazareth and, why not, the worst dressed. A carpenter's life could only have been monotonous and worthless. Jesus must have been looked down on and ill-treated. That is why he must have been reminded of that phrase from a sermon of Fr. Huvelin's, "Jesus so took the last place that no one has ever been able to take it from him."

It is essential to situate Charles de Foucauld's conversion in terms of this inner movement, a movement to the extreme opposite of what his life had been, to what he wanted it to become. He always imagined Jesus as being just the opposite of what he was. So Charles set out to live what he felt was the poorest and most miserable life he could imagine. He remembered having seen a monk at the Monastery of Fontgombault whose sad, dirty and patched habit attracted him. This then became the model he sought to exemplify for him who had been so refined and fashionable. He could not have led a life that was simply poor. He had to be the <u>poorest</u>. He couldn't look for a lowly place. He had to have the <u>last place</u>. In his vocabulary he always uses the superlative: the poorest, the last place. It's not good enough that it be poorer, it has to be the most impoverished, not just a lower status, but the last place. In so doing he gave himself an ideal that did not exist and that was impossible to attain, but he didn't realize it. But it really was in the streets of Nazareth that he felt called to imitate the hidden life of Jesus at Nazareth. This is how and when Nazareth came to play such an important role in his life even if many years later he wrote to Fr. Caron[32], "I am an old sinner who, the

---

[32] Author of the book *au pays de Jésus adolescent*, Paris, R. Haton, 1905. In Chapter 5 he spoke of Charles de Foucauld whom he had known. Fr. Caron was also involved in the beginnings of the *Association of the brothers and sisters of the Sacred Heart of Jesus*.

day after his conversion, felt irresistibly called by Jesus to lead the hidden life of Nazareth."[33] In fact, it was two years later.

From then on the question became, "What must I do to lead the life of Nazareth? "Charles de Foucauld spent the entire year of 1889 trying to understand with Fr. Huvelin's help how to answer this call from God. He said they had eliminated all of the active orders except the Franciscans because of St. Francis' poverty. But they would rule out the Franciscans as well. There was no mention of the Carthusians even though he seemed pushed to a solitary life. In the first letter that we had to Marie de Bondy on September 20, 1889, he expressed his ideal as he saw it at that moment as he shared wither his most recent meeting with Fr. Huvelin. "Again we looked at my reasons for wanting to enter religious life: - to keep company with Our Lord, as much as possible in his sufferings -."

For Fr. Huvelin it was clear that a man of Charles' social class should enter a place like the Monastery of Solesmes and he was friends with the Abbot there. So he sent his directee to stay at Solesmes for a while. But Charles saw very quickly that he would never be able to live out his ideal of Nazareth at Solesmes. So he thought about the Trappists of Soligny. There was no question of going back to Fontgombault as it was too close to the chateau of Barre where Marie de Bondy spent her vacations. At Soligny he felt that the Trappist life corresponded to his ideal of Nazareth with its life of manual work.

But he wanted to find a Trappist Monastery that was more isolated. Fr. Huvelin spoke to him about a very poor foundation that had just

---

[33] *XXV Lettres inédites du Père de Foucauld* (to Canon Caron), Paris, Bonne Presse, 1947.

been made in Syria by the Abbey of Notre Dame de Neiges. Dom Polycarp, the brother of one of his friends[34] and someone he had great confidence in, was part of the new foundation. Father Huvelin was ready to entrust Charles to them. This monastery had the advantage of being the poorest one in the order and was very isolated. Charles only thought about going to Syria from that time, but he first had to go to Notre Dame de Neiges where he would have to make his novitiate. In October he wrote to the Trappists of Notre Dame des Neiges to see if they would accept him, agreeing to send him to Akbès, Syria. He did not present himself as a poor and ignorant man. One has only to read his letters to Fr.

Eugene to see understand what was going on:

> *"I find that your Order is where the Christian life and the life of complete union with Our Lord is lived. My desire is for that life in which it seems to me that Our Lord is as much consoled and glorified as he can be by men."*[35]

His final decision was made during a retreat that he made at the end of November at the Jesuit House in Clamart. At the end of this retreat of election according to the Exercises of St. Ignatius[36], it was decided that he would enter the Trappists on January 1st or during the first week of January. He took his time to bid his farewells to everyone but only told his sister, his brother-in-law and Marie de Bondy that he was leaving to join the Trappists as he wanted to see how things would go. Fr.

---

[34] *Cf.* Jean-François Six, *Itinéraire spirituel de Charles de Foucauld,* Paris, Seuil, 1958, note 25, p. 114.

[35] Charles de Foucauld, *"Cette Chère dernière place"Lettres à mes frères de la Trappe,* Paris, Cerf, 1991, pp.37-38.

[36] Ignatian method that he always used in making decisions and choices.

Huvelin asked him to put off his entrance quickly because of the cold weather. But it was also because his family, especially Marie de Bondy, as well as himself, needed time to get accustomed to the idea of such a separation.

The Day of The Greatest Sacrifice

Without a doubt, January 15, 1890 marked the life of Charles de Foucauld as no other day. Its importance cannot be stressed enough both in its humanity and in understanding the depth of the passionate love of Jesus that enabled Charles de Foucauld to make such an act. As it is easy to embellish such an event I will limit myself to citing Charles' own words. This allows us to see the importance that he placed on this separation from the world.

Few people were aware of his imminent departure:

> *"When I leave,"* he wrote to his sister, *"I will say that I am going on some trip without mentioning that I am entering or in any way think of joining religious life."*

January 13th he wrote to his brother-in-law and the next day, the 14th, the last letter to his sister:

> *"I leave Paris tomorrow. I will be at Notre Dame des Neiges the next day around 2 o'clock. Pray for me. I will pray for you and your family. Growing closer to God does not make us forget one another. I will write to you the day after I arrive at Notre Dame des Neiges. But after this first letter, you will know that my silence means that there is nothing new. And I will understand your silence in the same way. When we are so close to God and so filled with God we have trouble finding the little things to say of which letters are made.*

Is better to pray for those one loves and to offer with them the sacrifice of separation."

We could, as did René Bazin on page 100 of his book4, leave the rest of the page blank and skip directly to January 16th where we would find Charles had already arrived at Notre Dame des Neiges, skipping completely the day of January 15th. But on the contrary we will tarry over this day in order to give it all of the importance that it represented for Charles. In his notebook where he listed all of the important dates, this is the first. Maybe it is simply because it is in early January. But in another list of dates he seems to list a chronology as if marking the beginning of his life: "Left the rue d'Anjou Wednesday, January 15, 1890 at seven o'clock in the evening, (Feast of St. Paul the Hermit, St. John Calybite, St. Maur)."

We have a reasonably good idea of what took place that day from the many letters that Charles wrote throughout his life in which he alluded to it. It began with an early morning visit to Fr. Huvelin who was leaving Paris that same day. We know this from letter that he wrote to Marie de Bondy on January 14, 1894: "I continue my letter… It is 9 in the morning (in Akbes), 6:45 in Paris, the same time as when I last saw Fr. Huvelin after his morning Mass."

Charles and Marie assisted at the 9 am Mass in Our Lady's Chapel in the Church of St. Augustine where Charles had received communion that morning after having gone to confession in October of 1886. They received communion together for the last time and then returned to the house on rue d'Anjou where he stayed until about 3 in the afternoon. He left Marie to visit Fr. Huvelin at rue de Laborde as he had not been able to travel because of illness. A last conversation, a last blessing, a last goodbye. He then made a last visit in St. Augustine's Church, the last prayer. Charles returned to the house on rue d'Anjou at about 4 pm "for the last time." Three hours later he would leave for the train that would take him far from all those he loved. The hands of the clock seemed to race. At 7:10 pm Marie blessed him and he left the house in tears.

There was nothing extraordinary on this day. It was like so many leave-takings for convents and monasteries, for mission lands... restrained emotions, the painful separations from families, the sacrifice, the normal sorrow that would quickly be forgotten as the course of life took over. That would not be the case with Charles de Foucauld. He would never forget that day. We will not understand his writings, his manner of speaking about suffering or his prayer if we don't grasp the importance of this moment in Charles' life. Reading several of his letters on the anniversary of this date is convincing enough:

January 15, 1900:

"It is 6:55 in the evening in Paris. Ten years ago at this very hour I was sitting in your living room, my eyes going back and forth between you and the clock. How vivid that day still is for me!... I thought of it as I received communion this morning!.. I thought of you the entire day!... Ten years!... It seems like yesterday..."

January 15, 1906:

"It is 5 p.m. Sixteen years ago I was there with you. I can still see you as if it were happening now... I can still see the hands of the clock marking off those last hours. I can still see it..."

December 8, 1907:

"The years pass but rather than calming the pain of separation, it seems just as painful."

There is also a note from January 15, 1895 written in Akbès on the back of an envelope that he had received. Charles de Foucauld answered questions that he had asked himself using the famous hexametric method of Quintilien that he used whenever he tried to make a discernment in his choices: *Quis? Quid? Ubi? Quibus auxiliis?*

Cur? Quomodo? Quando?

"**Quis?** The sinner whom you have led by such grace and mercy.

Quid? Leave to 1. be able 'to love you with a greater love;' 2. lead the life that will glorify you the most, that is, the life that will lead to my own and my neighbor's sanctification, that is, the life that is most like your own; 3. to offer you the greatest sacrifice of which I am capable by leaving behind all that I love.

Ubi? In a non-Christian country, in a Trappist Monastery, far from all that I love.

Quibus auxiliis? With your grace, such grace! Thank you, thank you infinitely! … With the help of the prayers of Our Lady, Saint Joseph, Saint Mary Magdeleine, Saint John the Baptist, my guardian angel, of all the saints and of so many people who love me and have gone before me, of your servant Fr. Huvelin and so many other holy people… Through your example and that of Our Lady, Saint Joseph, Saint Mary Magdeleine, Saint John the Baptist; through the help of Saint Paul the Hermit and Saint Anthony whose feast is these days…

Through the example, strength and goodness of your servant and of Fr. Huvelin. Thanks to you and to them! Bless them and be Blessed!

Cur? To glorify you and console your heart as much as possible.

Quomodo? With pure intentions, obedience and courage... Dear God, enliven me with these until my death so that I might accomplish your will and give you as much glory as is possible! By offering myself entirely to you, praying for those I love and for all of your children.

Quando? At ten minutes past seven it will be five years... and today, O my God! With my whole soul I renew the offering of my entire self to you, to breathe only for you, to use every moment of my life in order to glorify you and to console your Heart as much as possible by the most perfect accomplishment of all that you want me to do! Amen. Amen. Amen."[37]

These same reflections can be found throughout Charles' life on this anniversary date, not just in the first years but fifteen and eighteen years later as well. They tell us that January 15th was the day of the greatest sacrifice for him in the sadness and pain of separation. On January 15th, 1900 he wrote to Marie de Bondy: "It was a sacrifice that used up all of my tears it seems because since that day I have never cried. It seems that I have no tears left!..."

More than any other, the letter that he wrote to his cousin the day after he left home for the Trappists expresses this pain:

> *"Where was I yesterday at this hour? I was there with you, saying good-bye, it was hard but sweet because at least I saw you... Twenty-four hours is such a small thing. I still have not understood that I bid you adieu forever. So little was able to separate us in the past. How can we ever be so completely separated in the future? But I know it is the truth. I desire it and yet cannot believe it.*

---

[37] Charles de Foucauld, *Voyageur dans la nuit*, Paris, Nouvelle Cité, 1979, pp 25-26.

At nine in the morning, at four o'clock, now and always I feel so close to you although my eyes will never again meet your eyes."[38]

The intensity of these last hours in the world made them a holocaust was that it was to be forever: "never again", "forever".

A note written in Nazareth seven years later on the back of an envelope (an extract of a letter or a draft) confirms the dominant emotion:

"Once I arrived at the monastery, I suffered greatly… not from the community. They were all so good to me… but the thought of my family tortured me; sometimes I repeated it to myself, always, always, never, never, live here always and never see them again… How good Jesus was in helping me with his sweet protection to overcome the obstacles of my family, the devil and myself."[39]

This note follows another where he wrote, "To say it in one word, leave everything, my child, and you will find everything."

The other aspect of this sacrifice was how total it was. This is very clear in letter to Marie de Bondy on July 16, 1891:

"On January 15th I left everything behind, but the embarrassing fact of my rank and money remained. It gave me great pleasure to cast these out the window."

Ten years later, on August 14, 1901 he told Henri de Castries:

---

[38] Letter from January 16, 1890 to Marie de Bondy, first letter published in Charles de Foucauld, *Lettres à Madame de Bondy*, Paris, Desclée De Brouwer, 1966.

[39] Charles de Foucauld, *Voyageur dans la nuit*, Paris, Nouvelle Cité, 1979, p.59, n.71.

> *"I tenderly loved what little family God had left me. But, wishing to make a sacrifice in imitation of He who had made so many, I left for a Trappist monastery in Armenia about 12 years ago."*

But there is also a more positive note to this day, something of an actual passage from death to life:

> *"It is the day that, in tears, I left my family eight years ago in order to be totally yours, my beloved Lord! You dried those tears: You made of that day a day of celebration, something of a day of birth, for to live for you alone is true life... It is a stepping stone between the day of our birth into this world and the day that we will be reborn in heaven through your infinite mercy..."*[40]

The day of birth dies natalis, in martyrology the day of death is the day of entrance into life. It is good to mention the number of "conversion" moments throughout Charles' life, "days of birth". Each conversion is like a successive birth into life, true life, as he says. He could write each one as the starting point of a new life. Jean Guitton was correct in presenting Charles de Foucauld as a "man who never ceased to be reborn."[41]

It is in this sense that January 15, 1890 was for him a passage through death that could only be truly completed by his physical death. It gave such importance throughout the rest of his life to thoughts of death and that final meeting with Jesus.

---

[40] Charles de Foucauld, *Considérations sur les fêtes de l'année*, Paris, Nouvelle Cité, 1987, dated Jan. 15, 1898, p. 105.

[41] *Le Figaro*, Déc. 12, 1982.

"Months are added to months and will lead one day to that final month."[42] Yes, death would be sweet not only because it would lead to that perfect union with Jesus but because it would also allow one to be reunited with those he had so painfully left behind.

January 15, 1890 marked an end, a consummation. The passages that we have cited could allow one to think that only the sentimental and affective dominated. It is therefore necessary to take another look at the profound motivation of such a wrenching sacrifice.

It all began with that first conversion. The three years before that moment, he lived in something of a new world, a world filled with faith. Everything looked different in this new light. The day that he accepted to see himself as a sinner and welcomed God's forgiveness a new life began, as he said in that letter to Henri de Castries on August 14, 1901:

> *"As soon as I believed there was a God I understood that I could do nothing else than to live for him alone. My religious vocation dates from the moment I believed. God is so great! There is such a difference between God and all that is not God!..."*

He felt he had to make a radical choice from the very first moment: religious life, all or nothing. He wanted it all and right away. He experienced his call as practically being unable to do anything else: the desire to live for God alone, the irresistible attraction to the One who would become ever more his beloved Brother and Lord.

As we have seen, Fr. Huvelin did not see things in the same way. Wise and intelligent counselor that he was, he wanted to see Charles

---

[42] LMB, July 16, 1891.

marry without delay. But Charles wanted nothing to do with marriage. He felt that he had been seized by Someone who wanted him entirely and Charles wanted to live for Him alone.

If his conversion had only led to his childhood faith, Charles could have easily fallen into militant fundamentalism or religious sentimentality. In fact, it had been meeting with the living God, with a close and loving God. The God to whom he had prayed, "if you exist let me know you," was encountered in a loving communion, a God who loves and who must be loved in return. This God took flesh and had a name: Jesus. Charles' real spirituality was centered in the person of Jesus, his God, his Lord, his Brother and, later in the language of the mystics, his beloved Spouse.

To his friend, Duveyrier, the young monk confided, April 24, 1890:

> *"Why did I enter the Trappists? That is what you are asking of your friend. For love, for pure love. I love our Lord Jesus Christ, even if it is with a heart that wishes to love better and more deeply; but I do love him, and I can't stand the thought of living a life other than his own, to lead a gentle and honored life while his was the most difficult and despised that there ever was. I do not want to go through life in first class while I love the lowest class. The greatest sacrifice for me, so great that everything else seems like nothing, is the separation forever with a family whom I adore and my true friends and to whom I am so deeply attached: I count about four or five as such friends and you are among the first of these. This tells you how hard it is for me to think that I will never see you again. The love of God and love of others is my entire life and I hope it always will be."[43]*

---

[43] René Pottier, *Un Prince saharien méconnu Henri Duveyrier*, Paris, Plon, 1938, pp.225-226.

He explained it differently to his cousin: he left to "be with" Jesus in a fellowship of every moment, "keep company with Jesus, as much as possible in his sufferings."

Let us not forget that this was his spirituality, and of the weight of meaning behind his words at that moment. Even if we are not very comfortable with this way of speaking we can understand what he meant. It is not just the language of an era. It is expressive of his temperament and of the sacrifice that he had made. Duveyrier, unbeliever that he was, was not able to understand the transformation that his friend had undergone. He worried, "He has such an elitist nature and I fear that he has either caught an incurable illness or has

been profoundly emotionally disturbed."[44] As if it were a kind of prophetic statement that he made to the Geographical Society, Henri Duveyrier used the words "incurable illness" and "profoundly disturbed". These words beg a question and the Muslim mystic Ibn Arabi provides a right answer: "The one who has the illness called Jesus will never be cured." It is only the strength of Charles' deep faith (that over the previous three years grew more and more into a passionate love) that can explain his willingness to embrace such a definitive rupture with everyone he held so dear and which he described in the painful terms that we have seen. Did he not write to Gabriel Tourdes on November 18, 1885: "We are both too philosophical to believe that anything in this world is final?" The miracle of his faith is that he was able to live this situation peacefully and joyfully until his death with admirable perseverance.

---

[44] *Op. cit.*, p. 220, letter à M. Maunoir du 18.02.1888.

Charles renewed his sacrifice when, several months later he left France for Akbès.

He should have stayed at Notre Dame des Neiges for two years to complete his novitiate there. But on January 26, the feast of St. Alberic, a monk remembered among the Trappists, he took the habit and began his novitiate under the name of brother Marie-Alberic. But to avoid being called into military service because of his status as a reserve officer he was authorized by the Trappists to leave immediately for Akbès. He informed his military superiors of his change of residence only after he had left the country and was subsequently dispensed from fulfilling his military service. We know from various sources, and he said it himself, that he also didn't find what he was looking for at Notre Dame des Neiges but put up with it while waiting to go to Akbès.

June 27, 1890 on the eve of his departure from Marseille he wrote to his cousin:

> *"I can see myself on the boat that will take me away tomorrow. I can feel each wave, one after the other, taking me further and further away... My only recourse is to think that each one is a step closer to the end of this life."*

The boat's departure was the visible sign of the greater separation that Charles wished to place between himself and his family. July 8th he wrote to his cousin, "Tomorrow I will be in Alexandretta and I will say goodbye to this sea, the last link to the country where all of you live and breathe." It was a genuine inner passage of separation and distancing.

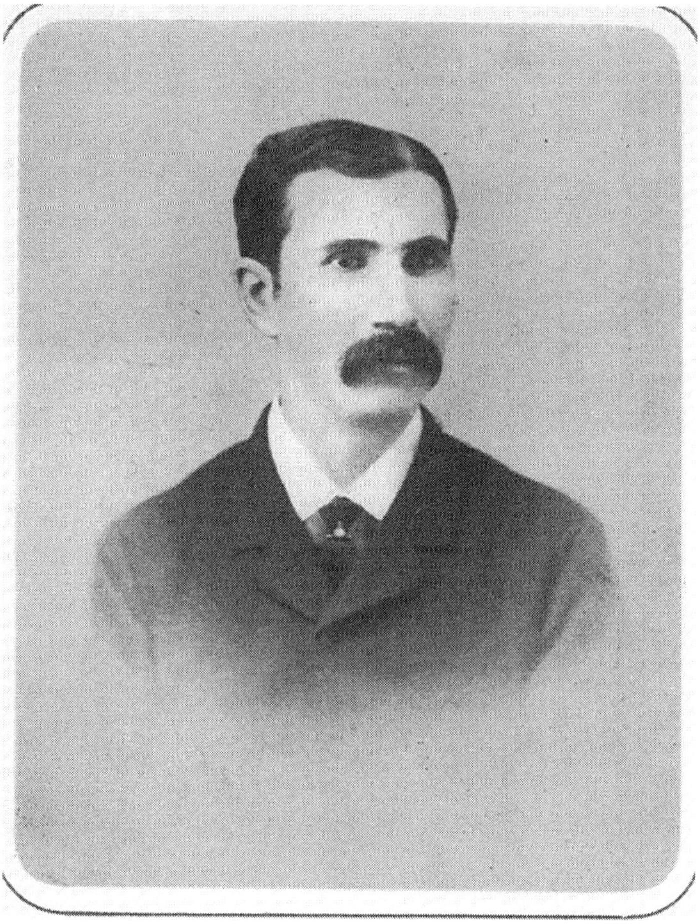

Seven Years as
A Trappist Monk

———∞·∞———

The seven years that Charles spent with the Trappists represent one of the longest periods of stability in his life. He spent the first six months at Notre Dame des Neiges and was in Akbès until September 1896. From there he was sent to the Monastery of Staouéli near Algiers for a few weeks, and then on to Rome.

So this was quite a long period of time. But it became clear that he could not find in Akbès, any more than at Notre Dame des Neiges, the ideal that he had glimpsed in the streets of Nazareth and imagined to be his calling. It would be hard to find a monastery any poorer than the newly founded Akbès where the monks lived in shacks as they worked to build a monastery amid a sea of mud. But for someone who was just arriving, who desired to live as poorly as possible in imitation of a Jesus he imagined to have lived in the very lowest place and the most extreme poverty, the very idea of building a monastery to settle into was contrary to everything in him. The ways of the world, as well as group living, went against his grain.

Charles' first letters from Akbès show him happily entering into the life of the monastery community. February 2, 1892, he made simple vows and the same day wrote to his cousin, "So now I no longer belong to myself in any way." He went as far as to say that he never felt happier in his life, a genuine spiritual euphoria, except maybe for when he returned from his pilgrimage to the Holy Land, having received such insight at Nazareth.

But very quickly that same year, and especially during the following year, he began to express criticisms about the Trappists because of the changes that their Constitutions were undergoing. At a General Assembly it had been decided that all of the Trappists would be united. Therefore, the Master General applied one common Rule of Life to all of the monastic communities. Brother Marie Alberic did not see this as a movement towards perfection. He preferred that each monastery be independent and have the freedom to follow the Rule as it saw fit in a desire for greater perfection. He felt that by applying a common observance for all, they would be obliged to adopt a "middle" course that would lead to mediocrity. When he finally read the text of the new Constitution, he noted that, despite it all, there were some positive points.

However, he became preoccupied with another question about which he wrote to Fr. Huvelin on September 22, 1893: "Some excellent modifications to the Order have been made following the Holy Father's directives: but these modifications and improvements will not keep evil from growing." Did he think that something like a virus had attacked the monastic life with all of its consequences?

> *"They are just distancing themselves more and more from the poverty and humility of the simple life of Nazareth that I came here looking for. I am in no way detached from this ideal and am so distressed to see Our Lord leading it alone without anyone or any group of souls in our Church seeking to live it with him, sharing out of love for him and in his love the blessed joy of Our Lady and Saint Joseph."*

If no one else was thinking of it, shouldn't he? He added in his letter to Fr. Huvelin:

> *"Would there not be a way to start a small congregation to live this life, to live only from the work of our hands, as did Our Lord. He did not live off of collections, or offerings or satisfy himself to direct foreign workers.*[45]
>
> *Could we not find a few souls to follow Our Lord in this way? To live by following all of his counsels, renouncing all private property, collective as well as individual. And consequently, and being against all that Our Lord was against, any lawsuits, arguments, claims over property and with a strict obligation to give alms. If we have two habits, then to give one away. If we have food to eat, to share it with those who have none, without holding back for another day…all of the examples of his hidden life and every counsel that came from his mouth… a life of work and prayer, not two kinds of religious as at Cîteaux but just one, as St Benedict wanted… Not the complicated Benedictine liturgies… But long hours of meditation, the rosary, Holy Mass. Our liturgies close the door to Arabs, Turks, Armenians, etc… who are good Catholics but do not know our language. I would so like to see these little nests of vibrant and working life, like that of Our Lord's, be established under the protection of Mary and Joseph. They would be close to all these isolated missions in the Middle East, to offer refuge to the people of these countries whom God calls to his service and love…*
>
> *Is this a dream, Father? Is it an illusion of the devil? Or is it an invitation from the Good Lord? If I were sure that it came from God I would do whatever was necessary right at this moment, not tomorrow, to enter this way. When I think about it, I find that it is perfect: To follow the example and counsel of Our Lord can only be excellent… And what is more, it is what I have always been looking for; it is what I came seeking among the Trappists; it is not any new vocation; if such a community of souls had existed several years ago I would*

---

[45] They had asked him to oversee the construction of a road. (LMB Feb 28, 1893)

have run to them right away, as you know… Since it does not exist and nothing is even close to it or replaces it, should we not try to form such a group?… It should be formed to spread it among the infidel countries, Muslim and others… I repeat, when I think about it I find it perfect… But when I think about the one who has this ardent thought, this sinner, this weak and miserable person, I do not see in him the stuff God ordinarily uses to do good things… It is true that once it has begun, if it comes from God, God will make it grow and he will draw other souls who are capable of being the first stones of his house, souls before whom I will remain in the nothingness that is my true place. Something else gives me the courage to take up such a task despite my misery and sinfulness. That is, Our Lord said that when one has sinned much, one must love much. So, Father, do you think that this comes from the Good Lord? I will act only according to your answer and advice, as you know, because a father always remains a father and you are such a father for me! You see how much I need you… This idea has been so strong for two months now that I could no longer keep from speaking about it with my confessor, Fr. Polycarp. I mentioned it to him two weeks ago but with many less details than I have with you. He advised me to let this thought sleep for the moment and not to worry about it until it comes up through some event… That is also what I thought to do but the issue will necessarily come up in little more than a year when it will be time for me to make final vows. For the moment, I try not to think about it but I am not very successful at that. At any rate, I needed to tell you about it and now that is done… I continue studying theology, very happy to study it I have written four whole pages about myself. It saddens and frightens me."

Unfortunately, we do not have Fr. Huvelin's answer to this letter but we do know that he advised him to wait and try not to think about it all and to give himself fully overdo living the Trappist life.

1894 was a peaceful time for him. On November 15, 1893 he had written to Marie de Bondy:

> *"I wait… I am in the same state as before entering the Trappists, trying to clean the slate of my own desires concerning this resolution I have such an ardent desire to follow him more closely… But is it his will? I do not know: but before trying another lifestyle I must know that it is his will… I am at peace as I wait for his will to make itself known."*

1895 was marked by several important events, not the least of which was the massacre of the Armenian population of which he wrote to Fr. Huvelin on January 16, 1896:

> *"My soul is in the same state as ever: same desires and feelings: nothing has changed since last autumn: with time it becomes ever steadier… I am not writing to you about myself today. You must certainly be aware of the horrors that have taken place in this area; in the monastery everything is quite calm and I am at peace as if the rest of the world did not even exist. But all the while at a short distance from us in Armenia there have been terrible massacres: they speak of 60,000 killed… and those who have survived are suffering terribly in the burnt-out ruins of their villages, stripped of everything, hungry. It seemed to me that the only thing that I could do for these unfortunate people was to write to you and tell you about their situation in case you would know someone able and willing to help them and whose charity you could orient in their direction."*

We see clearly that this man of action could not remain untouched by the situation and that he must do something right away.

February 2, 1896 brother Marie Alberic renewed his vows but he desired more and more the life of Nazareth. On March 19th, the feast of St. Joseph, he wrote to his spiritual director (the letter was lost) to tell him his thoughts about his upcoming final vows the following year and that he must decide about it. Fr. Huvelin answered on June 15th:

> *"I read and reread your letter… I have made you wait so long for an answer when you have been so thirsty for some response from me. But it seemed to me*

that you were not wasting your time there by studying theology, taking in sure and varied teachings, preparing your heart and mind through such teaching for a mystical life that is pure and without illusions. How deeply St. Bernard, as well as St. Augustine, were nourished by Sacred Scripture! His sure mysticism is like a flower born of religious truth! So, my dear child, you have not wasted your time!

I had hoped, dear child, that you would have found what you were looking for with the Trappists, that you would have found enough poverty, humility and obedience to follow Our Lord in his life at Nazareth. When you entered, I thought you would have been able to say, 'Here I find my rest forever.'... I am sorry that this is not the case. There is something too deep in you that moves you from within towards another ideal. Little by little whatever it is will lead you to leave this setting and you will find yourself on the outside.

I do not think that you can stop this movement. – tell your superiors at Staouéli[46]... simply tell them what you think – tell them how highly you regard their life and also of this invincible inner movement that has been working at you for such a long time no matter what you do, and of how it is taking you towards another ideal... Tell them, my dear child, your thoughts and feelings. I think you can do this... you should do so because a painful split is happening within your soul and you are no longer present to the life there

I am not making you wait any longer for an answer from me, you see, despite my own regrets and my own high regard for the Order you entered. I do not think that you have a higher calling... I do not see you better... oh no! But I do think that you feel called elsewhere. So I do not make you wait any longer. Show my letter to them – talk to them. Write to Staouéli. I would have wanted

---

[46] The Monastery of Akbès was no longer attached to Notre Dame des Neiges but to Staouéli, a flourishing monastery near Algiers, which was able to provide for it. Dom Louis de Gonzaga, brother of Dom Martin who was the abbot of Notre Dame des Neiges, had been the first abbot of Akbès before being named to Staouéli. Very attached to brother Marie Alberic, he did everything in his power to keep him with the Trappists.

to see you remain part of a family that loves you so much and to whom you could have given so much.

I am happy that they have entrusted these souls to your care."

He is not talking about novices but about two orphans who asked to enter the Order. Accepted as "oblates" brother Marie Alberic was charged with their formation. This partly explains why he began, around the month of May, writing meditations on theGospel,[47] taking passages that have to do with prayer and faith. Chronologically these are the first of his writings and, appropriately, René Bazin placed these meditations at the beginning of *Ecrits Spirituels*.[48] Everything else that brother Marie Alberic had written before this time, and he wrote. extensively during his years with the Trappists contrary towhat has been said, he burned. He later regretted this. We do not know precisely how much he wrote but these meditations were in little handmade notebooks and this one was number "6". Therefore, we can assume that 5 others disappeared.

These meditations are very difficult to date with precision as they contain neither personal nor liturgical references. In my opinion they must be dated around the end of his time with the Trappists of Akbès. We find in this notebook a meditation on the Our Father that he later copied into another notebook with the later date, allowing some to think that it had been written at a later date. But it was a word-for-word copy of the earlier text. In these early writings at the end of his commentary on the Gospel of St.

---

[47] Charles de Foucauld, *L'Esprit de Jésus*, Paris, Nouvelle Cité, 1978.
[48] René Bazin, *Ecrits Spirituels de Charles de Foucauld,* Paris, J. de Gigord, 1951.

Luke wrote a meditation on Jesus' prayer on the cross: "Father, I commend my life into your hands." What is called the "Prayer of Abandonmont"[49] is taken from this text.

After receiving Fr. Huvelin's letter, brother Marie Alberic submitted a formal request to leave the Trappists. He had already written his entire first Rule of Life[50] for those who would come to live with him on a 21 x 27 cm piece of paper folded in half. It is a fascinating text that he entitled *Congregation of the Little Brothers of Jesus*. It is strong and absolute and clearly shows his radical nature. When Fr. Huvelin received this document he answered the following on August 2, 1896:

> *"I am so sad, my child, and I blame myself for having given that decision ad duritiam cordis (against my better judgment) — I felt that things could not go on any longer as they were, given your feelings and the judgments that you were making about everything around you — not about the people — but the very lifestyle! The grace that I would hope for you, my friend and my child, would befor you to be able to be become very 'little,' to find some corner of the monastery in which to nestle down and to have the faith to believe that one follows the Lord and is close to him wherever one obeys and humbles oneself! Nazareth is wherever one works, wherever one submits oneself... It is a house that one builds within one's heart, or rather, that one allows the hands of the gentle and humble Christ Child to build!*
>
> *I am so upset by all of this, my child! If you are refused the permission that you are seeking, see in it the will of God and take it to mean that you should stay put, and, in the darkness, wait! I cannot see another way. Continue studying Theology. If your superiors tell you to try again, do it with a loyal heart. What frightens me the most, my dear child, is not the life that you imagine for yourself*

---

[49] *Cf.* Antoine Chatelard: "Le premier écrit spirituel de Charles de Foucauld",......

[50] Charles de Foucauld, *Règlements et Directoire*, Montrouge, Nouvelle Cité, 1995, p. 27.

if you were to remain alone, nor that of St. Alexis[51], as you say – but to see you founding or even thinking of founding something. I do not see you directing other souls, my child! Your rule is impossible. Have no doubts about what I think of it! The Pope hesitated to approve the Franciscan rule of life. He found it too demanding... But this rule... To tell you the truth terrifies me!

Life in the shadow of some convent if you must... but do not write a Rule, I beg you. See how much I suffer because of this, my child. When I wrote to you I had the feeling that things could not go on as they had. You had begun to judge the life that you had once embraced. You no longer entered its spirit. You no longer had the spirit of a religious but an independent spirit! This is why I have written you such a letter! I am so troubled by it all. Can you see? Open your heart to your superiors and take pure and simple obedience as a light. And especially, do not think of founding anything. If you are put off by the spirit of St. Bernard and the Trappists then lead another life... but do not try to attract companions – I beg you.

There in the Middle East, you could have given so much to the Order, have brought out the beauty, the firmness of the foundations, the greatness, haveserved it well in a thousand ways... have plunged yourself into it through mortification and, especially, humility. But you will never find enough mortification for your taste. You will always be wondering about things and looking for what comes next... You need to be on your guard against always being carried to the limit. It leaves you agitated and unable to settle anywhere. Only those hearts that are not given to extremes can live on the edge in that way.

Ah, your letter bothered me, my child! I thought that you would have continued to wait... Well, place yourself into the hands of your superiors.

Receive their decisions with simplicity. Study theology. And especially, do not try to find anything! I am very close to you... I pray for you with all my heart.

---

[51] Hermit model.

Show my letter to your superiors, my child!

Believe in my faithful, deep and painful affection for you in our Lord."

It's hard to put the photo of the manuscript in because the text is in French... But the text is Text of a Meditation of Br. Marie-Albéric from which was drawn what is called the "Prayer of Abandonment."

" 'Father, into your hands I commend my spirit.'

It is the last prayer of our Master, of our Beloved... may it be ours... May it not only be the prayer of our last moment, but that of all our moments.

Father, I place myself in your hands. Father, I entrust myself to you.

Father, I abandon myself to you. Father, do with me what you will.

Whatever you may do with me, I thank you; Thank you for all, I am ready for all, I accept all I thank you for all.

Provided that your Will be done in me, my God. Provided that your Will be done in all your creatures, In all your children, in all those whom your heart loves. I desire nothing else, my God.

I place my soul into your hands.

I give it to you, my God, with all the love of my heart, Because I love you And because of this love I need to give myself

To place me into you're your hands without reserve, I place myself into your hands with infinite confidence, because you are my Father."

The Act of Abandonment

⸻◆⸻

After receiving Fr. Huvelin's permission, brother Marie Alberic presented his request to be relieved of his vows and to leave the monastery to the Abbot General of the Trappists. Before any decision could be made, he was asked to go to the monastery of Staouéli for a time of discernment where Dom Louis de Gonzague was the Abbot. At the end of a month, (October 1896), he was asked to go to Rome to study for a minimum of two, maximum of three years. He left with Fr. Henri who would study with him.

One can read his first letters from Rome to Fr. Jerome, a young monk who sat next to him in choir at Staouéli. The younger man had become quite taken with this monk of such prestigious reputation, who had come from the Middle East and, being much older, seemed to be surrounded with an aura of holiness.

Having arrived in Rome he stopped writing the series of meditations on the Gospels that he had begun towards the end of his time at Staouéli. In a similar notebook (pages tied together with string and covered with newspaper) he began another series of meditations in a completely different style on the Old Testament, beginning with Genesis. These are much easier to situate than the previous series as he mentioned some of the difficulties that he was dealing with at that moment. He spoke about his solemn vows drawing nearer, of his desire to take the last place while, if he remained at the monastery, he felt they would promote him. We see in these meditations his desire to seek the

Will of God. On occasion he brings up his previous choices more explicitly:

> *"Poverty, abjection, penance, my only desire as you know, my God, is to practice them to the extent and in the manner that you would have me do... But what is the manner and measure?"*[52]

From the meditations dated December 25th, 26th, 31st and January 1st, he stopped these nearly daily reflections on January 15th. On this day, while continuing his classes, he began a kind of quasi retreat as he awaited the decision of his Trappist superiors. They had to decide one way or the other about his future as soon as the Abbot returned from a trip and before the end of the month.

Brother Marie Alberic must have promised to send copies of some of his meditations to Fr. Jerome. December 21st he wrote to him:

> *"Thank you so much for having the goodness to send me such an abundant supply of paper. I have already begun using it and will try to finish this little project as soon as possible. Thank you."* [53]

What project could have needed paper? Was it not at this time that he began to copy the meditations on the Gospels that he had written in Akbès into a new notebook[54], a clean, clearly written word for word copy with very few corrections?

---

[52] Charles de Foucauld, *Qui peut resister Dieu?*, Paris, Nouvelle Cité, 1980, pp. 64-65.

[53] Charles de Foucauld, *"Cette chère dernière place" Lettres à mes frères de la Trappe*, Paris, Cerf, 1991, p147.

[54] This notebook is in the possession of the de Foucauld family. Fr. Henri, who had kept it as a souvenir, sent it to Louis de Foucauld, thinking that Charles de Foucauld must have wanted

Around January 15, 1897, he finished this manuscript that contains his mediation on the Our Father. He made a separate copy of it on January 23rd. The same day he received authorization to leave the Trappists. For the next week he had to continue living as if nothing had changed in his life. No one at the monastery had been informed of the decision. On that same day he stopped writing his copies and dated what he had written with this date on which the Will of God had been so clearly manifested to him. After January 15, 1890, it is one of the key dates in his life. This January 23rd is not a Wednesday as he mistakenly wrote, nor a Friday as Bishop Jacqueline says in his collection of Charles' writings. Rather, it was a Saturday and the vigil of the Feast of the Holy Family. We read in his notebook, "The Abbot General informed me: Our Lord's Will for me is that I should leave the Order and follow him in abjection and poverty..." and in the other notebook where he had written about "leaving Anjou Street" he wrote:

> *"Received the decision of the Abbot General that the will of God is that I should leave the Order to follow Our Lord in his way of abjection and poverty. Wednesday, January 23, 1897, feast of the engagement of the Blessed Virgin with St. Joseph and vigil of the Feast of the Holy Family."*

To realize what this represented for him we only have to read what he had previously written in his meditations on the Old Testament:

> *"Blessed are you, St. Abraham! Blessed be you, St. Isaac, who let yourself be so gently bound upon the altar! Blessed are you for all ages, my God, you who bring forth such virtues among men! Love means to obey you, to obey you as they did, with the same swiftness, with the same faith, in those times when the*

---

him to receive it. In fact, this cousin was to have visited him in Rome at this time but was finally unable to go.

heart and spirit are shaken, when one's entire way of thinking has been turned upside down. Love is being ready to sacrifice to your Will, absolutely and immediately, all that one holds most dear, the sacrifice of the only Son, of that which is dearest to our hearts, that we cherish the most… Love means being ready to give all that one has in exchange for every suffering out of love for the Lord…"[55]

One can imagine that he was alluding to the sacrifice that he made on January 15, 1890, but there was more to it than that:

"That is what you did… St. Abraham! It is what You did, Oh Son of God, when you came from heaven to live such a life and die such a death!… My Lord and my God, help me to also do the same, according to your most holy Will. St. Abraham, St. Isaac, pray for me."[56]

In mid-January 1897 he relived the sacrifice of Abraham. He was ready to sacrifice it all: all that he had desired, all that he carried in his heart, and which was why he was asking to leave the Trappists. If ever there was a moment in his life when he had abandoned himself to the decision of another, this was it. It's what he wrote to Fr. Jerome on January 24th:

"This week I have really had to practice obedience. I still need to practice it, as well as courage: For the last three years I have been asking to change from being a choir monk to a lay brother, either as part of the Order or in another religious Order in the Middle East; I believe that this is my vocation; to have a lower rank; I asked this with the permission of my confessor: my superiors told me to spend some time at Staouéli before making any decision: once I arrived there, I was surprised to be told to go to Rome where I expected to be made to wait a

---

[55] Charles de Foucauld, *Qui peut résister à Dieu?*, Paris, Nouvelle Cité, 1980, pp.64-65.
[56] Op. cit., pp.64-65.

long time to receive my heart's desire, our good Father General asked to see me, examined my case, reflected about my vocation, prayed, gathered his counsel, and together they unanimously declared that God's will for me is that I should follow this way of abjection, poverty and humble manual work; the life of the worker from Nazareth that He himself has showed me for such a long time. Yesterday I received this news from my good and excellent Father General. I am greatly touched by all of his goodness towards me. .But where I really needed obedience was before the decision had been made. I had promised God that I would do whatever my reverend Father would tell me to do after having examined my vocation, and to do whatever my confessor told me. If they had told me, "You will make your solemn vows in ten days" and then, "you will then be ordained," I would have joyfully obeyed certain that I was doing the will of God. Since I was only seeking the will of God, and my superiors also were only seeking the same, it was impossible that God would not make known his Will."[57]

Charles immediately wrote to Fr. Huvelin with ideas for his future, and Fr. Huvelin waited until January 27th to write back:

"Yes, just as you do, I see you in the Middle East… I prefer Capharnaum or Nazareth, or some Franciscan house – not in their house – but only living in the shadow of their community – asking only spiritual support of them and living in poverty… on their doorstep… That is what I see, my dear friend.

Do not think about gathering other souls to join you, and especially do not give them any rule of life. Simply live your life and, if others come, share that life together, without any rules. Let me be very clear on this point."

---

[57] Charles de Foucauld, "Cette chère dernière place" Lettres à mes frères de la Trappe, Paris, Cerf, 1991,pp. 150-151.

He was able to find a religious house to live next to but would he be able to live without creating a rule of life for himself and for others?

On February 14th, he made vows of perpetual chastity and poverty into the hands of his confessor, Trappist Fr. Robert Lescand, promising to never have in his possession or for his use anything more than a poor worker might have. On February 17th this former Trappist set sail for the Holy Land, accepting the Trappists' offer to pay his fare on a cargo ship. He followed Fr. Huvelin's advice in a letter dated January 27th where he said, "accept with simplicity what is offered to you."

TO IMITATE JESUS OF NAZARETH

When he arrived in Nazareth, Charles de Foucauld thought he had finally found the place where he would be able to imitate the life of Jesus. He met a Franciscan who recognized him and directed him to the Poor Clare Monastery, letting them know who he was. The Poor Clares received him because of that recommendation although he was unaware of it. With his old blue shirt, he thought that he had passed for a homeless man. He took up residence in the shadow of this convent:

> *I am living in a little house within the enclosure of the sisters whose happy servant I am; I am all alone there It's a delightful hermitage, completely alone... I get up when my guardian angel awakens me and pray until the Angelus; When the Angelus sounds, I go to the Franciscan monastery, where a grotto marks the place of the Holy Family's house; I stay there until about 6 a.m. saying my rosary and attending the Masses It is tremendously sweet to gaze on the same rock walls that Jesus gazed upon and touched with his hands.*
>
> *At 6 a.m. I return to the sister's convent. I prepare the sacristy and chapel for Mass and pray until Mass at 7. I serve Mass... Then I do whatever they ask of me.*
>
> *If they have an errand for me to do, I do it, but that is quite rare; in general, I spend my day doing little things in my room near the sacristy: at 5 p.m. I prepare everything for benediction of the Blessed Sacrament on the days that this takes place*

Then I remain in the chapel until 7:30 p.m. Then I return to my hermitage where I read until 9. When I hear the bell that rings at 9 I know it is time for evening prayer; I pray and then go to sleep. I read during my meals which I take alone. The only people I see are my confessor, every week for confession, and the sisters on the rare occasions that they ask something of me."58

This period in Nazareth and in which Charles de Foucauld began calling himself Brother Charles is certainly the one which least resembled the life of Jesus at Nazareth. It is much more like what he began to refer to in Rome as the "life of Jesus in the Desert." In Rome he had, for the first time distinguished between the "three lives of Jesus": "Jesus in Nazareth," "Jesus in the Desert," and "Jesus' public life." Each person was called to imitate Jesus in one of these aspects of his life. For him, it was the life of Nazareth.

A great deal of importance has been paid to these distinctions of his, certainly too much. They did not last a long time since in 1901 he decided that there were four periods in the life of Jesus, each corresponding to different religious orders. It is difficult to see the difference between the life of Nazareth and that of the Desert as his descriptions of Jesus' life depended upon what Charles is living at the time.

We need to look at the word "Imitation"[59] which should be used rather sparingly. We must first look at the literary genre so that the

---

[58] René Bazin, *Charles de Foucauld, explorateur au Maroc, ermite au Sahara*, Paris, Plon, 1921, Letter to Raymond de Blic April 24, 1897, pp. 151-152.

[59] Chatelard, "Limitation de," *Jesus Caritas*, no. 267, 3 trimestre, 1997, p. 46.

reader does not become discouraged by the language that can seem naïve and obsolete, nor by a style that can seem overly dependent upon his will. It is important to recover the profound inspiration and original intuition that is hidden behind certain expressions, especially when Charles speaks of imitating Jesus.

In a document dated 1927 Bishop Nouet spoke of his visit to Charles de Foucauld's house in Tamanrasset: "When he had no visitors, he would go out in front of his hermitage just before nightfall." This little detail led the bishop to reflect, "One can be reminded of Jesus of Nazareth who, having finished his workday, would sit and rest awhile on a rock overlooking the village. Fr. de Foucauld who so loved the life of Nazareth did as the divine workman did."

This vignette illustrates my point well. We can ask ourselves who is the proposed model, Jesus or Charles de Foucauld? Who imitates whom? As we read Charles' meditations, we can ask ourselves this question frequently.

For Example, concerning poverty Charles has Jesus speaking:

"Remember my words and examples concerning poverty born in a grotto, raised in a poor house, the child of poor parents, living in poverty from the work of my hands until I began to spend my entire days preaching, then accepting to live from almsgiving, but only accepting what I needed to live, as poorly as when I was a worker." [60]

---

[60] Charles de Foucauld, *Crier l'Évangile*, Paris, Nouvelle Cité, 1982, p.120.

From where did he take this notion if not from the resolution that he made a year earlier as a vow?

Where did he ever get the idea that Jesus lived in a strict cloister with Mary and Joseph, having as little contact with neighbors as possible? Was it not what he expressed in the Rule that he was in the process of writing in Nazareth in 1899?

Where did he learn that Jesus worked eight hours a day? It seems that it was only as he was preparing to live in Tamanrasset in 1905 that he realized that Jesus had lived without cloister, without any religious habit, had few possessions and did not engage in extensive almsgiving. At that point he still saw Jesus living, not in the village but on its outskirts. Did he have to wait until the last year of his life when he moved closer to people in order to realize that Jesus lived in the heart of the village and not just near it?

Brother Charles successively constructed models for himself according to his need for one, according to what he felt called to live at the various stages of his life. He did not always escape an imaginative reconstruction. His way of expressing his desire to be like Jesus is like the story of the little boy who wanted to imitate Jesus in every thing but who refused to hang up his jacket when he came home from school.

His brother, in order to tease him, would say, "You know, Jesus always hung up his jacket when his mother told him to."[61]

---

[61] Hervé Linard de Guertechin, "Suivre Jésus est-ce l'imiter?", *Revue théologique de Louvain*, 15, 1984, 5-27, p. 16, note 21.

In the conclusion to the resolutions written in his Notebook on July 22, 1905, after having repeated seven times "as Jesus at Nazareth," he wrote, "Pray as Jesus did, as often as Jesus did... be faithful to the breviary and the rosary each day." We half expect him tosay, "As Jesus at Nazareth." He escaped the pitfall here but in other places we find such anachronisms.

It is impossible to paint a static picture of Jesus from the descriptions that his disciple provides us with. Has anyone succeeded in making an accurate, historical portrait of that Galilean? What does it matter that the "Modèle Unique" (A meditative, scriptural image of Jesus) resembles more what Brother Charles wished to be? The model is the same, but the portraits are different, sometimes complementary, and sometimes contradictory. Is this not how each one welcomes the Word of God in their daily life? It can never be norm that one dreams of attaining. Rather it is a life that one enters into little by little, reading the Word of God and welcoming it anew each day. Life forces us to read it differently than the day before, gives it each day a different shade of meaning that we overlooked the day before.

Suffering brings out an aspect that we were never aware of in the same way and love sheds a new light on images that left us unmoved.

Brother Charles did not have any illusions about this. But his faith suggested a kind of naïveté that was the fruit of the simple gift of spiritual childhood that helped him to move beyond pure rational thinking. He was simply trying, for his own benefit, to put his faith into words. Sometimes he was just trying to persuade himself that the choices that he was making had a solid foundation. For example, the day that he realized that ordination to the priesthood would resolve his dilemma he imagined Jesus clothed with the dignity of priesthood, while remaining humble: "I must <u>situate humility as Our Lord did, practice it as he did, and following his example, practice it in the priesthood</u>."[62] It is his way of lending legitimacy to his desires and justifying his practical decisions. His motivations matter little to us. It is up to us to use his writings as they were intended, "too some good for others" or to understand that they were often for his own personal use.

When Brother Charles speaks of doing some good for others he connected it with the vocabulary of imitation. He felt it was a duty to also be a good example for others to imitate. As much as he speaks about doing good by simply being who one is called to be, he cannot refrain from doing certain things purely as an example to them. In his mind this is what Jesus did. He explains certain actions of Jesus as being done only to set for us an example.

---

[62] LAH, 26.04.1900

Extract from the "Counsels" for the brothers and sisters of the Sacred Heart

Article 1. Imitation of Our Beloved Lord Jesus – The brothers and sisters of the Sacred Heart will make it their rule to ask, in all things, what Jesus would think, say and do in their place, and to do it. They will make continual efforts to become more and more like Our Lord Jesus, taking as their model his life in Nazareth which contains examples for every situation. The measure of imitation is the measure of love. – "If someone wishes to serve me, they should follow me," "I have given you the example so that as I have done, you also should do," "The disciple is not above the Master, but is perfect if he resembles his Master," "I am the light of the world. Whoever follows me does not walking the dark, but will have the light of life." – For the glory of God and the good of souls, the brothers and sisters will work to develop in others the imitation of Our Lord Jesus- Christ.

The Sacred Heart drawn by St Charles

THE TEMPTATIONS OF NAZARETH

It is necessary to linger a while in Nazareth [63] with Charles to understand his own humanity's depth. He had enclosed himself in such a special situation, one for which he was so little suited. No wonder that he was constantly in turmoil, tempted to be elsewhere, doing something else. In looking at the period of Nazareth through this somewhat negative lens of temptation and his desire to escape, we catch a glimpse of the depth of his character and of the role that Fr. Huvelin played as a spiritual director, one of the great spiritual directors of the nineteenth century.

The first Temptation: to beg funds for the Poor Clares

The first temptation came from his innate need to do something useful after eight months of inactivity, living in the Poor Clare's garden. He was led to understand that the sisters, especially those in Jerusalem, needed funds. As early as the end of his retreat of 1897 he came up with the idea to look for funds for them. Since Fr. Huvelin had recommended that he should obey the sisters no matter what they

---

[63] Fr. Philippe Thiriez, *Charles de Foucauld à Nazareth, 1897-1900*. This book can be obtained from the Monastery of the Poor Clares – Poste Restante – 16000 Nazareth, Israel, tel: 06.57.19.77.

asked of him, he felt that it was his duty to undertake this project. He shared his idea with Fr. Huvelin who answered him on December 9th:

> *"Oh, don't leave Nazareth. I see too many dangers for your soul in a life of traveling and soliciting funds... Devote yourself to living in that quiet little place where Our Lord worked. Do everything in your power to stay in Nazareth: you will be more useful to the mothers (the Poor Clares) in this way!"*

This first temptation lasted until the end of 1897. In his New Year's greeting of January 1st 1898, Fr. Huvelin insisted, "May your new year begin and end in the obscurity of Nazareth, in work and contemplation. It is my deepest wish for the sake of your soul." And, having received a letter from Brother Charles he wrote again on January 15th, "Yes, I deeply believe that the will of God for you is that you stay in Nazareth. It is there that Our Lord will allow to blossom that which he wishes to see grow in you."

The second temptation: return to the Trappists

The peace did not last long. In a very detailed review of life on January 15th Brother Charles admitted that he was often tormented by pride. It had nothing to do with pride but was again a symptom of his need to do something and be useful. It was the beginning of the second temptation:

> *I must tell you that lately, especially on the anniversaries of joining the Trappists and my profession (Feb 2), I am often tormented by thoughts of pride: Sometimes find myself thinking that I could have done some good by staying with the Trappists: two more years and I would have been the Superior: with the grace of God I could have done some good in that little monastery of Akbès that is so well situated for the sanctification of the monks and the local people... I see clearly that this is a temptation: I do not have the qualities to be a Superior,*

neither the authority, the firmness, the clear judgment, nor the experience, the knowledge, the insight, nor anything at all... and the spirit of the Trappists, as it is actually lived, does not correspond to my own call in my shack, at the foot of the tabernacle in the Poor Clares' chapel, in my days of work and my nights of prayer, I have everything that I looked for and desired these past eight years. It is so clear that the Good Lord prepared this place for me, that this is what my eyes were looking for... It is that imitation of Our Lord in obscurity and poverty... But the temptation is there."[64]

He saw clearly that this was a temptation, one of the devil's tricks. This life should have been enough for him as it was for Jesus. But there was nothing to do. The temptation was there. Should he stop reading the theology books that seem to encourage such temptation to greatness? Should he read the philosophy books with the danger to ambition that they represented? Should he discontinue using the breviary? So many false problems and useless questions. The real issue was his need to do something. The Poor Clares in Jerusalem would like him to come there. Should he go and help them?

He could not see that his real problem was one of needing to do something.

February 1st he wrote another letter to Fr. Huvelin telling him how happy he was to be in Nazareth, to read and meditate, but that the desire to return to the Trappist Monastery was still there: "As I told you before, sometimes I think about returning to the Monastery... something is pushing me in that direction: I do not know if it is grace or temptation." For him the desire to leave Nazareth was not one of taking back that which had been given but a desire to go further in

---

[64] LAH, 16.01.1898

giving himself: "I do not want to take anything back, but to try to hold on to everything and to move further ahead."

But instead, the isolation in which he was living became something negative: "it seems to me that it is better to work for the benefit of others, even if that is a struggle, than to be satisfied and by myself..."

The fact of feeling comfortable where he was turned against him: "I am too comfortable here." The temptation was to see his life as becoming bourgeois and therefore to see that working elsewhere as much as possible in the service of God would be better. These "vague thoughts" are typical of temptation. He continued in the following letter:

> *"When I consider what are the best ways in which I could serve God the most, it seems to me that 1- I could do no better than returning to the Trappists ; 2- that God would have me be in a Trappist Monastery of the Middle East, 3- that I should yet remain a while in this dear and blessed Nazareth…"*

Without waiting for answers to his first two letters, Brother Charles wrote a third, longer letter on March 3rd, repeating what he had already written in case the other two letters had been lost. In order to communicate what he felt, he spoke not only of something that was pushing him, "something outside of himself" (he uses that expression three times in the post script of his letter of Feb. 1) but also "as if, from the outside, his soul had been hooked, someone had used a crook over it the hook had awakened in him the desire to work for the Good Lord."

He felt that in his happiness in being in Nazareth that he was useless, without giving anything back. He used the words "do", "work" and "results" ten times in just one page. On February 1st he hit on the keyword, "efficaciousness." Let's take a look at the three or four rough spots or holes that allowed the hook to take hold:

1. the desire to work for the good of souls.

2. The desire to be ordained a priest. This was the first time that this came up if we disregard what he wrote in 1896 at the Armenian Massacre around Akbès. Why priesthood? To participate in the work of God;

3. the prize was to be found in the sureness of monastic obedience, the best defense against all temptation.

4. the mission of the Trappists, the work they accomplish for the world; in Muslim countries one cannot work more effectively than by founding Trappist Monasteries, "centers of light and virtue." On March 3[rd,] he wrote to Fr. Huvelin, "It is up to you to see if this impulse, these hooks are a temptation or a call."

In his response of February 19th, Fr. Huvelin had only mentioned the last of these:

> *"Yes, live, live (to say long-live Nazareth would sound strange) Nazareth in everything Yes, remain there We will see about the Trappists later on – maybe– but you need to be nourished in Nazareth for a while yet. The Master gives you all that you need to build yourself up there! I have nothing to say about the Trappists for the moment… in any event, that idea would have to prove itself and become more solid. Believe me when I say that what you are experiencing in Nazareth is the sign that God wishes you to remain there."*

Brother Charles had been so sure that Fr. Huvelin would be delighted to see him return to the Trappists that he had allowed himself to become quite elated by his desires. When he read Fr. Huvelin's letter his balloon burst. He immediately wrote back, March 8th:

> *"I was like a boat with all of its sails unfurled: when I read your letter the sails came down and now the boat is still in the water without any apparent movement and ready to remain so indefinitely."*

Abandonment became concrete, within human reach, and the Will of God showed itself through another person.

> *"It is so sweet to recognize the will of God I have 'commended my soul into your hands,' do with it as you see best for the Consolation of the Heart of Jesus… it is all that I desire, absolutely all."*

But then he added, "My only sadness is to see so many souls that are being lost or are suffering." We can hear him saying that he is not doing anything for them. The battle was nearly over. The questions that he asked at the end of his letter seem small in comparison.

We can do a parallel reading of this period with his *Considerations sur les fêtes de lane* that he wrote between November 1, 1897 and November 1, 1898. During the month of March, month of temptation, and until Easter every meditation, whether on the words of Jesus or his actions, end with the same resolution underlined several times: "Obey your Director."

From March 14th-21st, without ever leaving his shack in Nazareth, Brother Charles followed Jesus to Ephraim, to the banks of the Jordan River, where he had withdrawn to pray. During this retreat Brother

Charles wrote long reflections about obedience to one's Spiritual Director.[65]

This temptation lasted for more than six months during 1898. It is still there on June 17th, the Feast of the Sacred Heart.[66] On June 24th he wrote his thoughts about Nazareth[67], and again on June 29th:

> *"Be careful about temptations to ambition, no matter what form they take or through whom they come; do not let yourself be led away from imitation of the hidden life of Jesus, away from sharing that life, through any consideration, counsel, thought or person: Only one person has the right to command in my name, your Director: 'He who hears him, hears me.'"*[68]

Throughout these six months Charles wanted to remain the little brother of Jesus, present in the heart of the Holy Family of Nazareth or at his feet during his public ministry but was constantly fighting temptation: that of ambition or exaltation, that of running away from the present moment instead of doing that which was the most perfect at every moment:

> *"Imagine for a moment the frightful ingratitude of desiring anything other than the life of Nazareth, so complete and so perfect that Jesus deigns to bestow upon you with his own hand. You will be tempted away from this life that is so beautiful and so divine; the greater the gift that Jesus has given you, the more the devil is jealous, the more he will use the most subtle or violent tricks to take you away from it; he will whisper in your ear and in the ears of others; but 'no*

---

[65] Charles de Foucauld, *Crier l'Evangile*, Paris, Nouvelle Cité, 1982, pp. 84-89.

[66] Charles de Foucauld, *Considérations sur les fêtes de l'Année*, Paris, Nouvelle Cité, 1987, pp. 440 sq.

[67] Op. cit., p. 455.

[68] Op. cit., p.464.

one is tempted beyond their strength'; Do not be surprised by temptations, nor surprised by contradictions: the more your life is like Jesus' life, the less the world will understand."[69]

In his meditations on the Gospel from that same day he wrote two more pages trying to convince himself that he must live only in the present moment and not in the future.[70]

---

[69] Op. cit., p 465.

[70] Charles de Foucauld, *La Bonté de Dieu*, Montrouge, Nouvelle Cité, 1996, p.174.

From a letter to Father Huvelin – Pentecost 1899

My beloved Father,

This little retreat has come to an end. The Good Lord is pleased to have it end in a profound peace…. facta est tranquillitas magna…. This phrase sums up the state of my soul since my last letter…. I admire God's goodness and that invincible and never flagging patience with which He leads me by the hand, repairs my faults and brings all to a good end… This retreat which began in such temptation, with such troubles, in anguish, ends in overwhelming peace…

The Third Temptation: The Jerusalem Dangers

By July 1898, we find Brother Charles battling what we might call the temptation of Jerusalem or of visibility. If we look at it from that angle, it is fairly clear that Nazareth and Jerusalem are at opposite ends of the spectrum. This temptation came from outside. The Abbess of the Poor Clare community of Jerusalem, Mother Elisabeth, was curious about this phenomenon of holiness that she had heard so much about. She arranged for Charles to come to Jerusalem. She had almost managed to do so the preceding October but in his letter dated September 16, 1897 Fr. Huvelin was very negative about such a proposition: "You should remain in obscurity, in your simple place, practicing obedience, burying yourself in this life. I am very clear about this, my child, and you can say that I said so." When he heard that Brother Charles had not gone, his letter from October 16th reflects how glad he was about the decision: "I am so happy that you have remained in Nazareth; I was quite worried about you being in Jerusalem." What would be cause for worry? We shall see how right his intuitions were.

On July 8th the sisters asked Brother Charles to take a letter to Jerusalem. He didn't see that it was a pretext. An ailing Fr. Huvelin learned about it through two letters that have been lost. He wrote from his sick bed on August 26th, not hiding his preference for Nazareth but accepting what was presented as an urgent situation. Mother Elisabeth suggested that Brother Charles remain in Jerusalem and gather a group of companions there. His absence from Nazareth lasted only 4 days.

A second visit to Jerusalem of five months began on September 11th. As Mother Elisabeth had rekindled the idea of gathering companions, he began thinking about a young man he had known in Akbès who had left the Trappists. At the end of September Brother Charles traveled to Alexandretta to find him but he had no desire to leave his mother to follow Brother Charles. Back in Jerusalem he wrote to Fr. Huvelin on October 4th and shared his disappointment. Fr. Huvelin responded on October 15th, "I am <u>so happy</u> that this man did not wish to follow you I am deeply convinced of this Remain in the shadows of the monastery of Jerusalem, just as you did in Nazareth – in the <u>shadows</u>. That is the right word. I was so glad when you were there where God had led you."

But at the same time Brother Charles was in the process of writing a new rule[71] of life, having rediscovered his desire to found a community. On October 15th, in fewer than ten sentences, he wrote to Fr. Huvelin about starting a new community following the rule of St. Benedict. But by the end of October, he had already abandoned St. Benedict for the less structured rule of St. Augustine: "A few souls gathered together to live the life of Nazareth a little family, a little monastic home, very small and simple; nothing Benedictine about it."[72]

Fr. Huvelin saw Jerusalem as a risk to the life of obscurity and hiddenness, to living in the "shadows" about which he had spoken, and he was correct to be worried about it. The danger was Mother Elisabeth. She was not like the abbess of Nazareth who had developed a great sisterly affection for Brother Charles. She was a mother. He did not simply see her as "a beautiful soul" but as a saint with the "cool head and fiery heart" of Theresa of Avila. Had she not been the founder of five monasteries, including Périgueux, Paray-le-Monial, Nazareth and Jerusalem? With her unstoppable character, she wanted to start dressing him as a religious instead of in his blue work shirt, see him ordained a priest and then make him chaplain to the Poor Clares. She wanted to see him gather a group of followers and felt that, at the age of forty, it was time to leave the life of Nazareth and begin the work of evangelization. We know this through a letter written to Fr. Huvelin where he recounts

---

[71] "I began writing this rule twenty months ago when I went to Armenia to bring that child back…" LAH, 20.04.1900.

[72] LAH, 22.10.98

the dialogue between "she" and "I" and "she" and "I," an almost word for word account of their conversations.[73]

The early monks had warned their disciples against two things that could threaten their desert life: "The monks should be as wary of women and of bishops as they are of the devil."[74] In the abbess the two threats were combined in one person.[75] It was only in January of 1899 that Brother Charles received a tardy response from Fr. Huvelin about this latest project. He had not known what to answer. The letter is dated December 30th. As with the idea of returning to the Trappists he gave a clear answer. "Stay where you are!... Keep to your solitude, silence and total obscurity Stay put, stay where you are. Tell the Mother Abbess. Wait for the sign that will surely come." Such was Fr.

Huvelin's answer to the "perplexing" avalanche of propositions that Brother Charles had made. By the time Brother Charles received the answer, however, he had already written two Rules, one provisional for the time that he would still be alone and the other for when there would be several brothers with him. They were dated January 6th, Feast of the Epiphany.

At the same time he invented a vow of "cloister" prohibiting any travel for the service of others. He saw this as the only solution to the Poor Clare's requests for his services. They had already asked him to

---

[73] LAH, 15.10.1898.

[74] Cassien, Inst. XI, 18.

[75] The bishops traveled throughout the desert looking for priests among the monks.

travel to Nazareth with a Dominican priest but this had been postponed.[76]

On February 20, 1899 Brother Charles returned to Nazareth with the resolution to remain there. Who made this decision? As soon as he heard the news Fr. Huvelin rushed to send his approval, writing on March 13th:

> *"I am so glad to see you back in Nazareth! With my whole heart I tell you to remain in Nazareth! I was so sad when you left this dear nesting place, and it is with joy that I tell you to return."*

When we read Brother Charles's letter of February 8th to Fr. Huvelin, written before he left Jerusalem, one can think that it was simply time for him to return:

> *"I am so miserable! If you knew how backward I am, how lazy, prideful, uncharitable, self-centered, unfocused and distracted I am by the smallest things!... To be in such a state at my age after having received so many graces; I am confused! ... I would so like to begin loving the Good Lord, but, alas, I am so far from doing so! Speak to me often, dearest father, because your words dome so much good and are so important to the poor thing that I am. I am nothing, powerless, incapable, really like a small child, but, sadly, not through innocence nor humility, but rather because I have so little wisdom and my soul is so ill-formed. I have not grown but have remained childish and spiritless."*

At this point he began a sixty-day retreat from March 19th to May 21st, Pentecost Sunday. In the middle of this retreat "*in angustiis,* a time of temptations and trouble," he received a note from Fr. Huvelin dated

---

[76] Cf. LAH, 22.01.1899.

April 27th. It was a response to a lost letter that must have been full of still more projects for the future:

> *"Do not torment yourself with phantoms, strange visions, the "for how longs"… do not worry yourself. Stay where you are. Stay! Nazareth has been good for you, has filled you with good things. I can find nothing better to tell you."*

The retreat ended peacefully with Brother Charles having made a resolution to remain in Nazareth with "the worker, the Son of Mary" and in thanksgiving:

> *"I cannot thank the Lord enough for having inspired me to make this retreat, to have led me back to Nazareth, for having directed me in such an incomparable way through you, beloved father, through the difficulties of this past winter, to have so gently led me back to my vocation through you, and pulled me away from the dangers of Jerusalem… I will not go to Jerusalem again… I will try to learn the lesson of this experience to cling more faithfully and with greater thanksgiving to my blessed vocation."*

This letter to Fr. Huvelin dated Pentecost Monday, May 22nd, marked the end of the storm provoked by Jerusalem and all that this city represented as opposed to Nazareth.

It was the end of all his projects. There was no longer any question about foundations, priesthood, becoming the spiritual director for the Poor Clares, or wearing a religious habit. This state of peace lasted quite a while but unfortunately all of the letters from this period were lost. It is only through the letters written by Fr. Huvelin that we have an insight into what Brother Charles must have written at that time. These letters give us the heart of Fr. Huvelin's message to Brother Charles. On July 18th he wrote:

> *"Yes, the silence, yes, the silence of Nazareth – one is well placed in Nazareth to live a life of obedience in silence – and what is the good to be done? One accomplishes good by who one is, much more than by what one says… one accomplishes the good in being of God and for God! Yes, stability… yes, esto ibi! Remain there, gather moss there and allow the graces of God to penetrate, grow and become firmly rooted in the soul. Keep away from agitation and perpetual new beginnings. Indeed, we are always just starting but at least in the same direction and in the same way."*

And on August 14th:

> *"What a joy that you are really at your place, that you are happy, that you finally have the life that you desired, the life of Nazareth, inside as well as outside."*

And October 26th:

> *"Be aware of how sinful you are and humble yourself. Lose yourself in your trust in God. The love of God exists despite all of our misery. Do not worry about aridity. Wait for God's time."*

This peace lasted until February 1900. In a letter from the 8th of that month Brother Charles again thanked Fr. Huvelin: "It is you who defended me from the temptation of instability, returning to the Trappists, of priesthood. I would have succumbed without your help!" The remainder of his letter gives us a good insight into his relationship with his director concerning the theme of "temptation", even in the little things:

> *"I want to tell you about two temptations that have distracted me for quite a while: I always chase them away as being temptations but they always come back. I am telling you about it to free myself of them because I know that as soon as I tell you about a temptation, I am delivered from it: I am often tempted*

to read a bit of Saint Thomas… and also to try to procure the small Bible edited by Fr. Vigouroux in several languages to read it."

These two new temptations are therefore theology and exegesis!

The fourth temptation: a better place elsewhere

This fourth temptation is situated within a short interval in March of 1900. It sprang from a desire to run away from "this sweet nest at the Poor Clares" where he felt so cozy and protected. He had no shortage of reasons for wanting to leave the Poor Clares.

"I see how very artificial my situation is here: I am completely useless to the Poor Clares; the work I do is not work at all (he was painting icons); I serve and yet do nothing; worst of all, they know who I am and that makes my situation artificial and undefined."77

On top of that, his relationship with the Abbess had become problematic. She wanted to hold on to him and paid him special attention. There had been little mention of this until recently as the letters he spoke of were left out of what was published. But it is one of the major reasons that he wanted to get away from there. It's a classic temptation: to believe that a change will solve all of his problems. To live Nazareth more fully he must go elsewhere. This *elsewhere* presented itself under two forms, each quite different from the other.

His first idea was to go to a nearby village, not a town, where he could live alone and unrecognized. [78]He thought that he could "settle

---

[77] LAH, 26.03.900

[78] He had already imagined something like living in a cave at the top of the Mount of the Olives near Jerusalem, 08.02 1899.

in some field in the hills overlooking Nazareth <u>to carry the cross of Jesus</u> in <u>poverty and work</u>."[79] But these ideas were vague and episodic as he expressed in a letter dated March 22:

> *"More than once I have thought about leaving here and finding a place where I am really, and will remain, unknown But I would only do this in order to more deeply bury myself in a life of obscurity, a humble and abject life of prayer and work ("I've been thinking about asking the Sisters of St. Vincent de Paul to let me work in one of their hospitals in the Holy Land to help care for the sick)80 …"*

His second idea seems to have sprung from his idea about working in a hospital. He had heard about a poor, elderly widow whose son had wanted to enter a monastery but had remained with her to care for her. He allowed himself to become caught up in this situation, which indeed could have had a simple solution not requiring his intervention, as events would later show. But this never occurred to him. He saw it as a call and a means of escaping his present situation. His salary could be used to care for the widow. In a letter dated March 26th he laid out his plan in detail, showing how it was his vocation and the will of God for him. He only had to wait for Fr. Huvelin's permission. But another event cut short this latest idea which only lasted a week.

However, it is interesting to listen to his reasoning about this new way of imagining his future. This strange plan was totally opposed to his previous idea of living off in the hills around Nazareth.

---

[79] LAH, 26.04.1900
[80] LAH, 26.03.1900

His life as a nurse or orderly in a hospital would be completely different. He would lose everything, but it would be on behalf of someone. Had he never thought about doing something <u>for someone else</u> until now? Certainly, he had done everything for Jesu sand now he justified this plan by saying that he would not be doing it for the widow, nor for her son, but only for Jesus. He really seemed to have little love for these people who were merely a pretext for him. But let us not be taken in by this type of reasoning that may seem stripped of meaning for those who are not initiated. To present a truth of faith, for example, "Whatever you do to the least of these little ones you do to me," one would have to deny the evidence we find in the acts and feelings.

Let us rather observe the chink in the ideological wall of the monastic enclosure that allowed love to flood Charles's heart. He always described his motivations with these keywords, "Do unto others what you would have them do to you… Whatever you do for one of these little ones you do to me." With such reasoning he was sure of himself and sure that his logic was sound and therefore from God. But he had to wait for the confirmation of obedience. And, as he wrote, he was convincing himself as well. He does not see any subtle temptation that would make him abandon his course. He saw his idea as being in such conformity with the Gospel, so supernatural, so full of faith, hope and charity, that it appeared to him as "the priceless treasure." He had no hesitation about it: this life of work in service of the sick would resolve all of his problems.

One can ask what happened to the values that he attributed to the life of Nazareth, of contemplation, silence and solitude? He was already defending this new form of contemplative life. It may have been a passing and untried vision, but a prophetic vision nonetheless that opened new horizons. It would only be partially realized in his own life, but those who would later enter this way of Nazareth in his footsteps can find in it a confirmation of their choice and a word of encouragement.

> *"I don't think that prayer will suffer and anyway it is not the sweetness of prayer that one must seek but faithfulness to His Will… He will give me the grace to see him in the sick poor and be aware of his presence in the midst of working in the hospital."*

Yes, the hours of prayer would be fewer, but they would be richer: "I spend so much time in prayer now, but so poorly." At any rate, "My soul will gain so much through such a change." The Poor Clares would also gain: "My departure [...] from them will do them more good than all the time I spent there in fasting and prayer."

His argument was so convincing that he thought that Fr. Huvelin could only approve of it. Unfortunately, he did not have the time to respond before another temptation followed quickly and made Brother Charles forget all about this project. We can be sorry that he missed this occasion, this "priceless treasure," for still another mirage. He would never have another opportunity to work for a salary, not only in serving others, but working in a hospital.

The Fifth Temptation: The triumph of "willfulness" under the appearance of "devotion" and "piety."

Who would dare to use such words if they were not the very words of Fr. Huvelin himself in a letter dated May 20, 1900?

This was the most serious of all the temptations. It had multiple consequences as Brother Charles had reached such a level of hyperactive creativity that he was ready to listen to any voice to get out of

Nazareth. This could have been a good thing but it also could have led him away from his vocation of imitating the life of Jesus in Nazareth.

This last temptation, or illusion, played itself out over a shorter period than those of returning to the Trappists or of going to Jerusalem. But it could have changed the course of his life, taking him not only far from the original idea, but in the opposite direction. It can be presented by summarizing two months of feverish correspondence with his spiritual director and four months of his life when he believed he was "taking care of God's work." His letters with Fr. Huvelin during this period take up fifty pages in *Lettres à l'abbé Huvelin*. In the longest of these letters, he says that he was only sharing part of his thinking on the subject. The "hook" was able to take hold this time through his zeal and his daredevil character that was always ready to attempt to do what no one else had succeeded at. He wrote: "Several times they have tried to obtain title to the blessed and holy site (the Mount of the Beatitudes) without success I feel impelled as I have never been before (that would mean more than when he explored Morocco, more than when he entered the Trappists or left again, more than for founding a new Order) to acquire this holy place and establish a tabernacle. It is such a good thing that I have no doubt that it is not the will of God." Again, he interpreted his own desires as being the will of God.

To purchase the site, he had to find the money to pay for it, quickly and secretly. He would go through Fr. Huvelin to ask for this money first from his sister, then his cousins, Catherine de Flaking and Marie de Bondy, and then other persons if necessary. Once the site would be bought, it would have to be given to another congregation. But which one? He saw eight possibilities. And if no one wanted to own it this would not be a sign that he should give up his idea. No, it would mean that he would have to settle there himself and therefore he should become a priest and therefore he should prepare for ordination. He would have to find another solution for the widow and her son, taking up alms for her. He wrote all of this on March 30th. Fr. Huvelin only dealt with the financial side of the question and could not see how to reconcile this new idea with the one before it, that of working as a nurse for the sake of the widow. When the family wisely refused to give him the necessary funds, Fr. Huvelin thought that Brother Charles would give up the idea and did not write further, not knowing what else to say about the whole business. But the humble Brother Charles did not take his family's refusal as a sign from God to abandon the project. To the contrary, he interpreted it to mean that he must find other means, poorer and more difficult means, and should go begging. The family was so horrified by the thought of this that they ended up giving him the money as a loan.

He spent the night of April 25th in prayer before the Blessed Sacrament in order to make a formal discernment. He wrote out his thinking in the form of a draft of a letter that was 20 pages once printed.[81] On the 26th he copied the essential parts in a six-page letter to Fr. Huvelin: "My vocation is to imitate as perfectly as possible the hidden life of Our Lord at Nazareth…" He had to find a way to make the purchase of the Mount of the Beatitudes fit into his vocation. He therefore had to demonstrate how all of the virtues of the hidden life could be better practiced on that mountain rather than in Nazareth at the Poor Clares. His letter continued:

---

[81] Charles de Foucauld, *Crier l'Évangile*, Paris, Nouvelle Cité, 1982, pp. 131-149.

> *"I will give you a shortened version so as not to tire you: As I look at prayer, the love of truth, abjection, penance, courage, obedience to God, the total desire to seek God's goodness, recollection, the love of God, imitation of Our Lord and hope, I come to the conclusion that I would be better off there than here…"*

Brother Charles seems not to realize that this new way of imitating Jesus as a priest, doing good works and administering the sacraments, has nothing to do with the life of Nazareth. It just shows how easy it is to justify one's choices by saying that it is "Nazareth." But it doesn't matter. The Holy Spirit was pushing him towards something as yet unknown.

So for Brother Charles, now the Mount of Beatitudes had become the best place to live his ideal of "Nazareth." Priesthood was no longer simply a necessary means for having the Eucharist. He now saw the dignity of this special character as a better way of living humility as Jesus lived it:

> *"It seems to me that, all other things being equal, to practice the abjection and poverty of Our Lord as a religious or priest, is a more beneficial way of living these same virtues than as a layperson."*[82]

So now his "monastic dream" was becoming a unified whole out of an amalgamation of these two "necessary" elements (Priesthood and the Mount of the Beatitudes). In the letter from April 26th to Fr. Huvelin he referred to the rule that he had written for the *Hermits of the Sacred Heart*. He had begun work on it twenty months before, finished writing it a year before, made two hand-written copies of it and not spoken about it to his spiritual director since that time. Now he said that he would be

---

[82] Op. cit., p.134.

sending him a résumé of this rule. Then it would be up to Fr. Huvelin to tell him how to put it into practice.

Upon receiving this letter Fr. Huvelin did not hesitate to give Brother Charles a definitive and categorical "no" in a letter dated May 4th: "Stay in Nazareth with God as my witness I cannot tell you anything else." He might not have been against the idea of working in a hospital or of ordination. To the contrary, he had hoped that Brother Charles would be a priest. But the boiling, exuberant and impatient tone of the letter convinced him that these projects were not of the Spirit. Fr. Huvelin was so ill that he was unable to hold a pen and he was very worried about Brother Charles. He would worry even more when he received the next two letters as matters were speeding out of control. He received three letters the same day and could only observe, "It's as though a cannonball has been shot. Who can stop it?"

It seems that in his naïve zeal the hermit of Nazareth had been taken in by a financial scam. It was not the first time, but this time it was with other peoples' money. He decided that it was impossible to back off from it and, in his usual way of wanting to finish what he had started, he wanted to see the business through even at the risk of losing his way. He refused to see the risk and found himself unable to get out of something, all of his own making, in which he found himself embroiled. It would be a costly affair for his family and, indirectly, completely changed his life. It was a "decisive moment" that set him on a new course. Many have written and tried to justify Brother Charles' behavior at this time. But there was no excuse except for the thing that was pushing him, making him both blind and deaf to all else.

Not receiving an answer from Fr. Huvelin, he decided that it must have been because of a quarantine that had been imposed on the ships.

But Fr. Huvelin had not written, feeling that he had already said all that he had to say. His letter from May 4th arrived on the 17th and his explicit "no" did not impress Brother Charles in the least. He answered the same day:

> *"You should have received my others letters since you wrote on May 4th...They may have changed your mind about this Your "no" arrived too late, not because of my actions but because of unforeseen events..."*

He then added:

> *"Nazareth has not ceased to be a delight and a place close to my heart. But as I told you, I think that temporarily, for a little while, Jesus calls me to serve him on the Mount of the Beatitudes."*

He was totally unable to see that the whole business had been an extortion scheme. Raymond de Blic had finally given in to his brother-in law, the hermit's, repeated requests for money. He was never reimbursed, and it took years to clear up a very complicated matter.

In a letter dated May 20th, Fr. Huvelin no longer bothered with the financial question but maintained his refusal for the rest:

> *"I find your projects frightening I would rather see you purchase the Mount of the Beatitudes if you absolutely cannot do otherwise and that you then give it to the Franciscans and then let go of it I do not think that this idea of being a priest-hermit comes from God."*

In the meantime, Brother Charles continued making his own plans, hesitating whether he should be ordained in Paris or in Jerusalem.

As we have already seen, Fr. Huvelin's opinion was clear even though we can also read a sort of reluctant acceptance. He wrote:

> *"If, however, you feel an irresistible urge, take your Rule and throw yourself at the feet of the Patriarch of Jerusalem and ask him for light. I, my child, I don't have any with regards to this matter. I can only see objections and I fear there is a willfulness on your part, hidden under your devotion and your piety... The more I think about it, the more I see it that way Your cousin is also quite worried, as am I."*

As Brother Charles felt the urge to be irresistible, on June 22 he went to see Bishop Piavi, the Latin Rite Patriarch of Jerusalem, and presented his rule for the *Hermits of the Sacred Heart*. We know that he was quickly put out. He must have mentioned it to Fr. Huvelin in a letter that has been lost. On July 25th Fr. Huvelin answered the missing letter, delighted at the failure:

> *"It is exactly what I hoped would happen I saw Jesus' hand in the whole thing I no longer knew what to tell you. Your thoughts and ideas had become so confused."*

He was glad to think that Brother Charles was back in Nazareth. Unfortunately, Brother Charles did not receive that letter as he had already left Nazareth. He wrote to Fr. Huvelin from Jaffa announcing that he was on his way to Paris. He excused himself in the same letter for not doing as Fr. Huvelin had asked him.

Brother Charles did not take his failure with the Patriarch as a sign that he should renounce his idea of ordination, seemingly so contrary to his vocation. Although he was invited to try to see the Patriarch again he did not. Rather he saw in the refusal a sign that he should make the request in France to the Bishop of Montmartre. Finally, he was very happy that the Patriarch had refused him as he had been thinking for some time that he should go to France to "console" his sister and brother-in-law. It was a "new obligation" all the more that, in order to obtain the money, he had practically promised them that he would become a priest and it would be an occasion to come to visit them at that time.

When would it be possible? He didn't know. We don't know why he arrived in Jerusalem at the end of July and sailed for France on August 8th. We do know that the Poor Clares of Jerusalem had entrusted him with an errand in Rome.

Something that Fr. Huvelin said in a letter dated July 25th can conclude this chapter on the Temptations:

> *"I knew that the Master would lead everything. It was not a question of realizing an idea but of seeking the Will of God, allowing it to unfold gently and peacefully in abjection and littleness, that of Jesus, beginning in Bethlehem and throughout the long incubation period of Nazareth."*

On July 21st Brother Charles wrote to his sister. He used a phrase that was even more significant, and he probably didn't realize how much it applied to all that he had just lived. "Do not attach much importance to the events of this life, nor to material things; these are merely dreams dreamed during a night at an inn."[83] What remained of these successive dreams? Just one desire. He expressed it clearly to his sister in a letter dated July 10th. "My desire to receive Holy Orders is a strong as ever, but all the rest is in doubt."[84] Did he really have to pass by such a lengthy and difficult detour in order to come to desire and ask for that which he had so obstinately refused for so many years?

---

[83] René Bazin, Charles de Foucauld Explorateur au Maroc, Ermite au Sahara, Paris,

[84] Op.cit., pp.178-179.

As soon as he arrived in Paris on August 17th he went to see Fr. Huvelin. Fr. Huvelin described the visit to Marie de Bondy:

> *"He had dinner, spent the night, took breakfast with me and then left for Notre Dame des Neiges and on to Rome. He was oddly dressed, seemed very tired and pre-occupied. I think he is ill. But he was very loving. He is very holy. He wants to be a priest. I told him how to go about it. He had very little money, too little, so I gave him some. He knew very well what I thought as I had sent him a telegram, but something even stronger is pushing him. Has a director ever really directed anyone? But I have no need to guide him. I can only admire and love him."*

They also spoke about where he would go after ordination. Why not Algeria? Fr. Huvelin preferred the Holy Land, Nazareth or elsewhere, as a priest living near a monastery, but not on the Mount of the Beatitudes. From Rome he wrote to Marie de Bondy on September 3rd:

> *"Following Fr. Huvelin's advice I am here in Rome for a little while before going to Notre Dame des Neiges to complete the preparations for ordination that I am beginning here… Father thinks that I should receive the sacrament of Holy Orders and offer the Divine Sacrifice despite my unworthiness… To be ordained in my current situation was, humanly speaking, difficult to arrange. The Good Lord has paved the way for me through the intermediary of the Abbot of Notre Dame des Neiges: he has offered me hospitality until my ordination, will see to preparing me for it himself, and arranged everything with the bishop… I cannot say how grateful I am to him*
>
> *There is no longer any question about me living on the Mount of the Beatitudes. I think I already wrote to you about that. Father thinks that after ordination*

I should return to Nazareth and continue living as a priest in the shadow of the Monastery of St. Clare that had so well received me before."[85]

His departure from Nazareth and return to France cannot be seen as acts of obedience. And Fr. Huvelin was not fooled by it. "He knew very well what I thought as I had sent him a telegram". It doesn't matter. Fr. Huvelin tried to look beyond the present situation and enter into a logic that he did not understand. In that same inexplicable logic Brother Charles wrote a year later: "I returned to France on the advice of my confessor so as to receive Holy Orders."[86] He really believed what he was writing in saying this since Fr. Huvelin approved of it later. Chronology doesn't matter so much in autobiographical accounts of vocation! "The Will of God will be accomplished: whether through men or despite them, God will do for us what is best," he had written to his sister on July 10th. And so the "dreams dreamed during a night at an inn" came to an end. A new step was beginning in his life. He did not analyze what had happened. Was he even aware of that truth that Fr. Huvelin recognized in him, "Something even stronger is pushing him? I can only admire and love him."

Is it possible to decipher what this "something" was that had pushed him to understand such a complicated itinerary over the previous three years? It is not easy to do. But within these different temptations there are some elements that might shed some light on his journey.

---

[85] Achives de la Postulation, BACF, no. 142, april 2001, p.10.

[86] LHC, 14.08.1901.

The Trappists, Jerusalem, the Hospital and the Mount of the Beatitudes all represent an <u>elsewhere</u> as opposed to the <u>stability and rootedness of Nazareth, the burying of the grain of wheat in the ground.</u>

To do, to create, to work towards something, to serve, to be useful and to be more efficacious are all good and legitimate desires. But they were all contrary to the sovereign efficaciousness of Nazareth in apparent uselessness. This efficaciousness is continually reaffirmed in both the letters of Fr. Huvelin and those of Brother Charles.

Beggar, Trappist superior, hospital worker, priest at a Shrine and founder of an Order are not bad things in themselves. But for the hermit of Nazareth, they were all <u>dreams</u> that kept him from fully living the <u>present situation</u> in which he found himself, and that present situation could alone reveal the values of the life of Nazareth. Constant new beginnings are not reconcilable with the <u>continuity</u> that Nazareth demands.

Jerusalem, Priesthood, and the Mount of the Beatitudes would have placed Brother Charles in a situation of visibility that would have been contrary to the hidden life that defined the life of Nazareth.

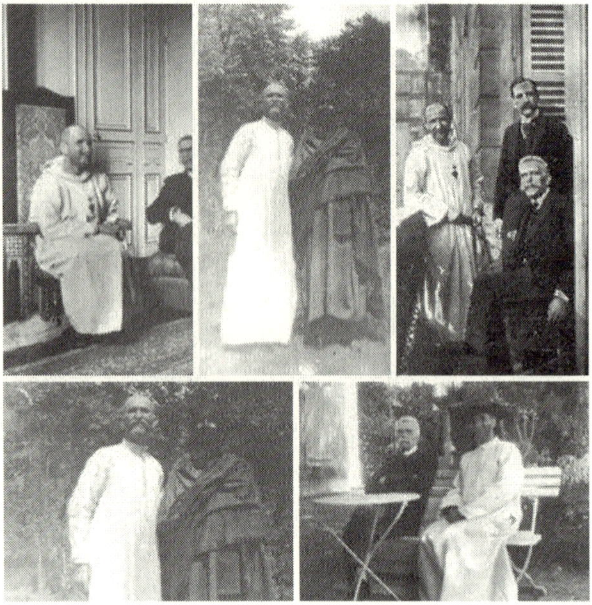

A Change of Direction

We find Charles de Foucauld in Rome where he spent the month of September 1900. Fr. Huvelin, worried about where his "errand for the Poor Clares" might lead, wrote to him on September 13th:

> *"Get yourself out of this business and these negotiations as quickly as possible. Do not get yourself involved in these money matters – I forbid it, my dear friend. Do not even mention anything to your cousin about borrowing money. Go to Barbary and give your sister the joy of seeing you. It would be so much better than having her go to Notre Dame des Neiges to visit you!… And now concerning the priesthood! Keep focused on it. Keep your eyes fixed on that – as soon as you will have finished with your errand for the Abbess of Jerusalem"*

When he finished his errand for the Poor Clares he left Rome for Bourgogne where he spent several days with his sister, meeting his nephews and nieces. He arrived at Notre Dame des Neiges on September 29th.

He continued his life as a hermit in a little room that they gave him in the northwest corner of the monastery and went back to using his Trappist name of brother Marie Albéric during his stay with them. He was ordained sub-deacon on December 22nd at Viviers. At the end of his retreat prior to this ordination[87] he wrote out his discernment process, as was his habit, in which he confirmed the direction of his life as he had seen it with Fr. Huvelin.

He wrote that he was a poor workman dedicated to the imitation of the hidden life of Jesus. He likened his duties of being a sub-deacon- the edification of souls and service at the holy Altar – to that of the wife who must love and obey her husband, care for the children and the home. But the question arose for him as to where he should carry out these duties:

> *"For the time being in Viviers. Afterwards, wherever my director judges to be the right place Wherever the Spouse calls me… Wherever he will be glorified by my presence… Wherever I can do the most good for souls… Wherever I can establish the hermits of the Sacred Heart, first of all in the Holy Land because it is Jesus' own country and because it is from there that we have received "every grace."*[88]

As we have already seen, this foundation, which had preoccupied him since 1893, began to take shape at the end of 1898. He had written the rule during 1899 and made two copies of it.

Where could he live out this Rule? With others maybe? At the end of 1900 he was again thinking about it. Since Fr. Huvelin had excluded the Mount of the Beatitudes as a possibility, what about Nazareth? But another idea presented itself in the form of Bethany, that cherished

---

[87] Charles de Foucauld, *Seul avec Dieu*, Paris, Nouvelle Cité, 1975; *cf.* retreats made at Notre Dame des Neiges before ordinations, pp. 21-83.

[88] *Op. cit.*, pp21-22.

place, "one of the holiest and most abandoned places." [89]Why Bethany? He had written in his meditations:

> *"Blessed are you among all other places on earth, Oh Bethany of my heart. You alone gave to the Savior of mankind what every other place refused."*

He had imagined it as "the only little corner where the Creator was well received: Bethany, the place of friendship, where people knew how to keep Jesus company."

However, it was no longer only these sentimental thoughts that held his imagination. A new thought took hold: Bethany was "the most abandoned of the holy sites." But how could he think in terms of abandoned places without thinking of other places that were far more abandoned than any place in the Holy Land? We see the first mention of this idea in the publication *l'Afrique Saharienne*. On August 22, 1905 he wrote to Fr. Caron in these terms:

> *"In my youth I traveled throughout Algeria and Morocco: Morocco – as large as France with 10 million inhabitants and no priest in the interior of the country, and the Algerian Sahara – seven or eight times larger than France and much more populated than they used to think with only a dozen or so missionaries. No other people seemed more abandoned than these."* [90]

He was seeing this land as a place where there was no one to love Jesus with the greatest love and where the *Hermits of the Sacred Heart* could do so much good.

---

[89] *Op. cit.*, p22.

[90] Letter to Fr Caron *XXXV Lettres inédites du Père de Foucauld* au chanoine Caron), Paris, Bonne Presse,1947, pp.13-14.

It was only a dream for another day but it reveals that a new thought was taking shape in the mind of the former explorer. He had gone to Akbès in 1890 in order to "go far away from all that he loved in a non-Christian land." He still wanted to find a place where he could have "cloister, silence, distance from all worldly affairs, a completely contemplative life." But he wanted to live in a "Mission Country." Did the countryside of Ardèche remind him of the Sahara? Did his chance meeting with a missionary Bishop in the streets of Rome reawaken his love for Africa? As the year drew to a close was he reminded of that Christmas of 1883 spent in the zaouïa of Tisint in southern Morocco where he experienced the first stirrings of religious sentiment? Maybe his recent meeting with Brother Augustine, a former zouave, at Notre Dame des Neiges rekindled some old memories from the Sahara. They realized that they had been in some of the same places in southern Algeria in 1881. And couldn't this novice become the first member of the hermits of the Sacred Heart?

Br. Augustine was also something of a character. He had wanted to enter the Monastery on January 1, 1900 believing it to be the first day of the new century. But he got lost in a snowstorm and only arrived on the 2nd. When Brother Charles went to Notre Dame de Neiges in August to ask the Abbot about staying there to prepare for ordination they met in the hallway. Br. Augustine wanted to speak with him and congratulate him on his book, *Reconnaissance au Maroc* which he had read or heard about. Brother Charles responded humbly, "Ah yes, that will do me a lot of good on the day of judgment." It was a spontaneous reaction that we will come back to later.

A new idea

During April and May 1901, a new idea presented itself to Brother Charles and he wrote to Fr. Huvelin about it, although the letters have been lost. We do, however, have Fr. Huvelin's answers to these letters and these give us some insight into what Charles must have written. He must have written at least twice in April. Fr.

Huvelin's letter of May 7th was a response and reminded us of letters written to Nazareth:

> *"Stay at Notre Dame des Neiges, my child, under the wing of Father Abbot. I stress this point in response to what you wrote in your last letter. This year of formation spent in the shadows of this blessed convent does not seem to be a lost year, far from it… you will be working for Nazareth there, filling the vessel where souls can come to drink – you will be strengthening the hands that others can lean on. It is not a renouncement of your mission to the Holy Land. It is a way of preparing yourself for it. Wait a year but don't give up your idea of going to the Middle East. It seems that the Good Lord is keeping this vision before your eyes – that of this Mission, of a family gathered around the Divine Master. To do this, my child, it takes maturity and preparation. This year will give you that. Whatever you do there you will be doing for the Holy Land that attracts you, that fixes your mind's eye and directs your heart."*

This is a significant letter since it is the first time that Fr. Huvelin recognized Brother Charles as having a double Mission: on the one hand to live in the Holy Land, and on the other hand to gather a family around Jesus in Nazareth. As they have always written about him, we cannot say that Fr. Huvelin was always against this idea. We can see that Fr. Huvelin's thinking also evolved.

From a letter dated May 29th we can see that Brother Charles must have made a still further proposition.

> *"Recollect yourself for the Mission that you seem to have received. Do not follow any other idea, not the one that you speak of, unless an almost invincible urge pushes you... A Priori, my dear child, I do not see indications for it. You will see after your ordination! There is a kind of active preparation there that I would not frown upon unless the urge that you feel is invincible – but apriori – I prefer to see you in the recollection of the cloister."*

This "other idea" could only have been the Sahara, where he could go to actively prepare himself for this double mission instead of remaining for a year at Notre Dame des Neiges. According to Fr. Huvelin, this is not an idea to follow unless "the urge that you feel is invincible."

By the beginning of June it seems that this "invincible urge" had taken root. More than ever he felt sent and sent for a special Mission. We have seen how many times he felt called to a mission while he was in Nazareth and each time he came up short. Was this another one of his illusions? Or was it a serious call?

This new idea came in April and brought with it a new way of reading the Scriptures. His reading was not limited to the Gospels. He also read the Acts of the Apostles, the Epistles of St. Paul and the Apocalypse. If we read through his numerous writings from this time and the notes and phrases that he copied from the Gospels, we already see the significance of the choice he made. Furthermore, from this selection he then made an even further selection. Some of the most characteristic phrases are:

> *" 'I have come to bring fire on the earth' – 'To save that which was lost – 'To bring light to those in darkness and the shadow of death – 'It is not the healthy who need a doctor but the sick – 'Go throughout the world and preach the*

Gospel to every creature' – *'As my Father has sent me, so I send you'* – *'I send you as sheep among wolves'.*"91

The hermits become brothers

This "new idea" also led Brother Charles to reread the Rule written in1898 for the Hermits of the Sacred Heart. In doing so he replaced the word "hermits" with "little brothers." This modification meant that he had to correct all of the passages that no longer corresponded to this new way of thinking in both copies of the Rule. His erasures, and insertion of "little brothers" for "hermits," are clearly visible on the original manuscript. This work must have kept him busy for some time since he was also writing French text of the Constitutions as well as translating these into Latin. We end up with the 40 paragraphs of the Constitutions in parallel with the 40 chapters of the Rule. He began each chapter of the Rule with a series of quotes from the Gospel. And he used the "Modèle Unique" that he had written in Nazareth as an introduction to the entire work.

The changes were much more than mere changes of titles. He necessarily had to make other corrections and sometimes glued little pieces of paper over certain sentences or half-pages. Other words now surfaced and took importance, in particular the word "universal." So we end up with "universal love" and "universal brother and friend." These same expressions appeared in letters that he wrote in the following months to speak of his new plans. We should note that the expression "universal brotherhood" was practically limited to this period at Notre Dame des Neiges in 1901 and the first few months at Beni Abbès (the

---

[91] Charles de Foucauld, *Seul avec Dieu*, Paris, Nouvelle Cité, 1975, pp. 77-78.

beginning of 1902). The most striking change of 1901 was that from "hermits" to "little brothers." Gone is the language of hermit and of being alone. From this point on he used the word "brothers" to speak of his future companions and "fraternity" to speak of their house. In the first Rule their house was to be called a "Nazareth" and in the *Rule for the Hermits of the Sacred Heart* it was a hermitage. Could he have better expressed his new sense of mission? The former Trappist wanted to remain a monk but the former hermit now wants to be a brother, brother of Jesus and brother to others. It is as though concern for others had become a concrete part of his project and would from this point on, be a motivating factor in his choices. In order to "be with Jesus," it was no longer enough to be "alone with him," to go "far from" everything in order to be with him alone. He had to do what was most pleasing to him.

And what Jesus wanted most was the salvation of all humankind.[92]

Is this new? No. We can find it in what he wrote to Henri Duveyrier on April 24, 1890, three months after he entered the Trappists:

> *"Each person is a child of the God who loves each one infinitely. It is therefore impossible to love, to desire to love God, without loving people The last commandment of Our Lord Jesus Christ just hours before his death was, 'My*

---

[92] The last quote, #74, from "edifying passages taken from pious authors" that he copied at Notre Dame des Neiges is from St. John Chrysostome: "The best way to be with Christ is to do his will. And above all else, Christ wants you to procure the salvation of your brothers." Homily on St. Matthew. He wrote this quote at the beginning of the Notebook that he began when he arrived in Beni Abbès.

little children, love one another; by this they will know that you are my disciples, if you love one another."93

The difference was that he wrote that from the cloister, thinking of those who were outside. And he thought mostly of distancing himself from them, forgetting them, thinking of them as if only a dream, as he wrote to Fr. Jerome from Nazareth on May 19, 1898:

> *"His will for you is that you should concern yourself only with Him. I do not mean in not loving others but loving them ardently for his sake. But for the moment, for the next several years forget them completely, see them as though they were merely a dream and, I cannot repeat it often enough, live as though you were alone with God alone in all the universe. Look upon people, all people, as not even existing."94*

His way of loving them and working for their salvation had been to give up seeing them, to not allow himself to write to them and to offer this sacrifice for their salvation.

From this point on, "others" were no longer an abstract concept but people towards whom he must go. Therefore, he had to leave where he was in order to be "close" to them, to enter into "contact" with them and develop close relationships with them. It was the appearance of a new vocabulary, to become their brother and friend.

It was no longer enough to love from a distance, to isolate himself in order to better love Jesus, in order to save souls more effectively. It was a complete and total change but hedid not yet clearly grasped it.

---

[93] René Pottier, *Un prince saharien méconnu Henri Duveyrier*, Paris, Plon, 1938, p.226.
[94] Charles de Foucauld, *"Cette chère dernière place" Lettres à mes frères de la Trappe*, Paris, Cerf, 1991, p.183.

Although Brother Charles accepted this new direction for his life, he could not imagine all of the consequences that it would entail. It took him the rest of his life to understand and see where it would lead him. Let us not forget that he still carried with him his Rule for the hermits and not be surprised that they no longer worked after a period of time.

Where to go?

He was ordained a priest in Viviers on June 9, 1901. Shortly afterward, in his written reflections about where he should go to establish the little brothers of the Sacred Heart he wrote:

> *"Not where there are, humanly speaking, the best chances for having novices and canonical authorizations, money, land or support. No, but to the place that is most perfect in itself, most perfect according to the words of Jesus, most perfect according to the Gospel, most perfect according to the Holy Spirit. There, where Jesus would go: to the "sheep that is the most lost." To Jesus' "brother" who is "the illest," to the most forgotten, to those who have the fewest shepherds, to those who 'sit in the deepest darkness."*[95]

It is full of quotation marks as the quotes came to his mind one after the other and led him to conclude that he must go first to Morocco.

It is the first time that he mentioned Morocco by name but is surely what he had in mind when he alluded to the Sahara the first time. He knew that there was no question about being able to enter Morocco but he thought of going as close as possible in the bordering region. Several days later he wondered about where he really had to go first.

---

[95] Charles de Foucauld, *Seul avec Dieu*, Paris, Nouvelle Cité, 1975, pp79-80.

"Would it not be better to go first to the Holy Land?" Going there first would help him to prepare himself. The answer was "no." It was clear and definitive. "It is necessary to go to the <u>land</u> that is not the holiest but to the <u>souls</u> who are in the greatest need." He compared people on the one hand to land on the other and expressed himself in terms of "lack" and "extreme drought" as compared to "great abundance." He then confirmed his thinking with the last quote as proof for him of the will of God:

> *"When you give a lunch or dinner, do not invite your friends, nor your brothers, nor your family, nor your rich neighbors… when you give a feast invite, rather, the poor, the crippled, the lame, the blind."*[96]

On April 8, 1905 he employed the same words to explain to Fr. Caron why he had changed directions:

> *"My last retreats before diaconate and priesthood showed me that my vocation to the life of Nazareth should not be lived in the beloved Holy Land, but among those souls which are the sickest, the sheep who are the most abandoned. This divine banquet of which I am the minister must not be presented to brothers, family and wealthy neighbors but to the lame, the blind and to the souls who lack priests the most."*

The change of destination was really a change of orientation just as when, in his youth, he decided to go to Morocco rather than to the Middle East.

Over the previous months Charles de Foucauld thought of this country that he was the first to have explored in different terms. When

---

[96] *Op. cit.*, p.83.

he had been 24 years old, he had had the audacity to plan an expedition and the courage to see it to its end, risking his life to do so. Should he not have the same audacity now out of love for Jesus rather than for the sake of his pleasure? Was this not a duty? Realizing that he tended to want to do things that no one else had ever done, he asked himself if it was not willfulness or pride on his part. He answered his question by quoting St. Theresa of Avila:

> *"No, because the effect, in this life, will not be honor or consolation but many crosses and humiliations: 'Either you will be looked down upon or I will be glorified. Either way you win."* 97

The only question left is *quando*. He contents himself by quoting Luke 1:39:

> *" 'Mary rose and went in haste.' When one is full of Jesus, one is full of love... Therefore, when I am reasonably ready and when, by the inspiration of the Holy Spirit, my director tells me: 'go'"* 98

As early as June 22, 1901 Charles de Foucauld wrote, with the Abbot, to Bishop Livinhac, superior general of the White Fathers, asking where he might go and to whom he should address himself.[99]

Where should he settle? This started a correspondence with Henri de Castries in which he addressed himself as to a dear friend, eight years older

---

[97] *Op. cit.*, p.83.

[98] *Op.cit.* p. 81.

[99] Charles de Foucauld, *"Cette chère dernière place" Lettres à mes frères de la Trappe*, Paris, Cerf, 1991, p.242.

than himself. In fact, he did not know him very well.[100] June 23, 1901 he wrote:

> "Where should I attempt this little foundation? someplace where onecan enter into relationship with the Moroccans some lonely oasis between Aïn Sefra and Touat No one knows this region better than you: And so I am writing to you and asking that you, who have always been so good to me, would please have the kindness to indicate where, in the far southern region, would seem best for a first little settlement."

We have already mentioned the about-face of Fr. Huvelin who wrote on June 26th, "I have reconciled myself to your idea about Africa which is so neglected." However, he still preferred to see him stay longer at Notre Dame des Neiges to prepare himself more thoroughly. On July 15th he wrote again:

> "Let yourself be led by this urge that keeps pushing you, my dear child. It is not what I would have dreamed of for you, but I believe that it is what God is telling you, since you are no longer able to stay at the Monastery. Go wherever the Master calls — I bless your intentions and the projects that will bring you closer to him while accomplishing his work on earth. I will do whatever I can to help you."

The same day, Dom Martin sent an official request on behalf of the newly ordained priest to Bishop Livinhac: "In my whole life I have never seen a man who lives in such a state of holiness."[101] Charles de

---

[100] Drawing from documents from the Archives (National, Historical Service of the Armed Forces, FondsPrivés) Michel de Surimain paralleled the movements of Henri de Castries and Charles de Foucauld andconcluded that the two men only met after 1884. BACF, # 131, July 1998, p.7.

[101] Charles de Foucauld, "Cette chère dernière place"Lettres à mes frères de la Trappe, Paris, Cerf, 1991, p.243

Foucauld clearly explained his intentions and plans in this letter. But in other letters we discover his deeper motivations.

It was not the nostalgia of the desert nor love for the land that was at the origin of this "invincible movement" that continued to push him to the point that he could not even pray without thinking of Morocco. He wrote to Henri de Castries on June 23rd:

> *"There are several among us who cannot recite the Pater without being painfully aware of the vast country of Morocco where so many souls live without "sanctifying God, being part of his kingdom, accomplishing his will nor knowing the divine bread of the Holy Eucharist."*

Did he not have a duty born of gratefulness towards those who had allowed him to "see something greater and truer than worldly preoccupations?"[102] He wrote to Fr.

Jerome on July 17th:

> *"It is not possible for me to practice the precept of brotherly love without consecrating my life to doing as much good as possible for these brothers of Jesus who lack everything since they lack Jesus. If I were in the place of these poor people who know nothing of the source of our joy in this world nor of our hope in the next, and if I were to become aware of my sad state, oh how I would wish that they would do everything in their power to pull me from it! What I would want for myself I must do for others: "Do unto others as you would have them do unto you."*

Several monks, happy to participate in the mission of someone they considered to be a saint, were mobilized to see to the material

---

[102] LHC, 08.07.1901

preparations: a portable altar, a tabernacle, wooden candlesticks, crates for shipping books, vestments, kitchen utensils. Marie de Bondy had been busy since September 1900 making a chasuble and other liturgical accessories. Catherine de Flavigny gave the chalice, ciborium, monstrance and many books.[103]

By August 22nd Charles had not received a response. He learned that Bishop Bazin had been named to head the apostolic vicariate and wrote to him. He wrote insistently, adding a further argument that he felt adequate to convince him of the urgency of his request:

> *"The memory of my companions who died without a priest during the expeditions against Bou Amama of which I was a part twenty years ago, strongly urges me to leave for the Sahara as soon as you will have accorded me the necessary faculties, and not a day later."*[104]

Upon receiving Charles de Foucauld's letters Bishop Guérin,[105] who had just been named apostolic prefect of the Sahara, wrote to ask for further information. As he had to leave Algiers to take up his new post in Ghardaïa in the South, he sent a telegram to NotreDame des Neiges asking Brother Charles to come quickly so that they could speak. Contrary to what René Bazin[106] wrote, he left without baggage and was ready to leave on the next boat. The baggage was left at Notre

---

[103] Charles de Foucauld, *Carnet de Beni Abbès*, Paris, Nouvelle Cité, 1993, p.66.

[104] Charles de Foucauld, *Correspondances sahariennes*, Paris, Cerf, 1998, p.27.

[105] The Apostolic Vicariat of the Sahara and the Sudan had just been divided into two, creating the Apostolic Prefecture of Ghardaïa. Charles de Foucauld later learned that a young White Father, Fr. Charles Guérin, just 29 years old, had just been named to head that Apostolic Prefecture. He would answer the two letters that Charles de Foucauld wrote introducing himself.

[106] *Op. cit.*, p.191.

Dame des Neiges to be sent on later if he remained in Algiers. Having written quite a few letters vaguely informing people of his departure, he took the train from the Bastide St. Laurent for Marseilles on Friday, September 6th. He stayed with the Blessed Sacrament Fathers there, made a day pilgrimage to the Saint Baume on the 8th, and left at noon on the 9th for Algiers.

Fr. Huvelin wrote to Bishop Guérin on August 25th as persuasively as possible:

> *"You will find in him heroic devotion, unlimited endurance, a vocation for the Muslim world, patient, humble and obedient zeal, enthusiasm and a spirit of penance without any severity or blame towards others."*

He wrote again a week later, on September 1st, in response to another question from Bishop Guérin: "How many times the same objections have come to my mind! I always come back to my experience with him and the test of time." He had written previously:

> *"His vocation has always drawn him towards the Muslim world. His time in Algeria, trip through the Moroccan interior, and years spent in Palestine have prepared him, toughened him for this mission. I saw this vocation come. I have seen how it has quieted him, made him more humble, more simple, more obedient [...] In my soul and in my conscience, I believe that it comes from God [...] There is nothing bizarre nor extraordinary. Just an irresistible force that pushes him, a hardened instrument for difficult work [...] Firmness of spirit, a desire to love and give himself to the very end, whatever the consequences – never any discouragement, never – a bit rash in his younger days but that has softened so much! Let him come and you will see!"*[107]

---

[107] *Op. cit.*, p.194

Fr. Henri who had become the Prior of Notre Dame de Staouéli wrote to Bishop Guerin on September 5th, sending along a letter he had received from Brother Charles in July:

> *"He is the most beautiful soul that I know; incredibly generous, he has taken giant steps in the way of sacrifice and has an insatiable desire to devote himself to working for the redemption of the infidels. He is capable of anything, except maybe of following overly rigid directives all that I can add is that, after having lived in close contact with him for six months, I was always deeply edified by his heroic virtue. He has within him the stuff of several saints. His very presence is an eloquent sermon, and despite the uniqueness of the mission to which he feels called, you can rest assured about welcoming him into your apostolic prefecture."* 108

Bishop Bonnet of Viviers also wrote on the same day:

> *"Fr. de Foucauld is a former brilliant military officer who gave up his career to give himself more completely to God in the priesthood. I ordained him; he is my subject and I consider it a great gift for my diocese to have had for a time a priest of his merit and character He has acquired here a reputation as a saint and our clergy take as a great grace, the joy of spending a few moments with him."* 109

Preceded by these recommendations and a reputation of holiness at which he would have been aghast if he had known of it, our Brother Charles set off, trusting in Providence to smooth the way ahead.

---

[108] Charles de Foucauld, *"Cette chère dernière place" Lettres à mes frères de la Trappe*, Paris, Cerf, 1991, p.246

[109] *Op.cit.*, p 245.

From distance to the nearness

We rejoin Charles de Foucauld on the boat from Marseilles to Algiers on September 9, 1901. He had again taken to using the name Charles of Jesus, and was dressed in a white tunic with the heart and cross emblazoned across his chest. Let us take note of a few points of his life's journey. It had been fifteen years since he rediscovered faith and he would live another fifteen years. This Mediterranean Sea that he was crossing was the geographic center of his life. To understand the meaning of this trip we can compare it to a similar trip that took him from Marseilles to Akbès in 1890.

The first trip took him as far away from everything as possible. The fifteen years that we have just examined all move in this direction: to distance himself as much as possible, to forget his past, his name, his work, his friendships, leaving behind family, house, belongings and his country. All of that was to follow his Lord, to be alone with him, to seek him where he could be found, that is, in the last place, and to offer him the greatest sacrifice possible. By renouncing the presence of the one who had given him everything, who had led him to God, he had offered the greatest possible sacrifice to his Beloved Lord. No other austerity could ever come close to the sacrifice that this separation represented. The joy of living with Jesus and for Jesus alone, the devotion to his presence and the seeking after intimacy with Jesus would never remove the suffering of this separation. It remained like an open wound for nearly twenty years.

He had the kind of personality that always went beyond the possible, seeking perfection in everything, employing all the strength of his will to reach the unattainable and infinite. He spent fifteen years of his life steadily moving in this direction: always to the lowest place, the furthest point, to be as close as possible, as intimately joined as possible to Jesus' heart. We have already mentioned his tendency to be excessive in what he undertook. Fr. Huvelin had warned him of the danger of seeking his perfection:

> *"You need to be warned against this constant inner movement towards that which has no end. It brings restlessness and keeps you from ever remaining in one place – this type of movement is only possible for those who are not given to excess."* 110

His tendency to excess had quickly led him to value as absolute some somewhat negative elements: renouncement, separation, contempt for the created order and a negation of the self to the point of self-destruction and self-hatred. This is what the trip to Akbès represented. It took him far away from everything to renounce everything.

As he made the trip to Algiers the movement was different, even opposite.

In the early years of his faith-life his desire to "be with Jesus" was characterized by phrases like; to go far away, to distance himself from

---

[110] *LAH*, 02.08.1896

everything that had been a part of his life, to separate himself, to leave himself behind to be alone with Jesus. In 1901 he realized that "to be with Jesus" meant "to do what Jesus wanted him to do." From that moment he wanted to move towards others to be <u>close</u> to them.

We can compare the "far away" of the first trip to this "towards" of the second: towards a country, towards someone. He was no longer preoccupied with leaving someone or something but with going "towards" someone. The "distancing" of the first was the opposite of the "closeness" of the second. From this point forward, he felt sent by Jesus to move towards others and no longer distance himself from them. Since he wanted to draw close to those who are "far away" people have often confused this going "far away" with the distancing of his earlier years. It seems that the movement in these two directions, that of distancing and that of drawing near, divides the last thirty years of his life into two parts.

As a consequence, we see that he began using new expressions. It was no longer question of simply being "alone with Jesus" but "to be with others," and therefore to draw progressively closer to them, to enter into a relationship with them, to have contacts with them and to create bonds with them. If we take an overview of the last fifteen years of his life, we see how this proximity grew and was expressed in the places that he chose to live as well as the type of houses that he built. It represents a new type of burying himself. It was no longer what he had imagined at Nazareth but meant burying himself among a people.

It meant that he wanted to be "small and accessible" to others. It meant a relationship of *brother* and not as a father to those with whom he drew near. It meant studying a language, allowing bonds of friendship and affection to tie him to a people. The keyword in all of this is "relationship." He sought to develop and nurture relationships with growing numbers of people, just as he had done and never ceased doing with Jesus.

We can see it as soon as his boat lands in Algiers. Fr. Henri, his Trappist friend, was there and Fr. Guérin, the young White Father who was assuming the role of Bishop and superior, and who would later become a friend. The proof of this can be found in the letters published in *Correspondances sahariennes*.[111] He also met a comrade from St Cyr, Commandant Lacroix of the Arab Bureau of Affaires, who was his best resource in deciding on where to settle as well as in helping him to obtain the necessary authorizations. As this comrade was there with his wife and daughter, Brother Charles was obliged to take a little plunge into the everyday life in the world. Madame Lacroix fixed special dishes for the one they supposed would have nothing else to eat once he left for the Sahara.

On the way to Beni Abbès he stopped at Aïn Sefra to thank the generals who had permitted him to settle there. He stayed with them. They gave him one of their mules to make the last part of the journey. He who had wanted to arrive in Beni Abbès on foot as a poor pilgrim traveled instead with an escort, and the Arab soldiers who welcomed him, kissed his burnous (his outer cloak). So many situations that the Rule had not made provisions for!

Some of the soldiers and several of the officers from Beni Abbès, would become his friends. Laperrine, who would later visit him and convince him to move further south, as well as some of the officers

---

[111] Charles de Foucauld, *Correspondances sahariennes*, Paris. Cerf, 1998.

stationed in the Hoggar and some of the Tuareg, also became his friends. These relationships played an essential role in his life not only because of the influence he had in others' lives but also because they influenced his life. In one way or another, all of these people contributed to humanizing this man who had such a tendency to try to be superhuman through excessive asceticism. [112]This process of humanization is part of the meaning of the Incarnation of God who became closer and closer to us through the humanity of Jesus.

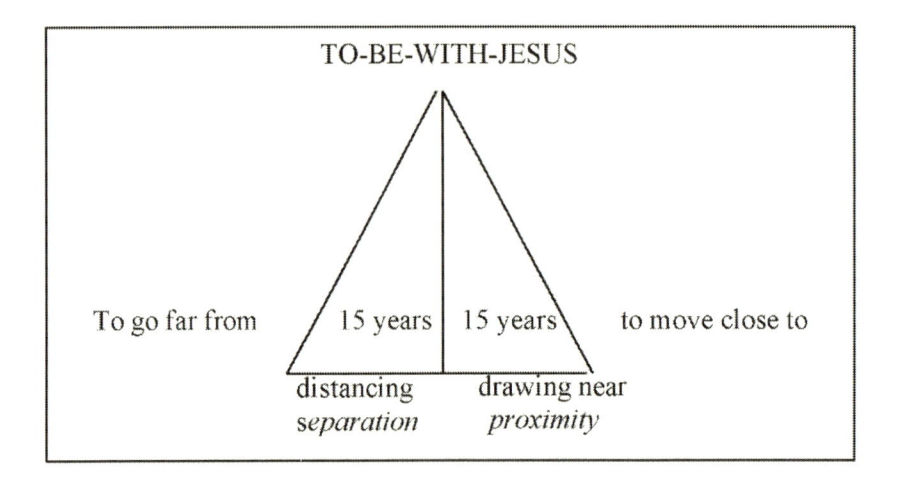

```
                    TO-BE-WITH-JESUS

                           /\
                          /  \
                         /    \
                        /      \
                       /        \
      To go far from  / 15 years | 15 years \  to move close to
                     /_____|_____\
                      distancing   drawing near
                      separation    proximity
```

This diagram outlines what we have just said about the life of Brother Charles. It can also help us to understand his devotion to the Eucharist. He essentially saw the Eucharist as the sacrament of Presence, in line with the teaching of the Council of Trent. This was the basis of a way of "being with." From the moment of his conversion at St Augustine's Church, from the moment of his conversion he entered

---

[112] Letter of Dom Martin to Bishop Guérin in *"Cette chère dernière place" Lettres à mes frères de la Trappe*, Paris, Cerf, 1991, p.281: "The intensity that he imposes upon himself seems so superhuman that I am afraid that he will drive his disciple crazy by the sheer tension of it before he kills him through excessive austerity."

into the presence of God, into a relationship with God. The cult of Presence was not so much that of the presence of God in one's soul, although this goes without saying. It was primarily the Presence of Jesus in the sacrament. Jesus was there is a kind of local presence. We can understand the language that he uses in this light because the goal was "to be with Jesus, "to keep Jesus company, to be as close to him as possible.

All of the negative aspects of distancing, separation and sacrifice, reflected the understanding of the Eucharist as a memorial of the sacrifice of Jesus, continually lived out in our lives. His continual reference to January 15, 1890 throughout this period stresses this aspect of the Eucharist: as a sacrifice offered in union with the sufferings of Jesus. It was a way of wanting "to be with him" in his sorrow and suffering.

This movement of closeness to others, of "going towards others," brings us to the third aspect of Eucharist as that of sharing, as a meal taken together, as the banquet brought to others. From the moment that he realized that he was the servant of the Eucharist, he had to bring it to those who did not know of such a gift. His desire to carry and plant the presence of Jesus was interpreted in a very physical sense. It was a question of erecting tabernacles in places that were further and further away. It should be said that this spatial notion would evolve and eventually let go of it. When he was left with an empty tabernacle, he stayed anyway, having only his own life to offer as eucharistic presence, a life offered and exposed.

This trip on September 9, 1901 marked a turning point, the beginning of a new orientation. He no longer dreamed of "solitude, alone with Jesus" in a hermitage someplace. Instead, while he desired to have companions in his mission, he accepted to live alone among these people. Doing something for them meant doing something for Jesus.

He arrived at a point of not worrying anymore about high ideals and an impossible life of perfection, but of letting himself be fashioned by the Spirit through the events and people in his life. This led him to forget about himself. One of the first resolutions that he wrote in his Notebook upon arriving in Tamanrasset in 1905 was: "Do everything in my power for the salvation of the peoples of these regions, completely forgetting about myself."[113] Rather than meditating upon forgetfulness of self, he did what God wanted him to do in the present moment, even if that seemed contrary to what he always called "his vocation." Fr. Huvelin never stopped encouraging him in this sense.

On May 18, 1902 he wrote:

"My dear friend, my dear child, be gentle with yourself. Remain humble and patient with yourself. Be less preoccupied about overcoming a need for sleep and with your need to worry about it. Your constant worrying about the best way to do things torments you. Remain peaceful so that you can receive the graces of God. If you have and hold onto a kind of self-hatred, let it be a hatred that is as quiet as deep water.

In his Diary of a Country Priest, it is easier than one might think to hate oneself, wrote Bernanos. Grace is to forget oneself. If we were to become dead to all pride, the grace of graces would be to love oneself as humbly as we love another suffering member of Jesus Christ."

We can wonder if Charles de Foucauld would get to the point of loving himself as God loved him. At least he would reach the point of

---

[113] Charles de Foucauld, *Carnets de Tamanrasset*, Paris, Nouvelle Cité, 1986, p.63.

no longer seeking to destroy himself and of becoming nothing. If he still alluded to it, it was in the terms that St. John of the Cross used to speak of letting oneself be ground by the events and problems of life, through hard work and numerous cares.

When he entered the Trappists, he had broken off contact with his family and friends. But already at Notre Dame des Neiges circumstances obliged him to renew contact with them. From that time forward he no longer worried about whether or not it was good to maintain relationships full of friendship and human warmth with everyone he met. We can be full of admiration when we read the thousands of letters that he wrote. No matter whom he was writing to, we find a very human man who had a lot of warmth.

He had renounced ever seeing his cousin again on this earth. They met again in 1909 after nineteen years of separation, never having lost that closeness between them. We must never forget that she was real support for him throughout that long and painful period of separation. Would he have been able to deal with such solitude without his correspondence with her and with others?

He had stopped writing to most of his friends out of love for God. He began again "so that we might help one another to live out the few years that are given to us in holiness and to help one another to live and die in the Heart of Jesus."[114]

When he arrived in Beni Abbès at first he tried to hide, but very quickly he did all he could to know what he was doing. If he was eager for

---

[114] Letter of March 2, 1902 to Dr. Balthasar

the military officers to take an interest in going to Morocco so that one day he might also go, then he had to speak about what he had seen there during his explorations. He got to the point of no longer trying to hide his name nor his past. This shows up in the way his signature changed over the years. After 1911 he signed "Br. Charles de Foucauld," and after 1913 he signed simply "Charles de Foucauld" or "Charles", or even "Ch" for his closest friends.

On August 19, 1900 when Brother Augustine had congratulated him for his exploration of Morocco, he had answered, "Yes, that will do me a lot of good on the day of judgement." But just a few years later he wrote the following, somewhat in the style of what Fr. Huvelin had written to him, to Massignon to encourage him to finish his work and write his book:

> *"If I have been able to do any good and to settle in the Sahara it is, according to Jesus, because I had been a military officer and had traveled through Morocco. God prepares things from afar and uses the good, the bad and the acts that are done without the least thought of him for the salvation of souls."*[115]

If this kept him from running after the always dreamed-for last place that he would have fashioned to his liking, it forced him to accept the place that God had given him. What is admirable is that he remained a humble servant despite this place, something that did not go unnoticed by his contemporaries.

---

[115] Jean-François Six, *L'aventure de l'amour de Dieu*, Paris, Seuil, 1993, letter to Louis Massignon, December 3, 1911, P.115.

We must never despair, neither for ourselves nor for others... however sunk in vice they may be, however much there seems to be not even the least glimmer of hope.. God is mighty enough for it... We are obliged to hope for everybody

Blessed Charles de Foucauld

Sep 24

BENI ABBÈS AND THE TIME FOR FRATERNITY

At this point Brother Charles felt that his Rule was in its definitive form and he left it with Bishop Guérin when he left for Beni Abbès. He wanted him to read it, meditate upon it and approve it. Several months later he received authorization to welcome others to live with him under this Rule of Life. Bishop Guérin's admiration for Brother Charles might explain why he had not looked carefully at the details of the Rule. He might even have thought of following Brother Charles himself. But if he had looked more closely at the Rule, he would have seen that it was impossible to live.

Brother Charles arrived in Beni Abbès at the end of 1901. His stay there was practically limited to 1902 and 1903, since 1904 was entirely given to traveling in the south. The first years are typically the period in which a newly arrived apprentice missionary, full of plans and generosity, will make every possible mistake. For Brother Charles, everything became a project to create. There were a dozen such projects at BeniAbbès which he listed for his Bishop. Among these was one of ransoming slaves.

During the first year, the more pious soldiers came every evening to listen to him and to assist at benediction. He read and commented on passages from the Gospel.

Although it only lasted a few months during 1902, he felt moved to create four or five brotherhoods of which the membership lists are still in existence. He considered himself among the Priests of the Sacred Heart of Montmartre, several of the brotherhoods being dedicated to the Sacred Heart. He was the only member of one of these groups and another had just one member, a Mister Abd Jesus, three years old. There are quite a few other such examples which give us some insight into his personality.

Among his many projects, that of ransoming slaves is the best known. His letters on the subject to Bishop Guérin and Dom Martin, Abbot of Notre Dame des Neiges at the time, are strongly worded and can not be read in just any context. They are the fruit of the excessive zeal that was his custom. On Sept 17, 1902 Bishop Guérin wrote to him, much as Fr. Huvelin would have:

> *"Concerning the question of slavery, my dear father, what can I say?*
>
> *More than on any other point I feel that I must tell you: watch out for your zeal, be very prudent, bring your sadness's to the feet of Jesus, but watch out about letting yourself be carried away by your zeal and acting on it. Slavery is certainly a social evil that we cannot deplore enough – and we will never be filled enough with the love of Jesus – In order to combat slavery, one must take into account the circumstances and the people involved and the place where one lives. One must be careful not to destroy the means of accomplishing a little bit of goodbye making a lot of noise that brings no results. That is Bishop Livinhac's thought on it. Making a lot of noise about what is presently happening in the South can only attract the kind of attention that will thwart what we are actually trying to do."*

Officially slavery had been banned throughout the French territories, including the colonies. But in practice, some of the military officers turned a blind eye and let the situation continue so as not to change local customs. This went on for decades, until independence and even beyond. In 1902, the White Fathers were feeling threatened with dissolution by recent laws passed in France. Because of this they reacted with prudence to Brother Charles' over-reaching zeal. He wrote back on September 30th:

> *"I will immediately obey the line of conduct that you have laid out before me... I must tell you one last time, so that the soul of the child has no secret from the father and is open, without any reluctance... - The explanations that you have had the goodness to give me with such affection, and which have such weight coming from you and Bishop Livinhac, do not leave me without regretting that the representatives of JESUS content themselves with defending behind closed doors (and not from the rooftops) a cause that is one of justice and charity."*

In his hasty zeal for a good cause he seemed to have forgotten that he had defined his mission as an announcement of the Good News not with words but in silence, by shouting it from the rooftops by his life, and not with speeches.

But we are not going to stop longer on this question of slavery which has been dealt with at length in most of the biographies of Brother Charles. Rather, we will try to understand the meaning and implications of the words that he used at the beginning of his stay in Beni Abbès in speaking of universal brotherhood.

Alexandre Duyck

Charles de Foucauld
Explorateur

Paulsen

"You asked me for a description of the chapel... The chapel – dedicated to the Sacred Heart of Jesus – is called "the chapel of the fraternity of the Sacred Heart of Jesus", my little home is called "the fraternity of the Sacred Heart of Jesus"... I want all of the inhabitants, Christian, Muslim and Jews and idolators, to see me as their brother, the universal brother. They begin to call this place the 'fraternity' (la Khaoua in Arabic), which is sweet to me... The inside of the chapel is plastered with dark gray very natural colored mortar (very dark pearl gray = pearl black); it is 4 meters high; the ceiling, or rather the roof, is flat made of large palm trunks, loosely covered with mats of palm branches.. it is rustic, very poor... " Letter to Marie de Bondy, January 7, 1902

THE UNIVERSALITY OF THE FRATERNITY

From the beginning of his time in Beni Abbès we find many quotes dealing with "universal brotherhood." In particular there is the letter he wrote to Marie de Bondy on January 7, 1902:

> *"You asked me to describe the chapel... The chapel – dedicated to the Sacred Heart of Jesus – is called 'the chapel of the fraternity of the Sacred Heart of Jesus.' My little home is called 'the fraternity of the Sacred Heart of Jesus'... I want all of those who live here, whether Christian, Muslims, Jews or pagans, to become accustomed to seeing me as their brother – the universal brother... They begin to call the house 'the fraternity,' (the khaoua in Arabic), and this is sweet to my ears..."*

He explained to his friend, Lacroix: "I chose that name because it says that I am their brother and the brother of every human being without exception or distinction." [116] We also saw that this word appeared in his Rule in speaking of his house. It is the primary meaning of the word and it is something new.

He wanted people to call him "brother Charles" because "khouia Carlo is the universal brother." He translated the words "brother" and

---

[116] Georges Gorée, *Les Amitiés sahariennes du Père de Foucauld*, Paris, Arthaud, 1946, tome II, p.26.

"fraternity" into Arabic, but no one ever used those terms regardless of what he said. In Beni Abbès as well as in Tamanrasset they only ever spoke about "the marabout." This is a French word with Arabic roots used to speak of Muslims who had received religious training and were considered men of God. When this same word was again used in Arabic, it was used only to speak of priests and consecrated religious men and women. The word come from a root meaning, "to tie together," to be bound to a person or a place, much as the word "religious" in French. Brother Charles was also satisfied with this name and used it himself. The word did not yet have the pejorative meaning that it later took on in Africa involving sorcery and witchcraft.

What did universal mean? He placed the accent on the word "all":

"all people, good or bad, friend or enemy, benefactor or torturer, Christian or infidel they will become 'all things to all people in order to save all' they will be universal friends in order to be universal saviors."117

The theme of universality was developed in chapter 30 of the Rule: "Charity towards those outside the community."[118] The Constitutions read:

"They will have no 'preferences among people'. May their universal and brotherly love shines like a beacon; for miles around may no one, not even sinners or infidels, be unaware that they are universal friends, universal brothers, who spend their lives praying for all people without exception and doing good.

---

[117] Charles de Foucauld, *Règlement et Directoire*, Montrouge, Nouvelle Cité, 1995, p.228.
[118] *Op.cit.*, p.235 and following.

May their fraternity be a haven, a place of refuge where each one, especially the poor and unfortunate, is welcome at any time, invited, desired and received; may it be as its name says, the house of the Sacred Heart of Jesus, from which divine love radiates throughout the earth, the burning Charity of the Savior of men."119

These texts were written while he was at Notre Dame des Neiges preparing for ordination. While there, he made the corrections to his Rule, changing from *hermits* to *little brothers*. As early as November 29, 1901 in a letter to Henri de Castries he called himself "the universal brother" in his desire that all people would find a brothering him. "All" meant first of all the poor, but it also meant all of the others without exception or distinction. And he added, "Pray that I might become the brother of all the souls in that country."

It is necessary to remark here. Nearly all of the numerous quotes concerning universal brotherhood date from 1901 and the beginning of 1902. After several months this vocabulary then disappeared from his retreat journals of 1902 and the following years. Already in 1902 these words and expressions were missing as he worked on the feminine version of the Rule for the Sisters who are no longer universal in their friendship.

So we need to see what the vocabulary of universal brotherhood meant for the marabout of Beni Abbès and Tamanrasset. Later, in 1908, as he worked on the *Directory*, he left out those expressions from the Constitutions of 1901 that we have taken as so characteristic of him: "universal friend," "universal brother," "universal savior."

---

[119] *Op. cit.*, p.87

Becoming a brother

We forget too easily that Charles de Foucauld's life, like that of each person, was a long process of becoming, an evolution. It sounded beautiful to call himself "the universal brother" as he arrived in Beni Abbès. His excuse for such pretense was to ask for prayer: "Pray that I might be the brother of all the souls in this country."[120] If these words do not appear in his later writings maybe it is because he became more realistic. When one starts as a universal friend, any particular love becomes a restriction to universal love. To become the brother of all, one must begin by becoming the brother to this one and that one, and one cannot love each one in the same way. He knew quite well that he did not love his cousin Catherine the same way he loved his cousin Marie. If Laperrine became his incomparable friend, that did not keep him from becoming real friends with Regnault and Nieger. He still had different friendships with warrant officer Joyeux and 2nd class Sureau. It is obvious, but we do not always think of it. And when we see him count his friendships among the Tuareg, we realize that he was not under the illusion of universality for too long. We can see it clearly in the following passages.

> *"A few sincere friendships with very diverse people, a few souls who really trust me, and friendly but not intimate relationships with many. It is quite something given how enormously distant these people have been from us."[121]*

---

[120] *LHC*, November 11, 1901

[121] *Archives de la Postulation*, letter to Fr. Laurain, November, 27, 1910.

"I spent all of 1912 here in this hamlet of Tamanrasset. I find much consolation in the company of the Tuareg. I can't tell you how good they have been to me, what upright souls I find among them. One or two are my true friends, something so rare and precious anywhere."[122]

"I have at least four friends here on whom I can count totally. How did they become attached to me? In the same way that anyone does. I didn't give them any gifts, but they understood that they had found a friend in me, that I was devoted to them, that they could trust me. And they in turn gave the same to me. Those who are good and true friends to me are Ouksem ag Oughar, the chief of the Dag Ghali, his son Abahag, Chikkat ag Mohammed (Dag-Ghali), a 66-year-old man who can hardly get around anymore, and his son, Ouksem ag Chikkat (whom I call my son). There are others whom I love and respect and on whom I can count for many things. But I can ask for advice, help or information from these four for anything. I know that they will always do their best to help me."[123]

This is far from the crowds that invaded his house in Beni Abbès when he distributed grain. To see sixty children and one hundred adults in one day was not necessarily being each one's brother. How can one have a deep relationship with so many people? Over time and through experience he learned what it meant "to be a brother" and "a brother to each one."

All without exception

To be a universal brother means not to exclude anyone. As he wrote his Rule in Nazareth his ideas about "the poor, the rich, sinners and infidels" were very abstract.

They were to give hospitality to all without ever refusing anyone, without ever giving more to one than to another, without ever making

---

[122] *LHC*, January 1, 1908

[123] *Archives de la Postulation*, letter to Garnier, February 23, 1913.

any differences among people. In Beni Abbes he was faced with flesh and blood people who daily came to his door and the idea of "not making any exceptions" daily took on a new and different meaning. The only universal love is that which is particular, the love of the person before us. It is not the thought of loving someone who is far away and whom one has never seen.

If it is difficult to become a real brother, it is even more challenging to become the brother of everyone, without exclusion. It would be to maintain the same errors that we find in some of the 'lives of the saints' to believe this was not without struggle and progress. The slave is his brother, but it is not so easy to, at the same time, be the brother of the master who wants to claim that child as his property. The Jews are his brothers, but Brother Charles also loved to read the book *Jesus adolescent* written by Fr Caron whose anti-Semitism comes through quite clearly. There are Whites and Blacks and the marabout's reactions are not the same in Beni Abbès and Tamanrasset. We are surprised to read that some of the officers, probably projecting some of their prejudices on him, said that Brother Charles didn't like certain groups of people. Is it true? At any rate, it makes us that much more attentive as we see how he learned to know and love these same people whom he may not have been naturally drawn to love, and was touched by their trust and affection for him.

Among the officers some were outright enemies of one another. It is not so easy in these situations to know that one is a friend to both. He met those who mocked him and those who ignored his opinions. Some put obstacles in his path. He did not have a very high opinion of crooked or who did not do their duty. Some found him rigid and intransigent. For the good of some he struggled against others.[124]

To be a universal brother was not an excuse for belonging to no one under the pretext of loving everyone.

> *"all people, good or bad, friend or enemy, benefactor or torturer, Christian or infidel they will see as a soul to save: they will become 'all things to all people in order to save all. They will hate the evil, but that hatred will not keep them from loving the person, carrying them all in their heart, even the most wicked, as in the Heart of Jesus; they will be universal friends to be universal saviors."*[125]

Maybe it is no accident that this passage from the Rule has the title "Courage in dealing with others" next to "Charity, peace, humility." It was easy to write such a passage in the solitude of a monastery. It was not easy to live it out among all sorts of conflicts in Beni Abbès and especially in the Hoggar, and even while traveling through the vast desert. We can question some of his positions only if we are humble. Who can say that they could have done better? We have to recognize the courage he showed in his options: he was not fooled by that other illusion about universality that can allow one to maintain a cloistered existence, whether moral or solidly built, that isolates one from the people and the conflicts that affect their lives.

---

[124] Already in 1902 he noted: "Conquer the natural hardness that I feel towards sinners, that distaste that I have for them, and replace it with compassion, interest, zeal and eager care for their souls." *Cf.* Charles de Foucauld, *Seul avec Dieu*, Paris, Nouvelle Cité, 1975, p100.

[125] Charles de Foucauld, *Règlements et Directoire*, Montrouge, Nouvelle Cité, 1995, p.228.

Those closest or those furthest away?

Suppose charity moves from closest to furthest, beginning with "family, friends, neighbors and acquaintances" as he mentioned in his last version of the Statutes for the Association. How is it that he felt called to go so far away for the rest of his life? The life of Nazareth could be lived anywhere even in one's own country and among one's own family. There is nothing in his definition of Nazareth that says where it must be lived.

But he turned it into a type of religious life and there is no doubt that he intended to live this life, with others, far away, someplace else, voluntarily leaving his homeland, accepting the cultural shift that this implied, and especially to live it among non- Christians. This is very characteristic of his vocation and ignoring it would diminish and disfigure his message.

In the beginning his motivations were personal. He wanted to go far away, leaving behind his roots and all that he held dear. It was a need born of his love for Jesus, the need to cut off every tie to anything in this world to offer to Jesus the greatest sacrifice possible: that of going far away and leaving behind everything that he loved. Inwriting his Rule, he supposed that those who followed him would share his motivations.

Only in 1901 did his motivations become more objective. "This divine banquet of which I am the minister had to be carried to the poorest…to the most abandoned…"[126]

---

[126] *XXV Lettres inédites du Père de Foucauld* (au chanoine Caron), Paris, Bonne Presse, 1947, April, 8,1905, P. 13.

His desire to see that no one was excluded became a call to go to those who were the furthest away, a preference for those who were most in need. But there, too, circumstances guided his choices. He felt it a duty to be grateful towards those he had met during his exploration of Morocco and felt it was his duty to think of them. They had become his closest neighbors because he had drawn close to them. In the same line of thinking, when he realized that he could not go to Morocco he felt it his duty to go to the Tuareg because they were far from everything and he found himself to be the only priest able to go to be close to them, these "distant brothers."[127]

In the same logic, when he urged his compatriots to step outside of their own little world in order to care for the people of Africa, it was because the colonial conquest had created a situation of urgent responsibility. Those who had been colonized had become their neighbors and the French had the immediate duty to do for them what parents would do for their children.

Brother or Universal

After his death, the words "universal brother," taken out of context, took on a much wider meaning than he had given it. It even became something of a posthumous title conferred on him from outside, rather than being his own words. We can see this in the encyclical *Populorum Progressio* (art.12):

---

[127] Georges Gorée, *Les Amitiés sahariennes du Père de Foucauld*, Paris, Arthaud, 1946, Lettre à Lacroix, December 15, 1904, vol II, p.39.

> *"It suffices to recall the example of Father de Foucauld who, because of his charity, was judged worthy to be called the "universal Brother" and who compiled a precious dictionary of the Tuareg language."*

It is like an official consecration of his worthiness as universal brother, making him *THE universal brother*, the perfect model of universal love as one who would never have loved except in a universal way. It became an abstract idea of which he was the concrete incarnation. Over time even "brother" became separated from "universal" to the point that they began to speak of universality: "in the spirit of Brother Charles, the great grace of the fraternity is its universality."

Furthermore, this notion of universality is most often associated with an international perspective which has nothing to do with Charles de Foucauld's way of seeing, nor that of most of his contemporaries. It is not easy to turn him into "a brother without borders." Instead, it is more useful for us to understand his nationalistic mentality and fervent patriotism, not forgetting his military formation or Alsatian background. We will be less surprised as we read the letters that he wrote during the war.

Simply because, on one occasion, he used the adjective "international" we cannot make universality the center point of his message, or because, one day, he said that he would be ready to go to the ends of the earth or because he once prayed for the people of Japan. No, the grace and charism of Charles de Foucauld is not universality. It is first of all fraternity, which is friendship, "friend and universal brother." To be the universal brother means to, first, be a brother before thinking about universality.

To be a brother

In Beni Abbès it was no longer a question of being a hermit of the Sacred Heart, the brother of Jesus or even of those who might live with him in the house he called the fraternity. It was necessary to be the brother of those who was outside. When he used the word brother, he thought especially of those outside the community rather than the fraternity members. It is true that he lived alone and did not have to deal with "community life" or worry about "seeing how they love one another." The light shed by the fraternities was first and foremost "see how they love."

To be a brother meant relationships of equality, excluding any attitude of master or boss, and that of father and benefactor. This must not have come naturally for a man who had been trained to command and organize. He did not always escape that temptation. It is not enough to "show that we are brothers, repeat that we are all brothers in God to enter into the work of fraternization," as he wrote to Henri de Castries on June 27, 1904. He was more lucid when he wrote to his cousin on July 3rd:

> *"We go from spring to spring in those areas most used by the nomads to pasture their flocks. We make camp right next to them, spending several days at a time in an effort that they come to know us and feel comfortable with us, in friendship. Although they receive us well it is not very sincere. They do it out of simple necessity. How long will it take before they feel the way they pretend to feel? Maybe never. And will they know how to tell the difference between soldiers and priests? To be able to see us as servants of God, ministers of peace and*

charity, universal brothers? I don't know. If I do what I should, Jesus will pour out abundant graces, and they will understand."128

So that they might *understand* he had to become "little and accessible" and to distance himself from the soldiers. This was the grace of his illness in early 1908. He became utterly powerless, incapable of moving, without defenses or strength, totally dependent upon the hospitality of those who could finally treat him as a brother. He had that irreplaceable experience of solidarity which meant not just giving to others but having to receive what others had to share with him. To be a brother is also to accept to be loved.[129]

Brother and Friend

Because of this event he began to live brotherhood through his friendships. He had so well described in theory how others should live as "universal brothers and friends." Through this experience of friendship, he was later able to explain what brotherhood meant.[130] His personal experience of friendship went back to his childhood. It would take another whole book to speak about these friendships which are so meaningful in understanding his life. He constantly referred to it, explicitly or unconsciously. When he spoke of his friendships with the Tuareg he had no other point of reference than how any friendship binds people together.

---

[128] René Bazin, Charles de Foucauld, explorateur au Maroc, ermite au Sahara, Paris, Plon, 1921, p.298.

[129] Antoine Chatelard, À Tamanrasset, une conversion de Charles de Foucauld." Cf. Jesus Caritas, #224, 4th trimestre, 1986, pp47-59.

[130] Charles de Foucauld, Règlements et Directoire, Nouvelle Cité, 1995, p.648,7.

Brother in all the little details

To be a universal brother did not mean only being a brother to souls, as he seemed to think initially, falling prey to his language. It was also not a question of global or generalized love. "If I love everyone, it is to tell you, very dear, dearly beloved friend, how much I love you, you my old friend, my chosen friend, the friend of my heart,"[131] he wrote to Dr. Balthazar on March 2, 1902.

It is good to recall here something he wrote in Nazareth. He must have practiced it in Beni Abbès and Tamanrasset, much as he did at the Poor Clares:

"Be infinitely delicate in our charity: do not limit ourselves to doing the big things but have that tender and delicate way of taking care of the details, that way that pours ointment on the hearts of others through the little nothings that we do – "Give her something to eat," Jesus said – In the same way with those who are close to us, address the smallest details of health, consolation, prayer and need, console them and ease their trouble through the smallest little attentions.

For those whom God places on our path, have the same tender, delicate attentiveness that brothers have for one another or that a mother has for her children, in order to console as much as possible all those around us; in order to be for them a consolation and a balm as Our Lord was for all those who approached him, whether it was for Our Lady and Saint Joseph, the Apostles, Saint Magdeleine or any of the others... He was such a consolation and sweetness for those who drew near to him; as much as we have it in us to do the same, we must try to resemble him in this as in every other way, so that as we

---

[131] Achives of the Postulation

pass through this world we might sanctify, console and relieve others as much as we are able to."132

We would have to tell stories from his life in Tamanrasset to illustrate this meditation on the Gospel. His letters also reveal the delicate attentiveness that was a trademark of his.

Prayer and universal salvation

If being a universal brother meant being a brother "for the entire universe" it must be said that only in his prayer, did he reach so far: "My God, may all men go to heaven! "This very universal prayer was not only evident while he was at Beni Abbès, where he wrote that phase at the top of every page of the catechism that was working on at the time. We find it from the very beginning of his religious life. In 1896 he made it part of the first Rule that he wrote:

> *"Each morning and evening they will spend a half hour in prayer, asking God's salvation for all men. It is what Our Lord so ardently prayed for throughout his entire life."133*

We find it again in his commentary on the Our Father:

> *"I make no request for myself alone: all that I ask for in the Our Father, I ask for the sake of God or for all humankind Forgiveness as well as grace is not asked for oneself alone but for all men."134*

---

[132] Charles de Foucauld, *La Bonté de Dieu*, Montrouge, Nouvelle Cité, 1996, pp. 124-125.

[133] Charles de Foucauld, *Règlements et Directoire*, Montrouge, Nouvelle Cité, 1995, pp. 28-29.

[134] Charles de Foucauld, *L'Esprit de Jésus*, Paris, Nouvelle Cité, 1978, pp. 32-33

In the Rule of 1901, the brothers were "universal friends, universal brothers, who spend their lives praying for all men without exception."[135] It was also the meaning behind urging all of his friends, priests and religious, to pray to the Holy Spirit three times a day, "praying for all men without exception." Shortly before his death he mentioned it again:

> *"Brotherly love for all men See a child of our heavenly Father in every person: be charitable, peaceful, humble and courageous with each one: pray for everyone, for every human being, offer one's sufferings for all."*[136]

This prayer for every human being is an expression of his anguish for the salvation of all people. His behavior, as well as his prayer, tells us that he was aware that all people could be saved and that he would meet all those whom he loved in the Kingdom of God. But his theology did not permit him to formulate his intuitions about this and this explains the discrepancies that we find between his writings and his actions.

Only one man was ever worthy of being called the universal brother. He is the someone who is the universal Savior, the only one capable of loving every person and each person as unique. He is the one whom Brother Charles once called, "Jesus, this older, universal brother."

As for Brother Charles, living with a small group of people, in a very limited part of the desert for just a few years, he learned something about brotherly love and friendship by trying not to exclude anyone. It is in this way that his life has taken on a universal dimension.

---

[135] Charles de Foucauld, *Règlements et Directoire*, Montrouge, Nouvelle Cité, 1995, p. 87.
[136] Charles de Foucauld, *Directoire*, Paris, Seuil, 1961, p.125.

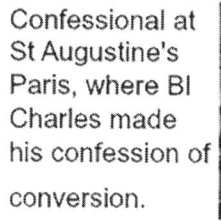

Confessional at St Augustine's Paris, where Bl Charles made his confession of conversion.

The first call to the Hoggar

In choosing to settle in Beni Abbès Brother Charles decided to go as far away as possible to be as close to Morocco as possible. After a while it became clear that the door to Morocco was firmly closed and that there was no real hope of ever going there. At the beginning of 1903 Laperrine made a detour to Beni Abbès on his way back from leave even though Beni Abbès was not part of his territory. He had heard that Charles de Foucauld was there and he wanted to see him again. Knowing the man that Brother Charles was, Laperrine thought he knew how to spark his interest in his ideas, all while respecting his vocation. He talked to him about his plans in the Hoggar region but did not convince him.

Back in his post in Adrar, Laperrine sent Captain Nieger on a mission that he explained later:

"In April of 1903 I met Fr. de Foucauld for the first time. After the first tour of duty in the Sahara that lasted nine months, my superior officer (Laperrine) left me entirely free to do as I wanted. At the same time he gave me strict instructions: Pass by Beni Abbès and go to see Foucauld who is acting the mason. He is building himself a hermitage that he never leaves. He doesn't eat. He lives from alms and still finds ways to ransom slaves that come from Morocco. He only thinks of Morocco, tormented by the memories of his youth.

He is very hard-headed and nothing will help him on that score. He needs to be convinced to come and join us. He could be the pastor of the Tuareg and would do so much for us'."137

During May Bishop Guérin visited Brother Charles, making a long detour by way of In Salah. At the end of this visit Brother Charles mentioned that he did not want to be pushed in the direction his Bishop would have him go.

On June 10th he wrote about his difference of opinion to Fr. Huvelin. This letter is significant because of the details that it gives us:

"The visit of this good and venerable priest has not changed my life. He keeps pushing me towards Morocco... I retain three things from his visit: first his admirable goodness, his holiness, humility and devotion... then, that he keeps pushing me towards Morocco. I would do my best to go but for the moment I just don't see an open door... then, he has a slight and subtle tendency to push me out of my life as a silent and hidden monk, my life of Nazareth, to that of a missionary. I will not follow this last one. To do so would be a lack of faithfulness to God who gave me this vocation of hidden and silent life and not that of a man of words. Monks and missionaries are both apostles but in different ways. I won't change this. I will keep to this same way that I have been trying to follow more or less as well as I can, which is generally not so well, for the last 14 years: the hidden life of Jesus, with others if Jesus sends them, alone if he leaves me alone."

At the beginning of June 1903, Laperrine was going through his archives in Adrar. Rereading the account of the Flatters massacre he

---

[137] Nieger, "Laperrine et le Père de Foucauld," dans *Construira*, 1923, C.XIII, p. 186.

discovered an anecdote that he thought might change the heart of the monk who seemed so riveted to Beni Abbès:

> *"At the time of the Flatters massacre, a Tuareg woman from a noble family took a marvelous stand against those who would finish off the wounded. She gathered them up and took them to her home where she cared for them. She also refused to allow Attisi, who had returned wounded from battle in Amguid against the Dianous,138 and who wanted to kill them himself, to enter her home.*
>
> *When they were well enough to travel she sent them back to Tripoli. She is now between 40 and 43 years of age, has great influence and is known for her charity."139*

Laperrine copied this text and sent it to Charles de Foucauld. The effect was immediate as we can see from what he wrote about it in his Notebook and letters. On June 18th, he wrote to Bishop Guérin, recopying the text from Laperrine and adding:

"Commandant Laperrine is trying to get her a medal from the Women's Union of France. If he can gain her trust through this he will later put her in contact with you and the White Sisters.

The Holy Father is the universal father just as JESUS is the universal king.

The Holy Father, as JESUS, is king and father to the Tuareg. Could we not ask him to give a little fatherly encouragement to this woman, his

---

[138] The Dianous were the men under the leadership of Lieutenant Dianous who had escaped the massacre at the Flatters Mission.

[139] Charles de Foucauld, *Correspondances sahariennes*, Paris, Le Cerf, 1998, p.191.

daughter and subject? If you feel this is appropriate, write to Fr. Burtin, Commandant Laperrine and anyone else you feel should be told.

At any rate, it would be good to develop closer relationships with the Tuareg, taking advantage of every opportunity… and it would be desirable that the Holy Father's gesture be the first."

On June 21st he recopied in his Notebook [140] the report that Laperrine had sent him, adding:

> *"Isn't this soul ready for the Gospel? Would it not be appropriate to simply write to her, telling her that the charity that she continually practices and with which she sheltered, cared for, defended, and repatriated the wounded of the French mission some 22 years ago, is known to us and fills us with joy and thanksgiving to God."*

In this same vein he wrote a draft of the letter that he wanted the Pope to send: "I am sending a copy of the draft of this letter to Bishop Guérin, asking him if he wants to send it himself or if he wants me to send it – offering at the same time – if the relationship should develop – if I remain alone – if it seems to be the Will of God – to go on foot to visit this woman."

There are many "ifs," but the idea is beginning to sprout. The same day he continues in his Notebook:

> *"It seems to us that it is the right time to edit a short version of the Gospel that can be translated into Arabic and especially into Tuareg… We will begin this today."*

---

[140] Charles de Foucauld, *Carnet de Beni Abbès,* Paris, Nouvelle Cité, 1993, pp. 70-71.

And on June 22nd he wrote: "If there were a way to found little houses elsewhere, instead of fraternities; for myself alone, or one or two or three brothers only, I think that this would be the way to go," and he went on to lay out three plans: A, B, C.

And so, in the few days between June 18th and 22nd we see that he became progressively involved in this project: first to write a draft, then to write himself, then to make a casual visit, then to edit a translatable version of the Gospel, then to plan for some houses in case he would have to settle elsewhere. These thoughts tormented him.

On June 24th he decided to write to Bishop Guérin about it to put his soul at peace:

> *"I am writing to you after much hesitation… Two things made me decide to write: the first is that in leaving the decision to you and Fr. Huvelin, I am only giving and offering myself even more to God. He will decide: "He who listens to you listens to me."… The second is that if both you and Fr. Huvelin say "yes" it is urgent to act as quickly as possible since the doors that are open to me today, thanks to the presence of a good friend in the Oasis, might be closed tomorrow.*
>
> *Since you have told me that you cannot make any foundation in the Oasis for the moment, and are not able to send any solitary Priests, since on the other hand you would like to see me visit Taghit once or twice a year, since I am still alone. No door seems to be opening towards the West:*
>
> *Would it not be better for the sake of souls and pleasing to the HEART of JESUS, that I ask my friend from the Oasis for permission to settle in Aoulef, or further South if possible, as close to the Tuareg as possible, in a place where, all alone, I would be safe, and able to learn the Targuie language and be able to prepare a Targuie translation of several books? (I would like to translate the Holy Gospel into Targuie language and writing)… If he said yes, I would go*

and settle into a little cell, two meters by two meters with an oratory of two meters by five, and lead a solitary life there, but without enclosure, trying to: 1) develop closer and closer relationships with the Tuareg (visiting them as often as possible), 2) Translate the Holy Gospel into their language (using M. Weber's work for a starting point), 3) Visit at least once a year the Posts in Adrar, In Salah, Timimoun, Beni Abbès, Taghit and others where there are Europeans to administer the sacraments, choosing to go there at the time of the big feast days that stir even the most indifferent hearts, 4) Making frequent stops along the way, having time to speak with the locals and to do a little of what you had suggested that I do.

If you say yes, if Fr. Huvelin to whom I have sent a copy of this letter says yes, I will write to my friend and leave as soon as he also says yes."

Fr. Huvelin received this letter at almost the same time as June 10th where Brother Charles wrote about not wanting to be pushed into a missionary life by theBishop. Fr. Huvelin was quite ill by this time. His encouraging response shows how he understood that it was impossible to keep Charles de Foucauld from following his inspiration. He also knew that, from such a distance, he did not have the light to make a judgment in such a situation. He wrote on July 5th: "Follow your inner conviction, go where the Spirit leads."

But Brother Charles did not wait for the answers as there was a rush and on June 29th wrote to Laperrine about his plan, asking for his permission. The Commandant was only waiting for this. The next day Brother Charles wrote again to Bishop Guérin explaining his haste and the reasons for which he wrote to Laperrine before receiving the Bishop's answer:

"In my last letter I believe I told you that I only wrote to you after much hesitation. Yes, every change and movement frightens me, makes me dizzy and panicky; I am afraid of making a mistake, and I am afraid of not being able

to accomplish the thing; At the same time I am afraid of being under some illusion and of my own natural laziness; together they make me panic before any vital action...

Usually the fear subsides as soon as I place myself in the hands of my director in a spirit of abandonment... From that moment a profound peace reigns and all hesitation ceases.

That is what is happening to me now. Before writing to you and Fr.

Huvelin, I was fearful and hesitant. Since I sent those two letters, the very same day, I am peaceful, joyful, filled with quiet confidence and a lively yet quiet, desire.

I simply and desire – while waiting for Morocco to open, if it opens – to go to the Tuareg people, in someplace where I would have sufficient safety... Here there are enough people, Muslims, who have heard the Christian doctrine; Those of goodwill have all been able to come, all have been able to learn; Those who want to see it have seen that our religion is all peace and love, that it is profoundly different from theirs: Theirs prescribes killing, ours loving...I have no companions. Morocco is not opening. I can do no better for the salvation of souls which is our life here below, as it was the life of JESUS "Savior," than to go to bring to as many souls as possible, the seed of divine doctrine. I would not do it through preaching but through simple conversation – and especially by going to prepare and beginning the evangelization of the Tuareg by settling among them, learning their language, translating the Holy Gospel, entering into friendly relationships, as much as possible, with them...

If JESUS wants me to have little brothers of his divine HEART, he can send them to me there. For however long this might last, I can travel north once a year, go to confession, stop in all of the military posts along the way and speak with the local people while we travel.

Fearing that he might have to travel and the consequent delay, I am writing to my friend from the Oasis by this same occasion to ask his permission to settle 'as deeply in the heart of the Tuareg region as safety permits, a safety due to his recommendation and protection, to learn the Tuareg language and to translate several works into that language'... I do not have the right to commit suicide and it is not the way to make JESUS known to souls. It is necessary to join courage with prudence, not be imprudent nor fearful.

If you say no to this desire of mine, which I more and more believe to be God's will, nothing would be easier than to tell my friend that I will not go for the time being.

If you say yes, all I have to do is leave, taking advantage of his presence and friendship... Several things seem to tell me that he will not be there for long, which is why I have hurried... God has given this opportunity, as it is also he who I believe has placed this desire in my heart.

I have said absolutely nothing to anyone else than you, Fr. Huvelin and my friend from the Oasis about my desire to go to the Tuareg... I ask you to also remain silent about it.

If I do go, the Fraternity, where I will spend a few days each year, will be closed in my absence and the garden rented out: nothing could be simpler."

We can see that his plans were becoming clearer and slightly modified. He no longer mentioned Aoulef and answered the objections that Bishop Guérin would surely raise before he even had a chance to ask. He also addressed the suggestions that the Bishop had made to him and resisted until this point.

On July 15th, having received Fr. Huvelin's response, he wrote a third letter to Bishop Guérin:

"I have just received an answer from Fr. Huvelin. It is yes: 'Follow your inner conviction, go where the Spirit leads. You will always find the solitary life

wherever JESUS recollects you in him to give you to souls. Yes, I approve of your letter to Bishop Guérin: he will decide what is best!'

I have not yet received your answer or the one from the Oasis. If both are "yes" I will leave as soon as possible to not lose this opportunity.

My idea would be to spend the major part of the year among the Tuareg, leaving only as necessary once a year to visit the garrisons where you are not able to send a priest, and to go to confession myself...."

On July 22nd he received Laperrine's answer. Brother Charles wrote a fourth letter to Bishop Guérin, writing with a surprising insistence that betrayed his impatience.

He did not pray to St. Magdeleine that the will of God be manifest.

He prayed that she would inspire Bishop Guérin to say yes:

"The answer from the South came today. It is also yes, very probably at least: 'I will take care of you. It might work, but in two stages. You can make the first visit to Aqabli where there is no garrison and where you will have a front-row seat for learning Tuareg. Then, once you can speak enough and have become known to the caravan drivers, we will let you go... I will write to M. as I do not want to send you to his territory without his permission... With prudence, I think that your program can work without fearing any danger.'[141]

---

[141] Laperrine did not want to send Foucauld to this the territory of this officer, who was known for his fanatic anticlericalism, without an introduction. Laperrine did not know that Métois had passed through Beni Abbès, visited Brother Charles and proposed that he come and settle in his sector.

I will answer that this two-step approach suits me perfectly… It is quite wise… Aqabli is an excellent first step. I had said that I wanted a place where there was no garrison.

It is St. Magdeleine who brings me this yes for her feast day. May this desert mother also inspire you to say 'yes. It seems that it is now up to you whether the divine tabernacle would be established in the extreme South and that each year all of the posts and garrisons that you are not able to serve, including Taghit, would have the benefit of Holy Mass and the sacraments.

I am deeply grateful for these two yeses that came so quickly, and I await yours, beloved and venerated Father… If I receive it, I think that I will not leave immediately. Besides the fact that, as you see, I am awaiting another decisive letter from the South, I would like to finish reading St. John Chrysostom and to spend two or three days in Taghit… But I will let myself be guided by circumstances, according to what I hear from the South… wanting only to do, as much as possible, the work of the heavenly Father, true daily bread and all that is necessary,"

He finally received the Bishop's letter, dated July 9th, on July 25th. Bishop Guérin, who had not received the last two letters, expressed his surprise and a certain mistrust of his projects. He did not want to give a firm and definitive no and asked for time to reflect:

"What can I tell you, dear Father. I consider you more Moroccan than Tuareg and I hesitate to see you distance yourself from Morocco.

If the situation would change, shouldn't you turn towards the West or Figuig? A little more patience: I am truly confident that Providence will show the way."

Brother Charles wrote immediately, on the 25th, his fifth letter to the bishop. He argued:

"Concerning Morocco and the West, in my opinion, for me, going to the Tuareg does not mean renouncing Morocco but rather preparing myself and doing, for the time being, what is most useful.

Figuig, no, that is not my place... And, to tell the truth, Figuig is not Moroccan. Still, Algerian Population centers and supply centers for the nomads would be good places to open schools and dispensaries: It is your vocation, your way of doing things, not mine...."

He felt that he had to leave for the South. He seems to us ready to accept anything as long as they tell him to go. Learning Tuareg could only be beneficial in terms of Morocco. In the South there may even be more chances of meeting Moroccans than in Beni Abbès! He forgot about the life of Nazareth and went as far as to say: "Then relationships with the indigenous people will be a good formation and will give me experience and self-assurance in terms of <u>mission and evangelization</u>," which Bishop Guérin must have liked hearing.

He continued his argument, more and more insistently:

"Well, I find that it is good to take advantage of opportunities, of the actual goodwill, and on the other hand, not to leave this big country abandoned while waiting for doors to open elsewhere... Let us go now where we can go. When doors open elsewhere, we will go there. Each day has trials of its own: let us do today whatever is best! In every moment, one after the other that makeup life, take advantage of the grace of the moment and the means that God gives us; nothing prepares us so well to receive future graces than to use well the grace of today...."

It is exactly the spirituality of the present moment that he had discovered in reading Fr. de Caussade.[142] Taken out of context, this phrase has a whole different meaning. It is not used only when one wants to do something that the superior does not wish to.

While Brother Charles was praying to St Magdeleine to inspire his Bishop to say yes, on the same day the Bishop wrote to him after having taken time to pray:

> *"I thought very much about you and prayed very much for you on this day that I know is a particularly dear feast day.*
>
> *With my whole heart I asked Jesus, through the intercession of his holy servant, to give you the grace and light that you desire to know the way ahead."*

Bishop Guérin did not want to give a definite answer without consulting Bishop Livinhac again. He later told him how perplexed he was by the unusual vocation of Charles de Foucauld: "An admirable obedience that is hardly easy to direct."[143]

Dom Louis de Gonzaga had had the same difficulty. He wrote, "It must be said, at the least, that the subject is pretty tenacious when it comes to his desires and will."[144] And Dom Martin had good insight

---

[142] Brother Charles wrote to a White Sister about the book of Fr de Caussade on December 24, 1904: "It is one of the books that helps me live the most. Under the title of *Abandonment to Divine Providence* it contains many other things; It is life giving." *Cf.* Charles de Foucauld, *Correspondances Sahariennes*, Paris, Cerf, 1998, p.957.

[143] Charles de Foucauld, *Correspondances Sahariennes*, Paris, Cerf, 1998, p.1012.

[144] Charles de Foucauld, "Cette chère dernière place" Lettres à mes frères de la Trappe, Paris, Cerf, 1991, p.154.

when he wrote to Brother Charles, "It seems that you too easily turn your ideas into orders from heaven when the goal is a good one."[145]

Maybe heaven had no other way of communicating its orders to earth. It's a bit what Bishop Guérin seemed to think as his letter continues:

> *"Ah, my dear friend, you ask for counsel, and you ask for orders! If it is easy to obey, it is not easy for me to discern God's ways and give you an order in the name of divine Wisdom.*

And yet, very dear Father, I will allow myself to tell you what I feel about your business in all humility. A project such as yours would need to be considered for a longtime: your immediate departure at this moment seems a bit abrupt and little in keeping with the habitual way that Providence works.

Furthermore, I cannot believe that such a departure is the will of Providence at this time of year. You would need to wait at least until October or November."

His negative response then went into all of the details. Difficulties on the level of material things such as supplies as well as for liturgy, the impossibility of such a solitary life, or living connected to a nomadic military patrol:

> *"Is it your place to drag behind what would essentially be a nomadic military column, you who always dreamed of the monastic life? I don't know.*

---

[145] *Op.cit.*, p.283.

You see, dear friend, I do not want to make any conclusions about the principle of the thing in itself. I want to take counsel and wait for some more evident manifestation of the Will of God. But I am much clearer about the prospect of an immediate departure I would not be quite so categorical if it were just a question of taking advantage of an occasion to go to Timmi to visit your devoted, old friend."

Then Bishop Guérin raised the question of the impossibility for Brother Charles to celebrate mass alone, without a server, since the authorization requested from Rome concerning this had not come. He continued:

"I have no trouble understanding how much these projects must stir your ardent nature. But with my whole soul I pray that God will help you not fall victim to an easy illusion.

Your presence in Beni Abbès has not been useless for the glory of God to this point: Both the French and the indigenous people have gained from it and by remaining longer, your influence will undoubtedly become even more efficacious.

You would like to take advantage of the presence of C. Laperrine whom you think may soon disappear from the scene – this is undoubtedly a consideration– but I don't know how easy it would be for you to penetrate the territories of Tidikelt and the Hoggar with Captain M. there."

Everyone knew that Captain Métois would never tolerate the presence of a priest in his territory. Bishop Guérin and a companion had been very poorly received at In Salah when they passed through. But, unknown to everyone, Charles de Foucauld already had an amicable relationship with this officer.

Brother Charles received this negative and disappointing response on August 1st. Did he not yet consider it an answer? On the 12th he wrote to his cousin, "I offered to go... I am still waiting for an answer from Bishop Guérin." On August 5th he had written his 5th letter to the Bishop, a short letter as he had little new to add.

> *"The letters with which I have burdened you recently fully explain my desires.*
>
> *What I am asking you is simply permission to find a way to penetrate the Tuareg region. Through my letters I have told you that my thinking is not to abandon Morocco but to do the best I can in the South – if the door is open to me– while waiting that you can send other workers, or until a door to the West opens. The door to the West is closed for now.*
>
> *You have seen that my idea is to take advantage of this time in the South to offer the sacraments once or twice a year in the various garrisons throughout the Oases."*

And to Bishop Guérin's major objection that it is the wrong time of year for such trip, he alludes recent combat:

> *"Captain Regnault left Beni Abbès on July 15th and returned the 30th.*
>
> *During that time he marched day and night, faced bloody combat, had the strap of his rifle pierced by a bullet right in his hands and saw five men around him either wounded or killed. You see that the soldiers of the earth, men, do not fear the season.146 Let us, soldiers of God, take our example from them and not make our Master have to tell us, 'The sons of this world are more astute than the children of light.'... I have always asked JESUS that I would not do less in his service than I did before for the sake of creatures...*
>
> *I am not saying that I want to leave immediately obstinately... Not at all. But there is only one thing that needs consideration: what is the best time to leave to*

---

146 Charles de Foucauld, *Correspondances Sahariennes*, Paris, Cerf, 1998, p. 213, note 1: "Father deFoucauld underlined the word "season" three times.

accomplish the 'work of our Father'... and leave at that moment whether sooner or later... The question of temperature is less for us than for Regnault... Only one thing matters the work of God...."

So when on August 26th he received an answer from Laperrine, he decided to leave "without hesitation" and without awaiting any other answer from his Bishop. He had the choice between September 5th and October 15th. He decided to take the first occasion and told Bishop Guérin of his decision in a letter the same day. It is very revealing of his practical and real conception of obedience:

"I received an answer this morning from my friend from the South who tells me that everything is arranged with Captain M.[147] and that all I have to do is come... that there is so much good to be done by allowing these souls to come to know us, in making contact with them... and that he is waiting for me and asks me to travel either with the convoy of September 6th or October 15th (leaving BeniAbbès at these dates).

I have not received any answer from you... Since it is possible to travel on September 6th thanks to Commandant L., Captain Regnault and the presence of a military convoy, I will leave on the 6th.

If later I receive an order not to stay in the South, I will not stay.

I am not leaving so quickly out of a lack of obedience towards you, beloved and venerable Father, but because the perfect obedience, and this is part of its perfection, sometimes means taking the initiative.

If I leave without hesitation, it is because I am ready to return without hesitation; as easily as I leave I will return.

I leave hurriedly because who knows if what is possible on the 6th will still be possible a month later.

---

[147] Métois

The convoys are highly uncertain right now. You know that Taghit has recently been under siege for 4 days by four thousand Berber.[148]

I think that I am doing for the best. If you want me to return here, write to me. I will return with the happiness of obeying JESUS: 'he who hears you hears me'... and I must also admit, deep happiness to regain the tabernacle of which I will be deprived for a particular time."

He added a post-script:

"Whether with the military or others, I will follow your recommendation scrupulously and will not in any way present myself as being sent by you, but acting instead by my initiative.

Keep this trip secret. I vaguely told my family that I would be gone for a while to another oasis, and, without any other details, they should continue to write to me in Beni Abbès. Only you and Fr. Huvelin know about this."

---

[148] Taghit was a garrison about 100 kms. from Beni Abbès.

Obedience and Initiative

"The most perfect obedience... means taking the initiative." Where did he learn this definition of the perfection of obedience? We can search through moral theology books that he may have used in his studies but it is more enlightening to recall what some of his friends thought about the subject, notably Laperrine who had just written to CaptainRegnault:

> *"My dear friend, I have authorized de Foucauld to come to Tidikelt.149 I don't have the authority to do so, but I hope to escape with the superior officers' backing and just a few threatening and insulting letters from the subdivision. It's funny how we can become accustomed to swift kicks in the... It hardly even fazes me anymore. I have a special folder for them and that's about it... Would you be so kind as to let me know if you have anything special to tell de Foucauld so that I will be the only one to suffer the insults?"150*

He thought that Captain Regnault had indeed received instructions about keeping tabs on de Foucauld, or at least some kind of orders concerning him. Documents were found in other garrisons noting that de Foucauld had stopped there and who had received him, proof that he had been under some surveillance.

---

[149] In the region of In Salah, north of the Hoggar.

[150] Georges Gorée, *Les Amitiés sahariennes du Père de Foucauld*, Paris, Arthaud, 1946, tome II, p. 60.

Lyautey, who would soon take over command of the subdivision, wrote in a similar vein in August of 1901:

> *"Ah, the initiative! Of all of the active virtues, it is the one I appreciate the most. What a joy it is to meet people who do not do established practice into dogma, people who know how to trample bureaucratic rules for the sake of common sense and progress."* 151

We cannot attribute such a spirit of initiative to Charles de Foucauld's military formation. He later reproached many officers for not taking the initiative. And we cannot limit the definition of an initiative to simply anticipating the decision of a superior in a given situation. This "active virtue" may bring us helpful insight for understanding something about his life. It is a distinctive personality trait of both Laperrine and Lyautey. It typifies a person of action, always ready to take upon oneself that which seems to be a duty, often an urgent duty. This duty necessitates acting before knowing the opinions or decisions of a superior.

We could reread Charles de Foucauld's entire life in the light of such a willing temperament, one geared towards action. We could bring out all of those instances where he felt it was his duty to want to do something, especially when it was a question of doing something that no one else had ever done, whether because no one had ever been able to do it or had simply never thought of doing it. It was such a part of his personality that it was never altered by unbelief, faith or any vow of obedience. He lived the different situations of his life with who he was.

---

[151] Hubert Lyautey, *Paroles d'action*, Paris, Armand Colin, cite dans *CCF* #1, p.128.

In this sense Charles' obedience was essentially a "submission of his judgment" with tremendous trust in the one who was given responsibility for guiding him. He often spoke of having a director of conscience and he recommended it to those who sought to live according to the Gospel. He was a person who needed to have someone to control him a little, to act as a brake. His spiritual director practically never had to make suggestions, push him or stimulate him. Rather, he always had to slow him down.

The times that he did not take the initiative are rare but significant. There was his conversion: the unforced initiative of taking the first steps on a path that should have been a slow process of coming to terms with faith. It led to a totally unforeseen and unplanned leap of faith instigated by Fr. Huvelin in St. Augustine's Church. He also needed to be pushed to make the pilgrimage to the Holy Land two years later. Although he took no initiative for it, this trip began a whole new and very personal way of discovery along the roads of Nazareth. It would lead him to commit himself to Jesus of Nazareth in a way that no one had ever dreamed of before. He had to invent and explore it as he went.

We can understand that someone who was so inventive and always ready to imagine, organize and plan things would live obedience in a particular way. It was a question of obeying God, of doing what God wanted of him and the question was always, "What must I do?" It was the question he asked his entire life. There were two parts to it: the "must" and the "do." The "must" was a desire that became a duty and imposed itself upon him as an inner need. It was an inner necessity that came from the core of his being, an inner need that he could not escape without denying something of who he was. It did not come from any external constraint but was a deep, inner urge that led to wanting to do something, provoking initiative.

On the one hand, obedience was a way of assuring himself that the desire, the thing that he felt he "must" do, was God's will for him. He did this through the mediation of another person to whom he confided himself, saying, "Tell me what is Jesus' will." He applied the words of Jesus, "Whoever listens to you, listens to me."

Two people played this role in Charles de Foucauld's life. The first was Fr. Huvelin who was a remarkable director. After his death, it was Father Voillard, general assistant of the White Fathers. But he had to follow orders and directions from many other people throughout his life: from superiors and confessors at the Trappists and in Nazareth at the Poor Clares. The details of monastic life and this "submission of judgment," as he called it, were always struggles for him whether it was a question of how to cut and stack the wood, doing studies, trips that he had to make or little jobs he was asked to do. The will of God was not in these things in themselves but through them he sought to submit his own will.

Obedience is also to be found in the thing that he had "to do." We can equate desiring, willing and doing. For Charles de Foucauld "doing" sometimes went no further than writing his ideas on paper. In another aspect of his personality, more often than not, there was a kind of fearfulness associated with the prospects of changes that were to take place in his life. We can understand this when he said, "Fear is a sign of duty"[152] and "It is one of the things that we owe Our Lord: never to be afraid of anything."[153]

Dom Louis de Gonzague had a monastic idea of obedience when he wrote to his brother, Dom Martin, on February 11, 1897 about the former brother Marie Albéric, "He could become a saint and I hope he does. But it will be his way and not because of obedience." It is clear that he neither had the same mind nor the same way of obedience. But there are many rooms in the Father's house and each one must find their path of obedience through the events and circumstances of life.

This brings up another aspect of his personality that needs mentioning before moving on. He had a remarkable ability to deal with new situations. Isn't this yet another type of obedience? The following year, Bishop Guérin recognized this when he said that Charles de Foucauld, "as with all those whom the Spirit of God directs, has a marvelous appreciation of circumstances."

"Providence speaks clearly"

On August 29th Brother Charles received an answer from Bishop Guérin dated August 19th and 21st. After consulting with Bishop Livinhac, the apostolic prefect finally gave in, with regret, and not without expressing some severe reservations. He needed not less than nine pages to explain that he felt that the trip was not advisable while he

---

[152] This phrase can be found in the first writings of the Fraternity and in the first Rules that were written. The first reference to it can be found in an article by Jean Lefranc in January 1917 in *Le Temps* and *L'Illustration*. During a conversation Brother Charles had asked the journalist if he were married. He answered, no, saying that marriage frightened him. Brother Charles would have answered, "Fear is a signof duty."

[153] René Bazin, *Charles de Foucauld, explorateur au Maroc, ermite au Sahara*, Paris, Plon, 1921, p. 127.

left Brother Charles free to leave. He felt that both the direction and timing were poorly chosen:

> *"For nothing in this world do I wish to change your mind if, after having seriously reflected on the remarks that I have shared with you in all simplicity, you still feel that God is calling you to leave now and that you have the necessary authorization.*
>
> *I also think that it is necessary, both in terms of the military and the local administration, that it be known that it is your choice to leave, that you do it at your own risk and that, in no way, are you sent by me."*

Brother Charles was only able to see in this the freedom he had been given to follow up on this project. He wrote to his cousin on August 31st:

> *"The authorization from Bishop Guérin came in the mail on August 29th… There is an excellent opportunity to leave: a military convoy is leaving (probably) from here on September 12th for that region… If I didn't believe with my whole heart that the words "sweet, painful, joy, sacrifice," etc., should be suppressed from our vocabulary, I would say that I am a bit sad to leave Beni Abbès: sad to leave the divine Tabernacle for a time, sad that I will be less alone at the feet of the Beloved, worried over my sinfulness and shortcomings, burdened by my laziness and inadequacy."*

At the beginning of September 1903 circumstances brought hesitation to his plans far better than all of the letters of Bishop Guérin. In mid-August, there had been combat near Taghit and Brother Charles understood that his first duty called him there. He was ready to leave for Taghit and understood that this could delay any travel to the South: "It is possible that the attack on Taghit, by itself or through its consequences, could keep me here or take me West."[6] But nothing came of it and he remained convinced that he should leave for the South.

Then on September 2nd there was a new conflict at El Moungar, thirty kilometers from Taghit. As soon as he learned of it, Brother Charles jumped on a horse and left for Taghit. He arrived on September 6th and remained there for a month caring for the wounded.

The urgency that he felt about traveling South began to wane and he wrote to Bishop Guérin on September 10th:

"My trip to Tidikelt has become problematic. I will let events lead me. There would have to be an unhoped-for peace for me to leave. I cannot leave amid such a troubled period."

September 15th, in a letter to his cousin, he pondered the very principle of leaving: "Will I later be able to carry through with the travel plans for the South? I don't know… I live day by day." However, on September 25th, he told her, "They say (it is not sure) that the Moroccans made a small raid in the far South, where I was hoping to go.

This would be the kind of thing to convince me to leave."

But on September 29th he definitively decided against leaving as he wrote to Bishop Guérin:

"I think I will leave for Beni Abbès in two or three days. I have decided against going to the Oasis as our regions are too troubled for me to be gone for the moment… and everything towards the West is such a hotbed that I think it is better for me to stay at the Fraternity, leading, in silence and prayer, the life of a little brother "at the foot of the tabernacle."

The same day, he wrote the same thing to his cousin, concluding, "I will lead my hermit life in silence and cloister."

It is exactly what Bishop Guérin advised him in a letter dated September 25th that he received upon his return to Beni Abbès:

> *"I can only approve of your decision to stay in Taghit or Beni Abbès for the time being. Your priesthood is more useful there than anywhere else and, undoubtedly, for a long time to come. Providence speaks right now; remain in the hands of Providence. When it is time to make another decision you can be sure that it will also make itself known.*
>
> *You have surely heard the rumors of an expedition to Morocco grow more realistic by the day. I have no idea what will come of it, but you must be attentive to the events."*

Those summer months had been full of heated struggles to obtain approval for his plans to travel to the South. They were full of the deep desire to go among the Tuareg that seemed to be the sign of the Will of God. Wasn't all of this but an interlude in his life as a hermit, a temptation or an excess of zeal?

THE SECOND CALL OF THE HOGGAR

And the first steps outside of the cloister

After the summer of 1903 that was so full of travel plans, and after spending the month of September in Taghit caring for the wounded, Brother Charles decided not to leave Beni Abbès. In October he went back to his life as a monk "leading, in silence and prayer, the life of a 'little brother' at the foot of the tabernacle"[154] and cultivating his garden. He thought that he would lead this life until he died, whether alone or with others. How long did that last? For only a few weeks. He could no longer tend his garden because of other things: linguistic work, planning trips, and getting involved in the social and economic organization of others' lives.

On October 30th he shared the depths of his soul with Fr. Huvelin:

> *"Yes, I will try to put up with myself… in fact, I feel a great lassitude, some kind of deep fatigue… I read when I am unable to pray; I do more manual work which is good and humble and seems to work; I try to compensate by working on becoming more charitable towards the poor, by becoming poorer, by trying to pray more fervently and allowing my heart to become warmer."*

---

[154] Letter to Bishop Guérin, September 29, 1903, in Charles de Foucauld, *Correspondances Sahariennes*, Paris, Cerf, 1998, p.230.

Was he feeling a kind of a letdown after all of the tension of the preceding months?

He continued:

"Seeing myself aging and beginning the downward slide is perfect joy: It is the beginning of that final dissolution which is good. I am happy and at peace I have definitively decided against traveling and settling in the South. After having prayed and thought about it as best I could, I think that I am more useful to the Gospel by staying in Beni Abbès which is such a central point between Morocco, Algeria and the Sahara."

It is also what Bishop Guérin had told him in a letter from October 20th:

"You can guess that I completely approve of your plan to remain in Beni Abbès or Taghit. It is really where you need to be for the time being! Providence takes care of showing where one's duty of the moment lies!"

He answered on November 2nd:

"I have decided against spending any length of time in Aqabli. I think it is best to stay here. It is a central point and close to Morocco... But if you cannot send a priest to the Oasis I will try, when things calm down a bit, to take advantage of a convoy to go to El Golea via Timimoun so that I can go to confession. By the same token I can offer the sacraments in the principal garrisons throughout the Oasis... Since you went that way in June there is no hurry so, unless there is an extraordinarily favorable opportunity to go, I will wait until summer... Communication with the North is more difficult than ever."

On the 24th he is more insistent:

"Do you think that you will be able to send a priest this year, that is 1904, to make the tour of the Oases of Touat-Tidikelt etc. for the sake of those who want to go to confession? I hope so. Many of the officers and soldiers who come

through here tell me that they wish that they did not have to be without a priest and the sacraments for such a long time... If you cannot send anyone, would you find the idea of me making such a tour sometime in 1904 to offer the sacraments, poor, very good or out of the question? (I have permanent military authorization) ... I will only go if forced by duty. My vocation is the cloister: I should only leave it for the sake of an urgent need

I will let things fall as they might and God will show me what should be done.

The only thing that I want to know is if you think I should make such a journey through the Oases. If so, I would need to decide ahead of time with my friends from the Oasis... I would prefer it if you were able to send someone else... You knew how much I am like a fish out of water when I am out of the cloister! I am not made to leave it."

During November, Brother Charles read and copied some passages from a little book called *Excelsior* by Fr. Crozier. On the 28th he wrote to his cousin:

"I am going to start my annual retreat for 1904 tomorrow, about 2 months earlier than usual; things are quiet now and I might as well take advantage of that as one never knows the future. I might be called away again to care for the wounded or otherwise impeded by who knows what."

In fact, on the first day of that retreat he was called to the bedside of two seriously ill soldiers in Taghit. He left in the middle of the night and didn't return until the morning of December 6th. He resumed his retreat the same day. He expressed his thoughts to Father Huvelin in a letter dated December 13th, the last day of his retreat.

There are two parts to this letter. He shared his routine examination of conscience in the first part, noting his general impressions and personal faults. There was only one question that pointed to a positive insight. It concerned the manner of sharing alms with the poor. He realized that he couldn't continue as he had been doing. His way of handling this issue would slowly evolve as he knew the people and what they were living.

The second part of the letter is more minor of a request for counsel than expressing the hermit's very complex feelings and desires. During his retreat he had received a second letter from Laperrine inviting him to travel south with them. It is the second call to the Hoggar. Forgetful of all of the resolutions and decisions he had made Brother Charles found himself in the same situation as the previous August. He tried to sort it out:

> *"I have a big question: It is about the trip that I had planned to make to the South, to the oases of Touat and Tidikelt, where a priest never goes, where our soldiers never have Mass, where the Muslims never see a minister of JESUS… You will remember that after receiving the threefold permissions from you, from Bishop Guérin and the military authorities, I was supposed to have left last September but was called to Taghit to be with the wounded there… Now that it seems quiet, should I carry on with that plan? This is a big question mark for me. I know in advance that Bishop Guérin leaves me free to do as I see fit: If Bishop Guérin were able and willing to send another priest, I would certainly not go: My duty would be to stay in Beni Abbès.*
>
> *But I don't think that he wants to send anyone; I even think that can't send anyone. On the other hand, because of some personal friendships I am able to go and I am probably the only priest who can go at this time, is able to go in the foreseeable future or until so many sad things change.*
>
> *In such conditions must I not go, establish a small place there that can serve as a base for a presence in the far southern region, a place that would allow me to spend 2, 3 or 4 months each year, taking advantage of the trip to administer the sacraments at the military outposts, and to let the Muslims see the Cross*

and the Sacred HEART and to speak to them just a little bit about our holy Religion?...

Should I not do this?

At the moment this has never been easier for me to accomplish. I have been invited and they await me.

My nature is extremely repulsed by the idea. I am ashamed to say that I tremble at the thought of leaving Beni Abbès, the peace and quiet at the foot of the altar, and to throw myself into travels, the very thought of which now fills me with such horror.

Reason also points out many inconveniences: leaving the tabernacle empty in Beni Abbès; distancing myself from here where there might (it is however not very likely) be combat; allowing myself to be distracted through these travels which are not good for the soul; do I not glorify God more by adoring him in solitude? Are not solitude and the life of Nazareth my vocation?

And after listening to all that reason dictates, I see these vast regions without a priest, I see that I am the only priest who is able to go and I feel extremely and more and more pushed to go: at least to go one time and then, according to the results, according to what experience will point to, to then decide whether or not to return.

Despite all of the objections of reason, and of my own nature which has a real horror of this absence from Beni Abbès, I feel extremely and more and more of an inner urge to make this trip.

A convoy will be leaving for the South on January 10th. Should I take it? At the moment it is easy for me and they are waiting for me. Should I wait for another convoy? There might not be another for several months, and I fear that it might not be as easy to leave later as it is now.

Should I not go at all?

My feeling, my clear opinion, is that I should go on January 10th. I beg you to write to me about this subject. I will obey you.

If I have not heard from you before January 10th I will probably leave.

If I hear from you, I will do as you say, whatever that may be. Write or send a telegram (Beni Abbès, by way of Beni Ounif, South Oranais), and I will obey your word as the word of Jesus. "Whoever hears you, hears me."

This letter brings out a triple distinction and throws light on this man's life who seems to be torn and at constant odds with himself. He compares "nature" which reacts and "reason" which speaks, but in the last analysis he is carried away by an inner urge, the "intense desire," the thing that he feels he must do.

Father Huvelin does not hesitate to recognize the action of the Holy Spirit in that which he calls an "instinct" that dictates Brother Charles' actions. "Go where the Spirit pushes you," he had written on July 5th. He is used to these discussions and has no illusions about the value of giving an order or a counsel. He never answered this letter.

The next day, December 14th, in a letter to his cousin one simple sentence confirms the change that has taken place: "It is not impossible that I leave around January 10th to make the trip that I had planned back in September… It is not sure yet." He spoke to no one else about it except to Bishop Guérin in a letter dated December 16th.

Compare this letter to the one that he wrote to Father Huvelin just three days before. The tone is completely different. There is neither hesitation nor question. There is no question of "nature" expressing itself, and if "reason" spoke, it was only to support what he felt in his heart that he must do.

"I received a letter from the South saying that they are waiting for me... All of the wounded and ill are healed... It seems that the Saoura and Zousfana are at peace for the moment... The sad events that are taking place in France lead me to believe that it will be impossible for you to send a priest to the South this year.

It seems to me very desirable that each year the sacraments be made available to our soldiers in the Oases; very desirable also that, at least from time to time, the Muslims of those areas see a minister of Our Lord. Therefore, I must seize this opportunity that is being offered to me to go now, while I have the necessary authorization, while it is so easy for me to go.

In keeping with what you and Father Huvelin wrote to me last September, I will probably leave with the next convoy (around January 10th or sooner) to go to Aqabli. They have written to me that there is a small survey expedition there and, with the help of God, I can set up a little place, something very small but which would make it possible for me to spend a few months there each year.

That way, I could divide my time between Beni Abbès and Aqabli, alone and cloistered in each location (for example, spending the summer in Beni Abbès and the winter in Aqabli) and taking advantage of traveling between the two to visit the garrisons and to see the indigenous people.

I am saying that I will probably leave, since obstacles can always arise... Furthermore, as I have just written to Father Huvelin about the matter and asked for an answer, he could always stop me by a letter or telegram. You also, my dearly beloved Father, you can put a stop to this, if not by a letter which might not arrive time, by a telegram.

My idea is to rent a camel to carry my baggage and me... I have a portable chapel which is in good shape... A significant thing that contributed to my willingness to leave is that I will have a catechumen to serve Mass for me... a young slave who was freed September 8, 1902, who spent seven months at the fraternity, receiving religious instruction; as well as hospitality... He left in April of 1903 but then returned just after your visit here... Since July he has resumed his place in the fraternity, conducts himself well, and of his initiative asked to continue his religious instruction. My idea is to bring him along to serve Mass and to help me for material things."

But Brother Charles had also to answer a letter that Bishop Guérin had written on December 18th. He waited until the last minute, January 10th, the day before leaving with the convoy to write:

"I waited until today to thank you for your fatherly letter of December 18th to tell you whether or not I was leaving for the South… Yes, I am going. Neither you nor Father Huvelin sent me contrary advice. I didn't receive anything from either of you: Therefore, I am leaving because it is very easy to go at the moment and later on maybe neither you nor I would be able to go.

I am leaving the 11th or 12th with a large convoy and an officer from the regiment of the Chasseurs d'Afrique from Touat, Mr. Yvart. God willing we will be in Adrar by the 25th. I am thinking of staying there for a short time only and leaving as quickly as possible for Aqabli. I will pay a short visit to In Salah whenever my old comrade tells me to go. His advice will heavily guide my decisions. I will spend some time in Aqabli to make some contacts and I will wait for your letters there. Then I will allow events to guide my decisions and, above all, whatever you write to me."

On January 4th Bishop Guérin answered Brother Charles' letter of December 16th, but it would take weeks to arrive. Seeing that he could not stop this trip, Bishop Guérin gave his permission, vaguely alluding to his hope that it would be decided otherwise. At the same time he abandoned his own plan to travel to the South that he had proposed 2 weeks before.

"You must be on the verge of leaving for the South! I just received your letter and am answering right away.

Leave, dear friend, if God pushes you to do so; I can only repeat what I told you several months ago. Without pushing you to go, I don't in any way want to place an obstacle in your path, if, having considered everything and in the present circumstances, you believe that it is a call from God. I even rejoice with all my heart for all the graces that the Divine Master deigns to pour upon these regions through your ministry, upon the indigenous people and upon the isolated Christians in all these garrisons!

If you have already left, this letter will hopefully follow you. It will probably reach you in Adrar.

But maybe, to the contrary, you will have remained in Beni Abbès. May the Holy Spirit always find you faithfully following his guidance! That is my final wish for you, a wish that I am always pleased to repeat."

While Brother Charles is busy making last arrangements for his trip we might make a few points. We might notice that, since October, there was never a question about the Hoggar or the Tuareg. In November his only goal seemed to be to visit the military outposts. By December there's a change. He began talking about going to Aqabli to set up a small house and then return to Beni Abbès. It was no longer simply a visit but a trip to make a real foundation. He would divide his time between Beni Abbès and Aqabli.

By January he was preparing a year's worth of provisions for the trip, hoping to go as far as In Salah before going to Aqabli where he would try to understand where things were leading. This remains a mystery to us. The next steps would be influenced by the advice of his old friend and by the orders of Bishop Guérin. At this point it is still not clear if this trip is a response to what we call "the second call to the Hoggar."

At the same time, Brother Charles probably had a good idea about what would happen during this trip. We are missing a letter from Laperrine which would give us clearer insight. But we know that Laperrine was preparing for a very long journey even though he did not have the necessary authorizations. He especially did not want the authorities to get wind of his plans. And so Brother Charles was also sworn to secrecy and absolute silence in his correspondence, since the wrong persons might read it. This also explains his silence with Bishop Guérin with whom he could not share certain information. Besides all of this, he knew quite well that he was the only one to take on such a mission and that none of the White Fathers would be authorized to do it.

That is also why he did not speak about the Hoggar or the Tuareg in his letters. He only mentioned Aqabli which he considered the relay point for going farther. If we reread his letter of July 22nd to Bishop Guérin we see clearly that he is envisioning this same project.

Through the "first call to the Hoggar" we learn something about Brother Charles 'understanding and practice of obedience. The "second call to the Hoggar" gives us further insight into this while, at the same time, opening a new page into the mystery of his vocation. And this is the most difficult question. Was his vocation one of solitude and cloister as he had written and believed? Was his vocation one of silence, solitude and inactivity which always led to introspection and languor?

Or was his call that of following his deepest desires? Was it to answer those things that called to him with the power of a direct order from God? Did he seek refuge in the cloister? Was it an evasion of this desire to go elsewhere? How does one distinguish one's duty at a particular moment from pretext? Brother Charles seems to be fully embroiled in all of these questions. He must choose but what criteria should he use to make his decision.

Brother Charles left Beni Abbès on the morning of January 13, 1904. He noted in his Journal:

> *"I have not received any answer from Father Huvelin nor Bishop Guerin about my trip to Touat, Tidikelt, etc. A convoy is leaving this morning in that direction. I have the possibility of joining it. No other priest would be able to go for a long time, maybe several years. Therefore, I think that it is my duty to go. This morning I have removed the Blessed Sacrament from the holy Tabernacle. I leave on foot around 8 a.m. Paul, the catechumen is going with me to serve Mass. We have a mule to carry what I need for the celebration for about a year."*

In a letter to Bishop Guérin dated January 10[th,] he described it further:

> *"I am leaving with the 18-year-old (because I say that I am 10yrs old) Negro[155] whom I mentioned to you who will serve Mass for me: I have a she-ass to carry the chapel and provisions; a young donkey that carries nothing; a pair of new sandals; two pair of canvas shoes... The convoy is composed of about fifty infantry soldiers. I will try to keep up with them; if I am not able, I will do as a bad soldier and asked to be allowed to ride one of the camels from time to time."*

---

[155] Paul Embarek

Brother Charles considered it very important to be able to make the journey on foot. In a letter to Bishop Guérin on June 3, 1904, he wrote:

> *"Yesterday we had an extended visit with two men from Tafilalet, two marabouts.*
>
> *They have heard about you and asked if you had visited Tafilalet. —No, he will go sometime, though. - Does he travel on foot? -No, by camel... This question from these marabouts made me think... They travel on foot leading their donkeys... We are disciples of JESUS and we want JESUS to live in us, "The Christian is another Christ." We never stop talking about poverty; They are disciples of Mohammed: Their question made me think."*

It was regret or a secret reproach concerning these good priests who traveled by camel. For the moment, in the name of holy poverty, he insisted on walking, as it was undoubtedly a more perfect way. It would not be long before he would come around to a more realistic and less perfectionistic way of thinking. But the journey was not difficult and the stages were short: Exceptionally, they would do 15 to 32 kms. Each day, as on this first day.

Upon leaving the beehive of activity that his house in Beni Abbès represented and entering the immense desert, was he entering the realm of Silence and the Absolute where he would meet God? We would have trouble finding those types of reflections in his Notebooks or his letters. We find this in Psichari and others but we should be careful about transposing them onto Charles de Foucauld, as is so often the case. He loves solitude but knows that he will not find it in a caravan. For him, the long journeys through the desert would always be a time of "ministry," life to which he did not feel called. He no longer enjoyed traveling but dreamed of a life like Mary Magdeleine's at the Saint

Baume. It was an idea that he dared call "his vocation." Without knowing it or thinking about it, by doing what he considered to be the will of God for him, he was experimenting with a life of union with God while sharing the life of others.

In a letter to his cousin on January 21st he naively described his first experiences:

> *"My trip is going well… So far I have been able to celebrate Holy Mass every day… I have visited many of the indigenous villages and been well received…*
>
> *-I don't think of alms and medicine as being so much temporal good as much as they are spiritual goods: They are a means to good and friendly relationships with the indigenous people, a way of breaking the ice, a way of learning to trust and become friends with me. When we come to a village, I ask who the four or five poorest ones are and give them some alms. I also let it be known that I am at the service of those who are sick, giving what treatments I am able… So far it seems to work well. In a week I have given out more medicine than in the two years I was in Beni Abbès where I gave several people some medicine each day…."*

Thanks to his Notebook, which has been published in part in *Carnets de Beni Abbès*, we can follow Brother Charles during this year of travel. He noted the distances traveled, the areas and villages visited, where they slept, the quality of watering holes and pastures, people that they met. His daily notes often turned to reflections on historical events, geography and frequently to spiritual meditations.

On February 1st he met up with Commandant Laperrine in Adrar and spent a week there. He received Bishop Guérin's letter from January 4th and answered it on the 9th:

> *"Beloved Father, I am delighted that I have come here. It seems to me that this little journey has been good for some of the Christians, and I hope for the indigenous people in the Saoura and the Oases… Far from regretting having undertaken this trip, I am more and more convinced that it was what the good Lord wanted and I am grateful that he let me know his Will. I pray that he will keep me faithful to it."*

Then he went on to write about his plans. The same day he wrote similarly to Marie de Bondy:

> *"I am delighted with this trip. From what I have seen so far, I realize that I had to make it; I thank God and ask him to make me faithful and do whatever he wants me to do… Tell Father Huvelin that I am happy, that I thank God, that there is more work here than I had thought, much more: Ask him to pray Jesus that I will be a good worker."*

These impressions are supported by what Laperrine wrote to Captain Regnault on February 19th:

> *"De Foucauld seems well; he is working hard at learning Tuareg… He should be in In-Salah by now and I plan to meet him in Aqabli where he will move into the house confiscated from Ag Guerradj156 (Asghar of the Taïtoq Tuareg) to immerse himself in the study of Tuareg, far from Europeans.*
>
> *I promised that I would take him along on our travels and if I see that he gets along with the Tuareg, I will leave him on his own; I'm sorry that he did not arrive 2 weeks sooner as he would have met Mousa ahg Amastan in In-Salah and could have left with his group.*

---

[156] Also known as Sidi agg Akaraji

I dream of making him the pastor of the Hoggar, chaplain to Mousa, maybe even chief of the village of Tadjmout which is comprised of captives placed under the protection of the Tuareg and, consequently, our protection.

His head works well and he understands perfectly that any such dream must be preceded by knowledge of the language; The Arabs are their hereditary enemies. We are a nuisance and unknown, but they hate us less than they hate the Chaamba.

If we live long enough, we'll see. In any case I was very happy to spend a few days with him again. Put into the context of adventure, the old Foucauld of Morocco resurfaces, and he is sorry not to have his sextant, maps, etc... Besides his alms, distributions of medicines, and prayers, I am sure that he will find the time to make a very interesting study of the country and the people (the Tuareg and their prisoner).

If I am not able to leave him in Tuareg country for some reason, I will leave him in Aqabli or at the camp of Tidikelt. But I prefer that he have some distance from us so that the people get used to seeing him without bayonets around him."[157]

From the outset Laperrine explained the situation to his friend: the submission of three of the six big factions that make up the Tuareg people. Brother Charles wrote in his Notebook on February 1, 1904:

"This news is somber. It shows that the entire Tuareg region which until now had been closed to Christians is open. Commandant Laperrine is ready to do whatever he can to facilitate my entrance into the region, travel, and installation. He has offered to take me along on his next tour of the region to visit his new subjects in Ahnet, Adrar and the Hoggar With this next tour, which should start in five or six weeks, he may even push as far as Timbuktu According to

---

[157] Léon Lehuraux, *Au Sahara ave le P. de Foucauld*, Paris, St. Paul, 1946, p. 53.

Commandant Laperrine and until any further information would become available, the best way to enter into relationship with them is through the distribution of medicine, vegetable seeds, and, when called for, alms; but the most important is to learn their language. Aqabli is the best place for learning Tuareg ("tamahaq") as all of the people there speak it and Tuareg caravans are constantly passing through. So it has been decided that I will go there and study Tuareg intensively until Commandant Laperrine comes to get me in several weeks to begin his next tour."

Brother Charles left Adrar on the 10th. He arrived at In Salah on the 16th and left on the 18th, arriving in Aqabli on the 20th. As planned, he settled in the house that had been confiscated from agg Akaraji. What did it mean for him to be "settled" someplace? Was it to place the Blessed Sacrament in the Tabernacle as he did the next day? Was it the pleasure of being stable in no matter what place he could call his own after 40 days of nomadic life? No, it was something else for him and he shared about it in a letter to his cousin on March 5th:

"I am still happy... among other sweet pleasures, there is one that I had been asking of Jesus since a long time: it is to be able, out of love for him, to live in conditions similar to what I experienced in Morocco for my own pleasure... Here, the conditions are about the same..."

But what about the shed where he lived in the Poor Clare's Garden in Nazareth or the hermitage in Jerusalem or his cell at Notre Dame des Neiges? This is an important revelation which relativizes his asceticism's of the previous years. At the Trappists he had complained that, "We are poor for the rich, but not poor like I was in Morocco."[158]

---

[158] *LAH*, Oct 30, 1890.

At the same time, it was not "La Sainte Baume" that he had sometimes dreamed of. But he was no longer preoccupied with that idea. In three different letters to his cousin, we learn more. On February 9th, "It's a center which can serve as my base for reaching out." On February 21st, "There is a lot that I can do here so I will stay here for a while." On February 27th, "There are often caravans from the south. That is why I am staying on here. In this crossroads there is much that I can do for the those coming and going."

In the language of the day this translates to reveal his apostolic preoccupation. And yet he did not go there to busy himself with all these people. He was sent there, a place where there were no Europeans, to learn Tamahaq, the language of the Tuareg. He wrote in his Notebook on February 21st:

> *"I started taking tamahaq lessons today with the help of Mohammed Abd el Qader. He is from Settaf and has spent a lot of time among the Tuareg*[159] *and also lived in Timbuktu."*

So he began what would become one of the primary tasks of his life. He might have hesitated if he had known what it would lead to. But he was far from imagining it. Laperrine, as we have seen, had a clearer idea. But he did not discuss it with Brother Charles. He was content to appreciate this monk whose natural temperament would translate itself into a sense of efficiency and a capacity for work that does not cease to amaze us.

---

[159] He wrote Tuareg without an "s" as it is the plural for of the Arabic word, Targui. But he quickly abandoned this practice for the more customary spellings: a Tuareg, some Tuaregs, Tuareg language.

Writing to his cousin on March 3rd he used a different vocabulary:

The populations of this region, like those of Morocco, speak Berber much more than Arabic. Berber is the ancient language of North Africa and Palestine, spoken by the Carthaginians, by Saint Monica whose Berber, not Greek, name means "queen." It is the language "loved" by St. Augustine as we read in his Confessions, since it was his mother's language. I had learned it a long time ago and forgotten it. I am trying to refresh my memory of it so that I can chat with everyone."

His work in Aqabli ended on March 14th according to his Notebook:

"Left Aqabli to travel with Commandant Laperrine. He plans to visit the populations that have recently submitted themselves and to push on as far as Timbuktu... Our itinerary is probably as follows: In Ziz, Ahnet, Adrar, Timissao, Attalia, Timbuktu; return through Adrar and the Hoggar... If it seemslike a good idea, we think that on the way back they would leave me with the Hoggar where I would settle down."

But on May 16th, in order to avoid problems in Timiaouin with a French column coming from Timbuktu, Laperrine decided to turn back towards the Hoggar. Brother Charles pondered the possibilities of settling in Silet, Abalessa or Tit. But on May 28th he wrote in his Notebook, "Less from fear of the Tuareg than from fear of certain French military personnel, Laperrine will not authorize me to stay in Tit for the moment, nor elsewhere in the Hoggar. We'll see later on."

On June 14th, rather than return north with Laperrine, Brother Charles chose to travel with Lieutenant Roussel who would spend several months in the northern Hoggar region. During this time, in June and July, he worked on translating the Gospels into Tamahaq.

Lt. Roussel's detachment returned to In Salah on September 20th. Two days later, Brother Charles left with a soldier as guide for Adrar, Timimoun and El Golea. He arrived in Ghardaïa on November 11th, with Bishop Guérin having met him along the way in Metlili. For the next six weeks Brother Charles stayed there, sharing the daily life, praying, enjoying the silence and making a nine-day retreat. [160]In speaking with Bishop Guérin he concluded that he was not cut out for traveling but stability in one place and would, therefore, return to Beni Abbès. He arrived there on January 24th after one year and 12 days of travel. He was worn out from the long marches[161] and the work.[162] He decided once and for all to stay in his cloister to be faithful to his vocation.

And yet just a few months later he would be back in the Hoggar. Why is this about-face? To understand we must look closely at what happened next.

---

[160] Charles de Foucauld, *Seul avec Dieu*, Paris, Nouvelle Cité, 1975, pp. 153-198.

[161] 5,994 kms. On foot or by camel in 377 days!

[162] Intensive study of Tamahaq, medical treatment of people that he met along the way as well as of the soldiers, outlines of their journeys, maintenance of his notebook full of detailed observations, correspondence, including 15 letters to Bishop Guérin and 20 letters or notes to his cousin.

Meditations from February 4th and 5th, 1905 at Beni Abbès

February 4

"My Lord I adore You during this flight to Egypt. Holy Virgin, St. Joseph, my mother, my father, unite me to You, make me share your love, your adoration, your feelings, your faithfulness, your perfection; like you, make me, without cease, be what pleases JESUS most, like you, make me console and glorify his HEART as much as possible… As you carried JESUS, now by day, now by night, over desert paths, in this cold season, thirsty, lacking enough food and clothing, in places infested with thieves and wild animals, are you sad, oh my Holy Parents? <u>What are your thoughts?</u> – We are flooded with joy, with grateful thoughts of adoration and love. Flooded with joy because JESUS is with us, is ours, is before our eyes and in our arms, and there is neither cold, fatigue, hunger, or suffering, grateful for the ours; that we see, touch, carry, know JESUS. In continual adoration of this beloved JESUS. And with all the love of our hearts.

Sacred HEART of JESUS, thank You for giving us this lesson, such a clear example of what You want for us. Following Your example, that of Your Holy Parents, Your servant, Your little brother, wishing to be another sign of You – arising in the night, as St. Joseph – fleeing wherever they were able to flee, in exile, he must flee in hunger, thirst, fatigue, cold, bad weather, difficulties along the way, danger, hardship, all the difficulties, all the sufferings, as the Holy Family – he must, despite all these difficulties, sufferings, be always like the Holy Family, and for the same reasons be flooded with joy, having only thoughts of thanksgiving, adoration ad love.

Lord JESUS, come into me. I adore You in Your flight to Egypt. Holy Virgin, St. Joseph, bring me to his feet. My God, I love You, I adore you, belong to You, and give myself to You. May it not be I who live, but You who live in me. At every instant may I be and do whatever is most pleasing to You; may it be the same with all Your children.

Amen. February 5th

My Lord, I adore You in the arms of the Holy Virgin as she flees to Egypt with you… Holy Virgin, St. Joseph, unite me to your thoughts, your hearts, your love, your feelings. I give you my heart, my Holy Parents; unite it to yours, make of it that which is most pleasing to JESUS… With what must it be full, at this moment, to be one with yours, with His, to be what He wants it to be, what He most desires it to be? - It must be full of love for the beloved brother JESUS; that love contains everything, he alone suffices, because from him comes all perfection: from this love will flow: thanksgiving to this JESUS who embraces flight, persecution, danger, hardship, for you; thanksgiving to JESUS who, by embracing them, forever transforms them for you into sweetness; unwavering resolution to always do, as quickly as possible, that which pleases JESUS the most, no matter the fatigue, danger, suffering, difficulties that represents; desire, all other things being equal, if it is the will of JESUS, to have a life full of fatigue, danger, persecution, suffering, allow all the trials to serve to be more united with JESUS through this resemblance; joyful in God, in JESUS, because JESUS is blissful, because He doesn't suffer, because He is eternally and infinitely happy; joy for you and for humankind, your brothers, because you possess JESUS in the Holy Eucharist and in your soul, that you possess him eternally if you so desire, because everything that happens to you will be willed by him for you, because at every instant of your existence in this life and in the other, you will do the will of this Beloved and He will be intimately and lovingly united in heart and will if you so desire, and that all human beings have the same happiness; adoration, continual contemplation of this Beloved brother JESUS who is at this moment, for you, in our arms... Oh my Holy Parents, fill me with these sentiments. I place my heart into your hands. Make of it what JESUS desires most.

Sacred HEART of JESUS, thank you for embracing so many crosses right from your crib, from the moment of your birth: flight, fatigue, long voyages, persecution, exile, cold, pain, thirst, danger, hardship, abandonment, all of the pain which your tender HEART suffers for your Holy Parents, shares with them, and inflicts upon them for us... thank you for later changing those thorns into roses, for hearts that love you: in sharing these sorrows with you they will become pleasures: to suffer with You, to resemble You, to share Your trials is the joy of joys for the heart of the one who loves You. To resemble, to imitate, is a violent need of love: it is proper to this union towards which love naturally and necessarily tends. Resemblance is the measure of love.

Lord JESUS, come into me. I adore You during Your flight into Egypt. Holy Virgin, St. Joseph, bring me to the feet of JESUS. My God, I love You, I adore You, belong to You, and give myself to You. May it not be I who live, but You who live in me. At every instant, may I be that which please You the most? Amen.

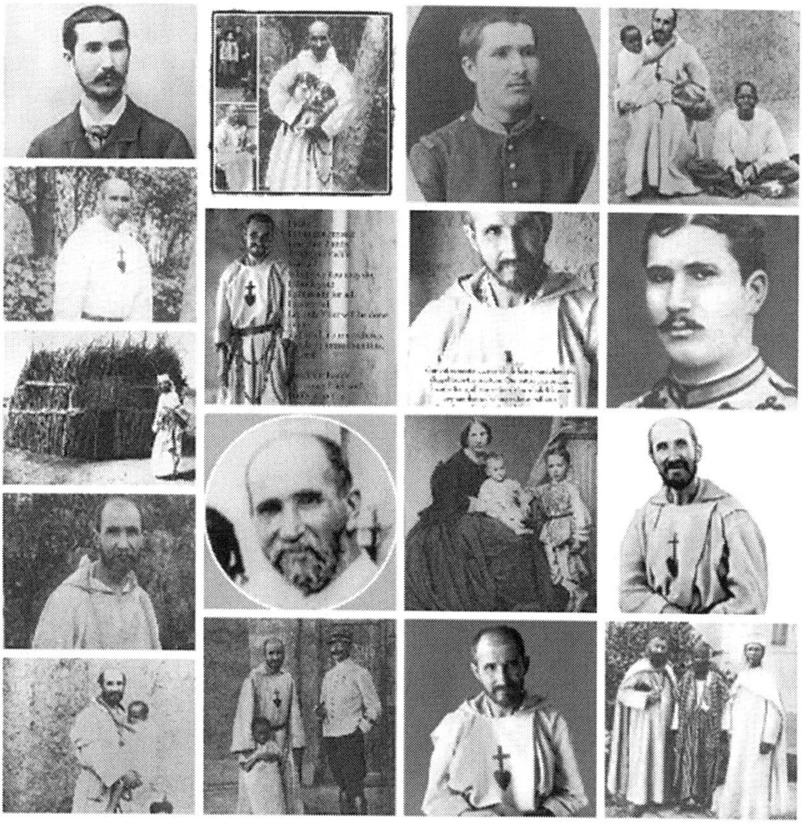

The Third Call to the Hoggar January 24 to May 3, 1905

We will follow Brother Charles day by day during the 100 days that he stayed in Beni Abbès in order to try to understand what was happening in him and analyze the circumstances that led to the change of direction. While this was one period in his life we can divide it into two parts: the first two months during which he was he was recuperating from the fatigue of his travels, and the last 40 days when he was feeling much better.

Three days after he arrived in Beni Abbès he heard that Lyautey had also just arrived. It was an unplanned visit and he only stayed about 36 hours. But during these few hours he encountered Brother Charles several times. While they had never personally met before, Lyautey was old friends with Brother Charles' brother-in-law, Raymond de Blic and his cousin, Louis de Foucauld.

Lyautey had arrived on October 1, 1903 as the General Commandant of the subdivision based at Aïn-Sefra. It was quite understandable that he would have been concerned about Charles de Foucauld's presence in what was part of the territory under his command. He had heard about this priest whose reputation for holiness was already quite well known. Contrary to what Brother

Charles imagined[163], Lyautey was not very keen about having missionaries who liked to make (OK) names for themselves. We know about his general mistrust through a comment that he reportedly made: "I wish they would send this little priest back to France. He is in the process of undoing the foundation of my policies with the indigenous people." Lyautey had clearly defined his approach in an article published in 1900 entitled, "The role of the army in the colonies."

Lyautey considered himself a "free spirit in questions of religion," meaning that he had great respect for the faith of others. He felt as much a sense of the (This is good) supernatural at the tomb of Sidi Cheikh, founder of the brotherhood, whose buried in the kouba at El-Abiodh-Sidi-Cheikh as he did in the chapel at Beni Abbès. He feared that Brother Charles' missionary zeal would run counter to this sense of openness. He needed to find out for himself. But Brother Charles had been gone on the expedition with Laperrine at that time, an expedition which posed a problem in Lyautey's thinking. So he had put off going to Beni Abbès. He also did not know his subordinate officer, Laperrine, very well except to know that he was, like himself, an independent type... Another reason to worry about the role that Charles de Foucauld might play on the expeditions.

So Lyautey's visit to Beni Abbès was probably not just luck (yes). His conversations with the humble Brother Charles must have reassured him. They developed a deep esteem for and trust in one another,

---

[163] "He must have met some missionaries while he was stationed in Madagascar. You will probably get a lot of support from him." Letter to Bishop Guérin, Nov. 24, 1903, quoted in *Charles de Foucauld, Correspondances sahariennes,* Paris, Cerf, 1998, p. 236.

mutually respectful of their different missions. Lyautey later described assisting at Mass on that January 29th with all the officers:

> *"His hermitage was a real hovel! His chapel no more than a miserable hallway of columns, covered with thatch! His altar was just a board! He had an image of Christ painted on cloth hanging over the altar, metal candlesticks! Our feet were in the sand. Well, I have never seen anyone say Mass like Father de Foucauld.... I thought I was in the Thebaide (I have no idea what the Thebiade is and it's not in the Larousse. Therefore it makes no sense to readers Do you know?). It was one of the most impressive experiences of my life." 164*

Lyautey was impressed by the monk and by the man. He came to like him, as did most of those who met him. They only began corresponding in 1908 but, unfortunately, Lyautey's letters, always quite interesting, have all been lost since Brother Charles did not keep the letters he received once he had answered. And we only have seven out of the twenty-one letters that Brother Charles wrote to Lyautey.

We also need to speak about Laperrine. During the months of traveling together in the desert a close friendship developed between them. Foucauld respected Laperrinein his agnosticism and Laperrine respected the monk's devotions. He understood his vocation to live as a universal brother, but he also knew how to use his various competencies. He recognized that his friend's humility and desire to be a brother to all was an essential presence in the process of pacification in the region. Foucauld discovered in Laperrine a deep sense of the common good and an overall interest in the people. These formed the basis of their shared vision for achieving progress in the country. A

---

[164] Georges Gorrée, *Sur les traces de Charles de Foucauld*, Lyon, Editions de la Plus Grande France, 1936, p.187.

total and reciprocal trust sealed a unique relationship that became one of his closest friendships. It was expressed through regular correspondence (more than 230 letters over 14 years); in the later years a letter each time the mail would go out every two weeks. That was as much as he wrote to his cousin, Marie de Bondy.

For the moment, he noted for himself and copied to Bishop Guérin and Sister Augustine, superior of the White Sisters in Ghardaïa, what he remembered of conversations with Laperrine concerning possible foundations of the Fathers and Sisters in the South. His naiveté was stunning. He imagined that his dreams could become a reality and believed that those who desired it could achieve the impossible. He wrote as if the White Fathers and Sisters had a whole entourage of personnel available for foundations throughout the south which should be made while Laperrine was still in charge. In his letter to Bishop Guérin he omitted the criticisms that the military made about the White Fathers. They complained that the White Fathers were a constant bother for the authorities, made big blunders, and involved themselves in matters that were not their concern. The Sisters, on the other hand, were always warmly welcomed.

While he was in Beni Abbès at this time, Brother Charles also received a visit from Captain Nieger, Laperrine's assistant, who was on his way to France because of his father's death. He had also become a "truly dear friend" during the long marches of the preceding year. "He is young, (just 33 years old), but I like him and have a lot of esteem for him."[165] He even asked him to visit Marie de Bondy on his behalf, something he

---

[165] *LMB*, March 21, 1905, quoted in Georges Gorrée, *Amitiés saharienes*, Paris, Arthaud, 1946, vol 1, p.285.

205

only asked of very close friends. Unfortunately, of the one hundred or so letters that he received from Brother Charles, Nieger only kept three, including one which Brother Charles wrote the day before his death.

There were also all of the other officers with whom he became close and who had been transferred. There was Captain Regnault, "the dearest friend of them all," "A friend and irreplaceable brother." There is also a whole series of letters that he wrote to various officers whom he had met over the year. Among these is a Lieutenant Bricogne to whom he would be "forever grateful" for the gift a tent in which to celebrate Mass during his travels. This officer would die on the front lines in 1916, hit by a shell. Brother Charles wrote to his wife several days before his own death, the last among many beautiful sympathy letters written by a man with a big heart who was faithful to his friendships.[166]

Another friendship is less well known, that with Sister Augustine.

They had only met three months before during his stay in Ghardaïa. Having read *Abandonment to Divine Providence* by de Caussade and another book, *Excelsior*, by Fr. Crozier that Brother Charles had given to her, Sr. Augustine began writing to Brother Charles. She shared about her difficulties and her desires for a life more totally given to God than what she felt she could live because of her present responsibilities. It is a series of very intimate letters which amount to spiritual direction, besides the discussions of foundations in the South. This very special

---

[166] There is a letter from Beni Abbès on January 28, 1905 written to Bishop Guérin whose mother had just died. Charles de Foucauld, *Correspondances Sahariennes*, Paris, Cerf, 1998, p.311.

collection of letters was unknown until its recent publication in *Correspondances sahariennes*.[167]

We could be led to believe that the bulk of his time was taken up with correspondence and seeing people. But that was just a very small part of his day. What was he doing that kept him from cultivating his garden, even when he would have had the strength to do so?

First and foremost was intellectual work. Brother Charles was able to do it despite fatigue and poor health because it was mainly a recopying his notes. "I spend my days following a monastic rhythm and in solitude; I replace manual work with copying my notes about the Tuareg language and other notes that I made during the year of traveling…."[168] As he finished a section, he would send it to Bishop Guérin, the first being a summary of his trip which he entitled, "Among the Tuaregs (Taïtoq, Iforas, Hoggar). May-September, 1904." He also wanted to make two or three copies right away of his translation of Holy Scripture in Tamahaq to help the White Sisters prepare themselves for mission among the Tuaregs. And he wanted to recopy his notes about how to travel in the Sahara[169] but other duties and his lingering fatigue prevented him from doing so during the first two months.

We also need to mention how concerned he was with missionary work. He had traveled for a whole year and he wanted what he had learned to be useful to others. He learned a lot and established some

---

[167] Op. cit., starting on page 954.

[168] *LMB*, Feb. 18, 1905.

[169] Charles de Foucauld, *Carnet de Beni Abbès*, Paris, Nouvelle Cité, 1993. This took up 23 pages of his notebook, pp. 115-138.

guideposts. He saw the urgency of this work but since he himself had renounced missionary activity, he felt that it was up to the White Fathers to carry on. He wrote pages and pages for all concerned, describing projects, organizations, and what he felt would be necessary for the accomplishment of these projects. This tendency to not only propose such foundations but to organize their setup was characteristic of his creative genius and his temperament.

Meanwhile, Brother Charles tried to live according to his Rule of Life which called for periods of meditation on the Gospel, either silent or written. However, throughout his life in the Sahara, he wrote very few of his meditations in contrast to his practice in Nazareth and when he was a Trappist. Only during this one-hundred-day period did he write his meditations, regularly and nearly daily.

He wrote these meditations[170] beginning on February 2nd until Easter. Except for the first entry about Jesus offering himself as a victim, the rest of the meditations from February have to do with the flight into Egypt. As we read them, we realize that we are reading Brother Charles' own experience of the last year of being on the move, including the fatigue that was a major consequence for him. He is both afraid of having to start all over again while being ready to leave again despite the fatigue. He did his writing in the evenings, imagining the scene and reflecting on what he imagined. He seems to have followed a method: 1) Placing himself in the midst of the scene that he imagined.

---

[170] Charles de Foucauld, *L'Esprit de Jésus*, Paris, Nouvelle Cité, 1978, pp. 165-286.

2) What do you have to say to me? 3) My response to you? All of his mediations end in the same way, with a résumé of his thoughts in other words:

> *"My God, I love you, I adore you, I belong to you, I give myself to you. Let it note I who live, but you who live in me. Let me be and do what pleases you the most at every moment, and may it be so for all your children. Amen."*

The important thing in his meditations was to unite himself with the will of Jesus to do what pleased him in this life. Was it in looking at Jesus that he would discover what he must do to please him? No. Concretely the process seems to have worked in the opposite sense. First of all, he saw what he should do, either through intuition or because he simply knew what needed to be done in his heart. This may simply have been Brother Charles being Brother Charles. From there he thought that in doing what he felt called to do, he would be doing what was pleasing to Jesus. From there he looked at the words and deeds of Jesus for confirmation of what he felt he should do. We should not confuse this process with Imitation's vocabulary, which he used to express his will to live in union with Jesus and to let Jesus live in him.

A forty-day period from March 24th to the beginning of May can be considered as a whole. It is the most significant time frame of this period, when he would decide which would change the direction of his life. It also coincided with springtime and the restoration of his health and energy. On March 29th he wrote to Mariede Bondy, "I have only gotten better and better since my last letter. I have no complaints. I have gone back to my regular activities." And on April 11th he wrote to her again:

"I am feeling surprisingly well. I have that great sense of well-being that one has after overcoming long-standing fatigue, that one feels once it is all behind one...

Don't think that the climate of Beni Abbès is bad. Rather it is exceptionally healthy."

Now we can look at the chronology of events to understand this new direction that he was about to take.

On April 1st he received a letter from Laperrine who invited him to make another trip to the Hoggar with Captain Dinaux who was planning on leaving In Salah at the beginning of May. On April 8th a second letter repeated the invitation. There is no reaction and there is no mention of it in his meditations. Brother Charles only answered Laperrine that he was not free to leave the region of Saoura before Autumn.

Only then would he decide among three possibilities: a life of travel, the cloister of BeniAbbès, or a cloistered life in Silet.

But in a letter to his cousin on April 11th he wrote:

"It is not impossible that I would be obliged to make a trip to the south... I don't think it is likely but I am ready if need be... I sent a telegram to Bishop Guérin, asking him to consult with Father Huvelin and to wire me back."

On April 15th he wrote in his Notebook:

"I am perplexed: on the one hand my vocation is the life of Nazareth on the other hand the Oases and the Tuareg have no priest and no priest is able to go there: not only am I allowed to go, I am invited."

On April 18th he wrote to Father Huvelin about his dilemma. He recopied this letter in his Notebook and the resolution that he had made during his retreat at Ghardaïa at Christmas time. We find his "dilemma" expressed therefore in his Notebook, to Father Huvelin, to Bishop Guérin and also in a letter to Marie de Bondy on April 19th:

> *"This was my dilemma: It is always so hard to see such a large country without a priest. It is hard on people, especially those whose faith is weak. And so it is that much harder to know that a priest has been invited and has refused… To make matters worse, those who extend the invitation are offended. Then when we later asked to go, they said that they had offered but we had refused and that the matter is closed. Nonetheless, I feel that it is the will of the Good Lord that I remain here and so I remain."*

Just the day before Brother Charles had written to Sister Augustine:

> *"I am in Beni Abbès and have no intention of leaving: Now that I am back within my cloister I do not see anything else on the horizon but to live out the hidden life of Nazareth at the foot of the tabernacle."*

During this time Bishop Guérin was in France and had met with Father Huvelin. He explained to him what was behind the resolutions that Brother Charles had made at

Ghardaïa and the decision that he had made. Father Huvelin brought up the usefulness of such a trip for the sake of the mission, especially in light of the immediate invitation to go. He concluded:

> *"So let him go! With the grace of God… at least let us leave him the freedom to judge the situation for himself on the spot. We are so far away and have so*

little information. But let him know that we are not against this new expedition, that we are even willingly inclined to accept the idea."171

On April 19th Bishop Guérin sent a telegram to Brother Charles which he received in the 21st. He was surprised to read: "We are inclined to accept invitation, leave you free to assess circumstances and opportunity." Having decided not to go, he received this telegram as an order:

"Sacred Heart of Jesus, you are so good to give me this very day, through the voice of those of whom you said, 'He who hears you, hears me' an unexpected order. It surprises my deepest self, throwing me into difficulties, trials and fatigue... How good you are, Sacred Heart of Jesus, to reveal your will to your unworthy servant, to let him know it infallibly through the voice of those of whom you said, "He who hears you, hears me."172

He wrote immediately to Laperrine, asking if there was still time for him to join the caravan. The next day, Holy Saturday, he wrote in his meditation:

"You are a useless servant: You must use all your strength, your care, and your ardor to do, not only all that he commands you to do, but everything that he even suggests; all that he is ever so slightly inclined to see you do; out of love, in obedience, by imitation. But as certainly as you must obey and work with all your strength you are just as certainly a useless servant: God could have others do whatever you do, or do it without anyone's help, or at least without you:you are a useless servant."173

---

[171] Charles de Foucauld, *Correspondances sahariennes*, Paris, Cerf, 1998, p. 337.

[172] Charles de Foucauld, *L'Esprit de Jésus*, Paris, Nuvelle Cité, 1978, p. 284.

[173] *Op. cit.*, pp. 285-286.

The meditations of this year end with the theme of the useless servant.

While waiting for Laperrine's answer Brother Charles made hasty preparations to leave. He wanted to finish copying the Gospels but he first had to send Bishop Guérin his notes on traveling in the Sahara. On the 29th he learned that everything was providentially arranged for a May 3rd departure. After sending bits and pieces of the Gospel in Tamahaq in two separate mailings the day before leaving, he took advantage of a good opportunity to leave for Adrar with Paul Embarek.

ON THE WAY TO THE HOGGAR
MAY 3RD - AUGUST 11, 1905

Brother Charles left Beni Abbès on May 3rd at the end of the one hundred days during which time he remained within the few square meters of his cloister. He had to hurry to rendezvous with Captain Dinaux who was leaving In Salah at the same time. He met the detachment on June 8th. Among the members of the expedition were: Professors E.F Gautier, explorer and geographer, and

R. Chudeau, geologist; M. Etienot, from the telegraph company; an interpreter and officer, M. Benhazera; a journalist, P. Mille; several non-commissioned officers and brigadiers, some Tuaregs with Sidi agg Akaraji, chief of the Taïtoq.

The expedition halted for three days and set out again on June 12th. The major event of the trip was the meeting with Mousa agg Amastan on the 25th. Captain Dinaux was a bit concerned about how the amenokal would react to this man traveling with the military. He wore a bizarre costume which included a red heart and cross sewn across his chest. But having already acquired certain ease with Tamahaq, Brother Charles served as interpreter and spoke directly with Mousa agg Amastan who remained with the group for about three weeks.

It seems that the two men had a reciprocally seductive effect on each other. The first information that we have of this is through a letter that Brother Charles wrote to Bishop Guérin on July 13th after Mousa had left the group:

> "Mousa, their chief, is a remarkable man. He is intelligent, with a broad vision of things, God-fearing, very pious. He is an honest man who truly desires peace and the common good as he understands it.... He is thirty-five years old, has lived a just life until now, and is very much loved throughout the country.... If he continues in this way we can expect much from him, through him, and for him He has a great desire to go to Algiers and even to Paris."

This request had an immediate effect on Brother Charles. He took it very seriously. While he recognized the inconveniences of such a trip, he saw it more so as an opportunity. He wrote to Bishop Guérin about it, including a detailed itinerary for Algiers and Paris, apparently paid for by the White Fathers. This monk who vowed himself to the life of Nazareth was incorrigibly and perpetually creative when it came to ideas for others. In October he brought the idea up again (an idea that he never let go of), even proposing that he could accompany Mousa, although he said that it wasn't his place to do so.

In his July 13th letter to Bishop Guérin he tried to keep to the present: "I am preparing a small Tuareg glossary and book of grammar for my companions and for those who might need one." In his postscript he mentioned a short-term project:

> *"I will try to prepare the beginnings of a mission in the Hoggar: but just a very small thing of no importance. Nothing big, like at Beni Abbès: Just a small hut and a couple of goats near a watering hole I have not decided where yet:*
>
> *Abalessa? In Amgel? Tit? Someplace between Tit and Tamanrasset? I'll see when I get there."*

He alluded to his hope, of which he was practically certain, that he would soon have a companion, a Fr. Richard from El Goléa. The year before he had hesitated to have him come, on the premise that their vocations were too different, Fr. Richard being a very active and apostolically oriented White Father. Now he was ready to go all the way to Algiers to meet up with him. But this companion was never offered to him.

Brother Charles wrote to his cousin:

> *It seems indispensable that I try to settle in the Hoggar and spend at least several months there each year... It seems to follow from Father Huvelin's decision to have me make this trip... I will do what I think best."*174

The same day he wrote to Father Huvelin, interrupted only by nightfall. He asked some important questions:

> *"I do not forget that your feast day is the day after tomorrow: St. Henry. My poor prayer will be with you even more than usual... The trip is going well, very well. I have met many indigenous people... I lack just one thing, myself... I am happy with everything except myself.*
>
> *Besides my countless faults, one thing pains me: ... I would like to be able, at least to some extent, to recite the Office, have the hours for prayer and meditation, the time to read Sacred Scripture, as when I am more settled ... But if try to do all that I have no time left to keep up with Tuareg, to study the language, to prepare as much as possible the way for those workers who will come after me... Since I cannot reconcile these two things, I am dropping the*

---

174 *LMB*, July 13, 1905, p. 138.

first and spending my time on the second, which seems to be what God wishes me to do the most… But although I think that I am doing the right thing, it pains me to lead a life with little time dedicated exclusively to prayer, neglecting the spiritual exercises which are good and nourishing. I often ask myself if my inability to reconcile these two things is real or the result of my own tepidness.

But since leaving Beni Abbès I have almost always replaced the Breviary by the Rosary – and sometimes having put it off until evening, it goes unfinished… During the marches I think of Jesus as much as I can, but alas, so miserably!

- The time which is not occupied by the marches or rest, is spent preparing the ways, trying to build friendship with the Tuareg and working on the lexicon. These translations are indispensable for those who will come to bring JESUS…

If I am wrong about this if I should stop doing things this way and find another, tell me and I will obey… Despite my regrets over this, unless I hear otherwise from you, I think that this is a good way to manage…

For the future I need your advice… I am accepted but I don't think that they will accept others… As long as other priests are not welcome among the Tuareg should I stay and settle for a good portion of the year? The more I think about it, the more it seems like a good idea. It is necessary to keep this door open until others can come; to make friends and develop trust; to make good impressions; to prepare the ground until the workers can come into the field; Since JESUS sent me here through the words of your mouth, it seems that I should continue to try to do His work until others can replace me

For the moment I am trying to prepare a little place among the Tuareg: not the beginnings of a place like the fraternity of the Sacred Heart at Beni Abbès; a simple hut without any land or garden where I can live my life of prayer and make wooden bowls and rope for a good part of the year, having as little land as possible.

Night has fallen. A Dieu, beloved Father."

Charles de Foucauld is unable to write three sentences without outlining some project that he has dreamed up. Point in fact: he never made any ropes or wooden bowls!

On July 20th the expedition turned north, progressing by steps of 25, 45, 50 or even 60 kilometers at a time. Mousa aag Amastan had set the rendezvous for a village called Tamanrasset.[175]

The Notebook that he began in Beni Abbès was completely filled by July 21st.

But he noted under the July 4th entry everything that happened until the 21st, including his decision, agreed upon with Mousa, to settle in the Hoggar. He began using another notebook in which he had begun copying the Gospel of Matthew in Arabic, meaning that he had begun from the back. He continued writing his journal from the front of this notebook, but also writing other notes in the back, such as names of poor people that he met and his expenses. So as we look at this notebook the two sections gradually converge in the middle. It is understandable that the editing of his *Carnets de Tamanrasset*[176] was no easy task.

The change taking place in Charles de Foucauld's life was not only symbolized by starting a new Notebook. His first entry in the new book, on the feast of St Mary Magdeleine on July 22, is one of the most

---

[175] At this time Charles de Foucauld was writing Tamenghaset. Later he would replace the gh by an r. For our purposes we have chosen to use the usual spelling, Tamanrasset throughout.
[176] Charles de Foucauld, *Carnets de Tamanrasset*, Paris Nouvelle Cité, 1986.

telling texts that we have of the evolution of his thinking about the meaning of Nazareth. We read:

> *"...no habit – like Jesus at Nazareth, no cloister, like Jesus at Nazareth, not living far from where others live but close to a village – like Jesus at Nazareth, not less than 8 hours of work [manual or other but manual as much as possible]–like Jesus at Nazareth. no large pieces of land, nor large house, nor big expenses, nor even large alms, but extreme poverty in all things – like Jesus at Nazareth… In a word in everything, like Jesus at Nazareth. Use the Rule of the Little Brothers as you would a holy book to help you live this life. Clearly distance yourself from anything that does not serve the perfect imitation of this life.*
>
> *Do not try to organize or prepare for the foundation of the Little Brothers of the Sacred Heart of Jesus: Alone, live as if you would always be alone. If you are two or three or several, live as if you would never be more numerous. Pray as Jesus prayed, as much as he prayed, always giving a very great place to prayer… Like Jesus, always give a great place also to manual work: it is not time taken from prayer but given to prayer; the time that you give to manual work is a time of prayer; faithfully pray the Breviary and the rosary each day; Love Jesus with your whole heart "dilexit multum," and your neighbor as yourself for love of him… Your life of Nazareth can be lived anywhere: live it where it will be most beneficial for your neighbor.*

On the morning of August 6th after having seen Abalessa again and the village of Ennedid, he decided to settle in Tamanrasset, sight unseen. He wrote to Bishop Guérin:

> *"I will probably settle in the village of Tamanrasset in the heart of the Hoggar region. I will sell my camels, build a small hut, place the Blessed Sacrament in the tabernacle and settle to stay at least through the autumn and winter… After a lot of thought, I prefer Tamanrasset which is quite central and at the same time not likely to be near any future military installations or a telegraph*

line... And I will stay instead of heading back north as I had initially planned. I am able to stay now, but if I leave I may not be able to come back.

This opportunity seems to be a gift from God which should be taken advantage of... I will build a very small house, two rooms, two meters by two meters, one a chapel and the other my cell."

So that day he decided not to return North with the military detachment but to settle in Tamanrasset, reserving the final decision for when he would see the place. This is the first time that he explicitly mentioned Tamanrasset. We are led to conclude that that this had been a topic of conversation with Mousa agg Amastan, who also had some ideas about this hamlet near to where he often made camp.

They stayed in the village of Tit, about 40 kms from Tamanrasset, from the 6th to the 10th of August. He wrote five letters there. The previous year, on May 26th 1904, he had hoped to settle there and noted his thoughts on the subject: either among the cliffs along the right side of the wadi where there was enough arable land to eventually establish a fraternity or on the top of the mountain:

The first place has the advantage of being immediately inhabitable. It would only take a little time and work to fix it up and easily accessible. It could easily become a fraternity if one were to be established there; ... the second place has the advantage of being far from people and noise and would therefore provide solitude with GOD."

After discussing the advantages and disadvantages of each, he continued:

> *May the Spouse tell me in which of the two places he desires me to settle today.*
>
> *Today and in the future, 'if you can, establish yourself in the first place, in the grotto which so resembles Bethlehem and Nazareth. You will have both the perfection of imitating me and that of charity. Concerning recollection, it is love that must recollect you in me and not distance from my children. See me in them and as I did at Nazareth, live close to them, lost in God. In these cliffs where I have led you despite yourself, you will imitate where I lived in Bethlehem and Nazareth, the imitation of my whole life in Nazareth, in charity towards those who live there and towards travelers because you will be accessible to them. It will be a charity towards your companion by lessening his fatigue.*
>
> *There will be recollection by avoiding the distractions of a lengthy construction on the mountain. There will be poverty by avoiding construction costs. There will be humility in having, as I did, a humble, poor and hidden dwelling, instead of one that will be seen from afar. Having more contact with others, there is the hope of doing better. There is the hope of having brothers come and live there, increasing and becoming a true fraternity. And finally, and this is enormous, you will quickly have the presence of the Most Blessed Sacrament in the tabernacle as you will soon be able to set up a chapel"*

If we put this together with what he wrote on July 22, 1905 on the feast of St Mary Magdeleine, we see that he had clearly taken a new step in understanding Nazareth, and the implications for his vocation. Brother Charles realized that the Rule that he had written in 1899, even though he had corrected it several times, was not capable of guiding life whose dynamic would henceforth be dictated by the "provisional." This "provisional quality" of his life is reflected in what are unusual words for him that we find in a letter that he wrote to Marie de Bondy on August 6th:

"I think that I will settle for several months, maybe longer, in the village of Tamanrasset in this area… I had tried to find a spot last year, without success; this year it looks like it will work .

So I will most likely settle there at least through the summer, fall, winter and maybe much longer: I will settle without making any plans: on the one hand, I am not the one to make any decision about it. That's up to Father Huvelin and Bishop Guérin; on the other hand, so many things happen, and we can hardly see what the future will bring! Will I go back to Beni Abbès? When?

…I really don't know…I will try to do for the best at each moment, without making any plans."

Settled in Tamanrasset

He arrived in Tamanrasset on August 11, 1905, having camped for the night just 20 kms away. He wrote in his Notebook:

"I have chosen Tamanrasset, a village of 20 campfires in the heart of the Hoggar mountains and of the Dag-Ghali, the major tribe of the area, far from any sizeable village. I don't think that there will ever be a military post here, nor telegraph, nor Europeans, nor mission in the foreseeable future. I have chosen to settle in this forsaken little corner, asking Jesus to bless this place where I hope to have as my only example his life at Nazareth. May he deign, in his love, to convert me, to make me into what he wants me to be, to help me to love him with my whole heart; To love Him, obey Him, imitate Him as much as possible in every instant of my life! COR IESU Sacratissimum…adveniat regnum tuum! Our Lady of Perpetual Help, carry me in your arms. Saint Mary Magdeleine, Saint Joseph, I place my soul into your hands."

Taken by the place and the climate, he wrote to Bishop Guérin on August 13th:

"Tamanrasset is in the middle of mountains at about 1200 to 1500 meters altitude. It is in the heart of the Hoggar region and will never become a big center, have a military garrison nor telegraph office, etc. It is isolated and does not have much water. There are about fifteen poor haratin families. It is in the middle of the pastureland where some of the Dag Ghali, the largest and most important tribe of the Hoggar, are always camped. The climate is perfect, like summers in Touraine or Anjou."

On the same day, Mousa rejoined the expedition, camped in the Sersouf Wadi which runs perpendicular to the Wadi of Tamanrasset. The amenokal was happy to learn that the marabout had decided to settle in this village rather than elsewhere and this confirms that it was his idea in the first place. Brother Charles wrote to Marie de Bondy the same day:

> *"Tomorrow I will begin to build my hut: I don't know how long I will be here... The Good Lord has made everything happen so easily that I see that it is his will... May it be blessed... It is no small grace that Jesus has given me in letting me settle here: For centuries it has been such a closed region!... I must be faithful to such grace and do the good that is expected of me...I will be the only European here. The authorities are convinced that there is no danger and that the country is completely submissive and peaceful."*

On Monday, the 14th, he began preparing the foundation for his house. He chose place a little apart from the other huts and gardens on the north side of the village.

From what he wrote we might be led to believe that all the problems had been resolved. But it is just at this moment that some difficulties became apparent. Mousa had called for a meeting of the Dag Ghali. Many came and they hardly shared the enthusiasm of the amenokal who had thought that it would be a simple matter for them to accept the presence of the marabout. Mousa obviously managed to convince them of the usefulness of his presence among them, but the Dag Ghali were not willing to share the water from their foggaras with this stranger. Captain Dinaux's notes give us some insight into the issue's complexity: a vegetable garden and fruit trees are not watered like a field of wheat or sorghum. We can only imagine the discussions on the economic impact that could have led to the failure of both Mousa's and Charles de Foucauld's projects.

On August 15th, a day when he did not work, Brother Charles wrote a beautiful prayer of abandon to the Mother of the Holy Family:

> *"Most Holy Virgin, I give myself to you; Mother of the Holy Family, help me to live the life of the divine Family of Nazareth. Let me be worthy of being your child, to be the child of St. Joseph, the true little brother of Our Lord Jesus. Into your hands I commend my soul, I give you all that I am so that you can make of me that which is most pleasing to Jesus. If I should make some special resolution, help me to make it. Carry me. I only desire one thing: to be and do what pleases Jesus the most at every instant. I give and confide to your care, Beloved Mother, my life and my death."*

Finally, Mousa gave in to the Dag Ghali, and proposed to the marabout that he abandon the idea of settling in Tamanrasset. Instead he suggested that he settle in Ennedid where they could dig a common foggaras (I can't find a word for this in Larousse). But it was no small thing to change the marabout's mind. He had chosen Tamanrasset and wanted to stay. The reasons that led him there blocked him from seeing any other solution. In the end a compromise was reached. They would move him to the other side of the wadi which was not Dag Ghali land. There he could dig a well and have garden without bothering anyone. He would furthermore be safer on that side since groups often camped towards the southern edge of the village. Paul Embarek, who had helped build the foundations on the north side, only remembered the security question to explain the move.

On the 17th, they chose a site with Mousa and began the foundations on the 18th. On the 19th Brother Charles set the first foundation stone to his house which would be six meters long and 1.75 meters wide. It was built with a combination of earth and stone.

Afterward he built a zeriba, a hut of reeds, (We have no idea of 'zeriba' in English…donc le petite phrase en plus) which was used as parlor, dining room, kitchen, bedroom for Paul, and for hospitality.

A new life was beginning, a new way of living Nazareth without a monastic enclosure. He was far from imagining that only eleven years later his short life would end in this village where he had come for some undetermined amount of time.

Life in Tamanrasset

—⧖—

Charles de Foucauld's life in Tamanrasset alternated between travel and times of settled life. Dividing the eleven years into five periods can give us a better overview of his life in the Hoggar. Remember that a long trip south and through the Hoggar in 1904, and a shorter one in 1905, preceded his time in Tamanrasset.

1st Period: August 1905 to July 1907   ® 23 months

TAMANRASSET	Trip to Algiers	Trip South
13 months	7 months	3 months

2nd Period: July 1907 to May 1909   ® 23 months

TAMANRASSET	1st Trip to France
18 months	5 months

3rd Period: June 1909 to May 1911   ® 23 months

TAMANRASSET	2nd Trip to France
18 months	5 months

4th Period: May 1911 to November 1913   ® 31 months

TAM	ASEKREM	TAMANRASSET	3rd Trip to France
3 months	5 months	16 months	7 months

5th Period: December 1913 to December 1916   ® 36 months

TAMANRASSET
36 months

During the first period, a trip north took him as far as Beni Abbès and then to Algiers. He started back with a companion brother whom he left at In Salah. He stayed there for a while before making another tour of the South which lasted until July 1907.

The second and third periods have a strange resemblance: both consisted of eighteen months of settled life in Tamanrasset and five months of travel in France.

The fourth period can be divided into 23 months of settled life, five of which were in the Asekrem, and a trip to France that lasted seven months.

Each of these segments lasted about two years. Only the fifth period would last for three years without travel because of the war.

We can only summarize these eleven years that would need to be treated in a special way due to the diversity of activity and the developed relationships.

1st Period

Having settled in Tamanrasset since August, Brother Charles quickly realized that he was not going to meet many people. He had desired this "very secluded life" in terms of all of the people he had left and of the contacts with the military which had brought him there, but were now gone. It was a whole new experience for him and he felt the pangs of isolation that deprived him of mail. Then, another form of solitude imposed itself. He had dismissed Paul Embarek whom he had considered as catechumen. Without him, he could not celebrate Mass, but he preferred to go without the Eucharist rather than keep Paul with him. In fact, Paul, a teenager, was utterly lost in a place so different from where he had grown up. His behavior left something to be desired in his employer's opinion.

But at least Brother Charles found himself amid a nomadic population with whom he hoped to develop a close relationship. It is what he must have wished for when he had met Mousa agg Amastan and felt that they had hit it off. But he saw almost no one: only a few of the poor nomads or gardeners from the village who came to his door. In a letter to Marie de Bondy on March 18, 1906 he wrote:

> *"The time since my letter of January has passed as a single day: I see no Christians and very few of the indigenous people: in winter the Tuareg, who are very sensitive to the cold and are poorly dressed, don't travel much; neither are they in any hurry to visit me: the ice has not been broken: it will take time… I have gone no further than a hundred meters from the chapel."*

Did he miss the "beehive of activity" of Beni Abbès? If he did, he had no intention of repeating that experience. He even made resolutions to limit the alms that he distributed since it only attracted large numbers of people. Besides, he had very little to give. He pondered his two experiences of traveling with the military. The camps were numerous, the villages welcoming, and it seemed easy to connect with people. But did he meet so many people simply because they covered such a vast territory? Was the welcome he received not simply the obligatory reception reserved for the military? Had he already forgotten that the village elders had refused to allow him to settle down among them in several places, living his life as a monk?[177]

---

[177] Charles de Foucauld, *Carnet de Beni Abbès*, Paris, Nouvelle Cité, 1993, pp. 150- 151 (July 29th and August 4, 1904)

So it was that he quickly realized that it would be up to him to "make a few visits in the villages and camps of the region to reach out to those who don't come to see me." But this was not possible. He was prohibited from traveling alone because of the insecurity of the region.

That explains why he had invited his friend, Motylinski, a specialist in the study of Arab and Berber peoples, to come for a visit, and why he was so impatient for his arrival. Motylinski would bring several months' worth of mail and Brother Charles would celebrate Mass again. Together they could travel throughout the region and see people since Motylinski traveled with a military escort consisting of six méharistes (a unit that traveled by camel).

As soon as he arrived at the beginning of June 1906, the two friends began studying. A hartani from Tamanrasset was their teacher during June and July.

Motylinski went to Abalessa from August 2nd to the 9th, most probably accompanied by Brother Charles. On the 11th, back in Tamanrasset, he was bitten by a viper and treated by one of the méharistes. He wrote to his cousin on the 16th: "I was able to be treated right away and so I don't think there is any danger… But my foot is very painful and it may still develop a nasty abscess."

He was therefore forced to give up the idea of traveling with Motylinski who was about to cross the Atakor region from West to East. The little expedition surely came across many camps as there had been good rains and the pastures were exceptionally green. Motylinski was impressed by the large numbers of people that he saw in those mountains and his reports to Brother Charles overestimated the numbers of people living there. Because of this, Brother Charles always kept the impression of large concentrations of nomads there. It gave birth to his desire to move to that region even though each time he visited it he saw no one. He thought that his experience was the exception.

As a result of his work with Motylinski, he found a new manner of studying the language. Until that point, he would translate from French into Tamahaq. Motylinski taught him to listen to the people, to analyze their way of expressing themselves, to write down their stories and to observe the way that they lived. Together they began collecting large number of texts which eventually became *Textes touaregs en prose* .[178] In Brother Charles eyes this would be the basis for any study of the language and a starting point for compiling dictionaries.

Even though his foot was not completely healed, he took advantage of being able to travel with his friend in order to go north where he felt that duty called. On September 12th, 1906 they headed for In Salah, arriving on the 30th. On Oct 1st he wrote to Marie de Bondy "My foot is nicely healed. Not only was I able to travel, but I walked a good third of the way." From here they went their separate ways, Motylinski to Constantine and Brother Charles to Beni Abbès. From Beni Abbès he continued on to Algiers to see Bishop Guérin. He started back with a companion, brother Michel. They traveled by way of Beni Abbès and then set off for the Hoggar. At the beginning of February 1907, they arrived at In Salah where he bought a house. There he finished his first French- Tuareg dictionary.

---

[178] Charles de Foucauld and A. de Calassanti-Motylinski, *Textes Touaregsen Prose (dialecte de l'Ahaggar)*. Alger, Carbonnel, 1922, (edited by René Basset). Critical edition and translation by Salem Chaker, HélèneClaudot, Marceau Gast, Edisud, Aix-en-Provence, 1984.

On March 7th he decided to send his companion back as he didn't think he would be able to go any farther. On the 16th he received news that Motylinski had died on March 2nd. The following year he published his first dictionary, which he had just completed, under his deceased friend's name even though Motylinski never knew anything about it. On the 18th he left In Salah for the Hoggar and points further south.

This third journey in the South took them close to the border with Mali. Spending time from April to July 1907 in the Tuareg camps, he collected 6000 verses of Tuareg poetry. He spent the next nine years working on these texts, translating them and situating them within their historical contexts.

On April 28th he wrote to Marie de Bondy: "I am very happy with this trip; we are going to see many indigenous people during the month that we remain practically stationary in this region. It is what I had hoped for." And on May 28th he wrote again:

> *"I take advantage of the presence of many Tuareg in order to get to know them and to document their language. I bless God for this trip and for these contacts. I have never had such close contacts before."*

This gave birth to the idea of settling 600 kms south of Tamanrasset in a region called Tin Zawaten, in addition to the idea that he came up with the previous year of settling in the mountains.

2nd Period

July 6, 1907 Brother Charles arrived back to his hermitage in Tamanrasset. "It is sweet to be back here; I am well received by the population, much more affectionately than I would have hoped; little by little they seem to trust me more."[179] And yet, shortly after his arrival he already wanted to go to In Salah because of his linguistic work. His thinking was to finish this work as quickly as possible since he felt that it troubled his life. At In Salah he could work with his teacher. But finally, he found a better one in Tamanrasset, a man by the name of Ba Hammou, of whom he wouldn't want to be separated.

Even though he made plans to travel, he spent the next eighteen months stable in Tamanrasset. This was surely one of the most important periods of his life in the Sahara because of his illness in 1908. We will come back to that later.

At the beginning of 1909 he returned to France for the first time since 1901. While in Paris, he visited Father Huvelin and shared his plans to settle in the mountains to the South of Tamanrasset. Father Huvelin, who had taken to leaving his directee free to follow the "instincts" which urged him from within, approved of and encouraged his plans. He was gone from the Hoggar for only five months, including rapids stopovers in Beni Abbès on the way to and for.

3rd Period

Brother Charles returned to Tamanrasset on June 11, 1909 and remained there for eighteen months. "I have picked up where I left off, as if there had been no interruption, except for more visits the first day." (*LMB*, June 14th) He had entered into the life of the people of the Hoggar and this eighteen-month period would be quite different than before. The mail had taken on some degree of regularity. There were

---

[179] *LMB*, July 7, 1907.

more frequent visits from the military as well as nearly daily visits from the nomads.

"My life has not changed in any way, cloistered life in Tamanrasset," he wrote to Regnault on April 11, 1910. But he wrote this at 200 kms from his "cloister," during the second of his trips during this period. The first took place at the end of August 1909. He wrote to Marie de Bondy about it on September 2nd:

> *"I am not writing to you from Tamanrasset but a neighboring village… Laperrine is spending two weeks visiting the villages and camps in the radius of 120 kms; I am traveling with him since it is an occasion to meet many people, which is very important."*

The goal was always the same but only served to fuel his desire to live among those whom he didn't see in Tamanrasset. On June 14, 1909 he wrote to Father Huvelin:

> *"The projects for the other two hermitages among the Tuareg, which you advised me to found, are in good shape. The goal is to create more relationships with the tribes. I can only thank God for it."*

Nothing had happened. He visited the Asekrem during the first two weeks of September 1909. On October 13th he wrote to Marie de Bondy about both projects: the first located 500 kms south and the second 100 kms east of Tamanrasset.

But on October 31st he wrote to her again from Fort Motylinski, asking for money to build two hermitages seemingly in different places: "one in the mountains about 60 kms from Tamanrasset and the other 600 kms southwest." They were the same places, but he had corrected his calculations. The first one must have been the Asekrem. It was built in May-June 1910, without him even being there.

1910 was a year marked by departures. His friend Laperrine returned to France and three other friends died: Bishop Guérin in Ghardaïa, Lacroix in Algiers, and Father Huvelin in Paris.

Brother Charles left Tamanrasset for his second trip to France at the beginning of January 1911. He had three goals: to meet his new Bishop in Algiers, to start a confraternity that he had been planning for two years and to do whatever he could to find companion. He was gone for five months.

4th Period

He wrote to Marie de Bondy on May 2nd during the journey back to Tamanrasset, sharing his projects for the future: "I should be in Tamanrasset by tomorrow. I'll spend about ten days there before leaving for the Asekrem where I will move into your country house." In fact, he only made it there on July 6th, accompanied by Ba Hammou. Besides the necessary books and manuscripts, they took with them enough supplies to last two people for sixteen months.

His table became piled high with thousands of sheets of notes, constantly reread, and corrected. When the first blast of cold weather arrived, he was surprised that he had trouble dealing with it and attributed his fatigue and fever on the lack of eggs and vegetables. Eventually he came to realize that the excessive amount of work was the cause. Ba Hammou did not wait until that point to complain. Ever since they had arrived, he groaned about it, and now he threatened to leave. At the beginning of December, Brother Charles finally decided to return to Tamanrasset and to stop working. He was exhausted.

They reached Tamanrasset on December 15th and he did not go back to work until January 1912. His time was totally taken now with prayer and with receiving visits from his neighbors who were now becoming old friends. That is what he told Marie de Bondy in a letter written December 25th. He had written to her to ask for financial help to ease the misery of those around him: "I found Tamanrasset and the people of the area in a frightening state of misery. I thought it my duty to give much more alms than I had anticipated."

After going back to work he wrote: "This dictionary is so long! The more I learn the more I see that I don't know. It is the story of each day." March 31st, he wrote to Marie de Bondy, "the dictionary is taking much more time than I had imagined; if my calculations are correct, it will take me another five or six months." But there was more to it than simply a dictionary and on May 16th he acknowledged, "I will not have really finished before three or four years." He worked less intensely as he was often interrupted by visits and he also was able to visit more easily in the village.

On April 28, 1913 he left Tamanrasset for his third trip to France. He took with him a young Aragous by the name of Ouksem, the second son of his friend, Chikat.

On September 28, 1913 they sailed from Marseilles. They were back in Tamanrasset on November 22nd, having passed by way of Algiers, Ghardaïa, El Golea, InSalah and Timimoun, both coming and going.

5th Period

After his trip to France he spent three very stable years in Tamanrasset both in his desire to finish his linguistic work and because of events that were taking place. It was quite different from the preceding periods in that it was totally linked to life in the Hoggar. Nothing seemed strange to him anymore. Despite himself, he was something of an attraction both to the Tuareg as well as to the Europeans who passed through the region. He often repeated how sweet he found friendships. But he was equally firm, even rigid, when it came to questions of the common good. That is what others said and what we see reflected in his letters. He also was attuned to what was going on around him, in particular the needs of Africa and the duties of Europe. He felt called to a universal mission and did not stop working for the foundation of the "Union" that he wished to found. He had managed to enroll 49 people during his last trip to France.

On September 3rd the mail brought word that Germany had declared war on France on August 3rd. Brother Charles kept working ten hours and forty-five minutes a day. He made steady progress on a clean copy of his Complete French-Tuareg Dictionary. January 1, 1915, he was on page 1,100. He finished on June 24th: a total of 2,028 pages.

We will not discuss this work[180] in detail here, but it occupied the majority of his time. And although he repeated that it was his duty to

---

[180] Antoine Chatelard wrote on this subject, "Charles de Foucauld, linguistor expert despite himself." Paris, INALCO, Études et Documents berbères, #13, 1995, pp.145-177. There's a list of the linguistic works of Charles de Foucauld in the annotated bibliography at the end.

remain in Tamanrasset, he began asking himself if he should not join in the war effort and join the soldiers.

At the beginning of 1915 he was again sick with scurvy, but recovered fairly quickly. He became preoccupied with the insecurity caused by raiding parties. He more and more felt the need for some kind of fortified warehouse or fort where the people from the village could take refuge. They began making dried bricks on June 9th next to the place where the chief of the Dag Ghali had chosen for its construction. The building began on August 17th. Paul Embarek, who had been working for him again since 1914, helped as well as the people from the village. They did it all themselves without any help or financing from the military. His neighbors asked him to move into it, and he did so on June 23rd, 1916. His permanent presence there would make it easier for them to use in case of need and he would also "be closer to them." He continued copying the Tuareg Poetry which he finished on November 28th, three days before his death.

But new threats were being felt from the Senoussi Brotherhood who were waging holy war from Tripolitania (northwestern Libya). Armed insurgent groups were on the move. It was one of these groups, operating around Tamanrasset on December 1st 1916, that would be responsible for Charles de Foucauld's death.[181]

---

[181] This last period of his life as well as the circumstances surrounding his death were developed in a recent book by Antoine Chatelard, *"La Mort de Charles de Foucauld,"* Paris, Karthala, 2000.

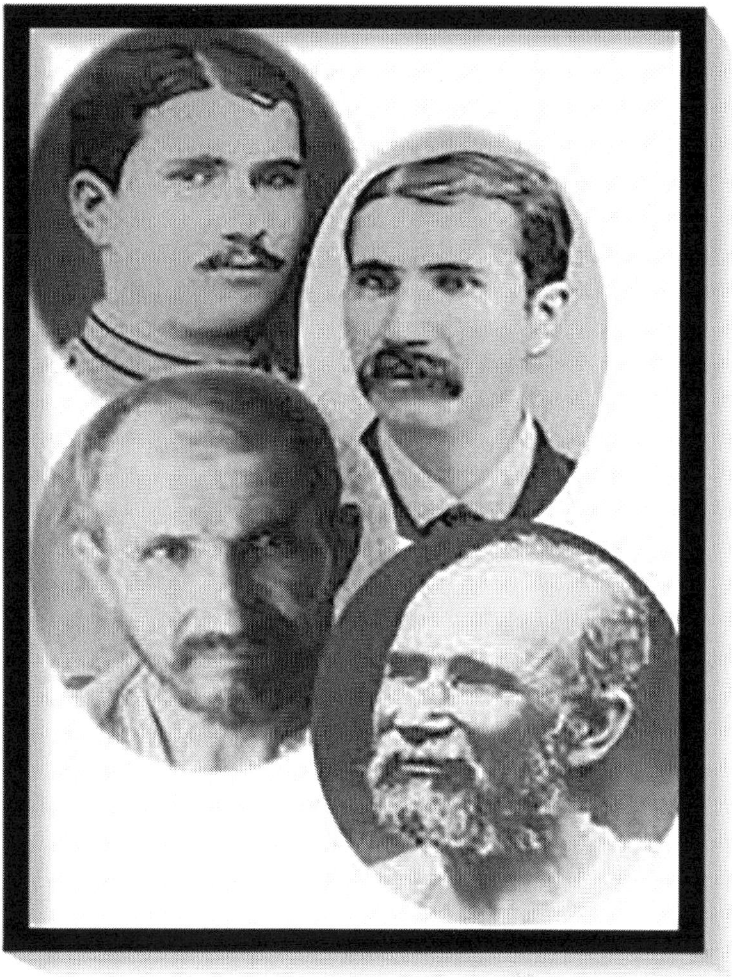

STRENGTH IN WEAKNESS

I want to spend some time on a very special moment in Charles de Foucauld's life in the Sahara. It represented a new experience for him. It was a consequence of a voluntary choice that he had made to imitate Christ in his poverty and to live close to men and women who were poor. It was an unanticipated situation of inescapable and dire poverty that led the hermit of Tamanrasset to take a further step towards communion with others.

Sickness

Monday January 20, 1908: He was living in his house to which he had recently added a room. It was now eight meters long by 1.75 meters wide. He had a chapel, his bed, his desk, his library and his papers. And now he was unable to move from his bed. The slightest activity left him unable to breathe. He felt that the end was near. He wrote in his Notebook, "Sick. Must interrupt my work. Jesus, Mary and Joseph, I give you my soul, my spirit and my life."

He was fifty years old, at the halfway point of his life in the Sahara (1901-1916).

He would live another eight years. Since the beginning of the year he had been very tired, slept poorly and had lost his appetite. He did not know what was wrong with him and blamed the cold, the heavy workload and lack of sleep. He had scurvy, a form of malnutrition that produces anemia. It is not surprising since his diet contained no meat, no fresh foods and not much in the way of vegetables. He had had a large enough stock of wheat and dates, but when he returned from his trip in July, seeing how hungry the people were, he gave away his provisions without keeping enough for himself.

> *"This has been a hard year for the country. There has been no rain these past 17 months. It means total famine in a country that depends on milk, where the poor practically only have milk. The goats are as dry as the earth and the people as dry as the goats."*[182]

We are reminded of a meditation that he had written in Nazareth:

> *"Share, share, share everything with them (the poor) and give them the best of what we have. If there is not enough for two, give them everything. We are giving to Jesus. And if, without dying, we become ill because of what we gave to Jesus through his members, what a blessed and happy illness it would be! We should feel happy, favored, privileged, graced by God; what bliss to be ill for such a reason."*

He had thought about just such a circumstance long before. Did he remember? According to his ascetical theories, the less one ate the more perfect one was. "Do not worry about one's health or life more than a tree worries over a leaf that falls," he wrote while in his hermitage at Nazareth. Now he was beginning to see things differently. On January 7th he wrote to Laperrine asking for provisions, including concentrated milk and wine. When Laperrine received his letter two weeks later at In Salah he understood that the situation was serious. He wrote to Bishop Guérin on February 3rd, "I'm going to yell at him and I give myself permission on your behalf to tell him that penance which leads to suicide

---

[182] *LMB*, July 17, 1907

is not acceptable."[183] He wrote again later, "I sent him a reprimand as I strongly believe that his exaggerated penances have played a big part in this fatigue, and too much work on the dictionary did the rest."[184]

The excessive amount of work that he was doing was a factor. Over the previous three months, he exhausted himself trying to translate the prose texts he inherited after Motylinski's death. He actually reworked the entire collection with Ba Hammou, "a very intelligent and talkative Tuareg," working from morning until night, about eleven hours a day. The student simply became exhausted by such a rhythm.

Consequently, during the month of January they were only able to work a few hours a day. Would all this work, the thousands of pages arranged on his table, remain unfinished and be lost?

Loneliness: solitude of the heart

There may also have been psychological reasons that contributed to his illness. Charles de Foucauld had only seen two Europeans over the last six months: M. Dubois, an ethnologist, visited in October, and a Lieutenant Halphen, in December. These were the only two outside visitors that he received in the course of eleven months. That meant that the mail was only rarely picked up, that those carrying the mail were not always very reliable, and that incoming mail was even less frequent. On January 7th he received the first and only letter from his cousin during this period, although she had been writing to him faithfully every two weeks. Deprived of the precious support of her

---

[183] René Bazin, Charles de Foucauld, explorateur au Maroc, ermite au Sahara, Paris, Plon, 1921,.

[184] Op. cit., p. 355.

affection, he renewed the offering that he had made many years before when they separated. He recalled that event in a letter that he wrote back to her:

> *"I am writing to you early on this January 15th, the anniversary of the last time that, side by side, we received the eternal Beloved. May we, dear mother, be reunited at His feet in heaven! You must feel how close I am to you today. I don't know if it would be true to say that I am closer to you than on any other day; I am very close to you every day; but today, it is with deeper emotion that I recalled the last hours of that day eighteen years ago, and with the hope that, despite my sins and failings, the Beloved will not eternally push me away, because on that day I did give him my all… May Jesus blesses you, my dear mother, may he give back to you the blessing that you gave to me that day, and may he be your eternal portion in the heavenly homeland!"*

The wound of separation remained as open as on the first day. He knew that he would never see her again and that the sacrifice would continue until the end. Had that end arrived? What gave him hope and peace was the knowledge that he had given to God, with complete detachment, the most precious thing that he could offer. He never sought to mitigate his sacrifice and he knew that God would accept him.

He had never felt so keenly the isolation that separation from his loved ones imposed. To understand the measure of such an absence we need to know how important correspondence was to him. It was the only way he had for expressing himself, of sharing and communicating but nothing from Father Huvelin, not one letter for the last two years. Solitude is very heavy when it is not desired. We should not too easily refer to what he wrote to his cousin two years before to reassure her about his lonely conditions. He knew, as he had known in 1905, that one is never alone when in the presence of Jesus in the Blessed Sacrament, the best friend with whom one can speak day or night. But at this moment he needed to hear someone speak to him, to hear the friendly voice of a brother or sister. He felt as alone as he had when he was in Morocco, when he felt death just as close as he did this day. "Never another Christian with whom to speak," he complained back then. There was no comfort in telling himself that now it was for the glory of God and not for his own glory.

Isolation

He was even more disappointed that none of his neighbors had come to see him during the last months. The village people, about forty of them who lived there and had their gardens, had quickly exhausted his possibilities of giving alms. They had no more reason to go to his place. The nomads who were scattered throughout the area because of the drought showed no urgency to visit him either, or it wasn't because of the cold weather, as he would have liked to believe. Out of discretion and especially because it was a principle for him, he did not venture beyond his own three little huts which represented his "cloister."

And yet he had come to these mountains to be with a people to whom he believed he had been sent. During the travels of the preceding years he had met numerous men and women where the pastures brought them together. He had pondered moving to what he felt might be a more central location: 600 kms further south near Tin Zawaten, or higher in the mountains where the coolness and the rain drew the nomads. All his efforts to draw closer to the people had been in vain and there were so few people nearby.

Even worse, his very presence seemed to have provoked an Islamic reaction.

Mousa agg Amastan, the amenokal of the Ahaggar, had also settled near the village. He was thinking of making Tamanrasset his "capital." With remarkable religious zeal he wanted to transform the village into a true Islamic center. He called for the Tolbas from Touat to come and teach the Koran and Arabic. In the eyes of the marabout, they spread ill-will towards everything French and Christian. Furthermore, Mousa began collecting money to build a mosque and a zaouïa.

Anguish over the salvation of others

In such a state of physical and emotional exhaustion, his worry over the salvation of others became a veritable anguish. He saw the powers of evil at work against him and his mission. He wanted to work toward the salvation of these men and women who were so close to him, and yet so far… and he felt unable to do anything more. He thought of an idea that came to mind during his last retreat in September: since priests and religious had not responded to his appeals or prayer, should he not reach out to the laity? Could he not get people thinking about their Christian duty towards the peoples that had been colonized? He even thought of having a book written about this. Now he began thinking of creating an association of laity and clergy who would help each other accomplish this duty. But would he not die before even being able to write his ideas down?

A Useless Life

Reduced to a state of utter powerlessness, he could only attest that his life and work had been a failure because of his own lack of conversion. Shouldn't he have chosen a more useful life, or a more favorable place for his mission? What did he come to do there? What had he done with his life for the last twenty years since his conversion? He had fled to the deserts of the Middle East to put as much safe distance as possible between himself and the world. To save his own life he had sought the protection of a cloister, then the obscurity and solitude of a hermit's life, far from others and the world, to live for God alone. God had brought him out of his sweet solitude to once again live among others. He believed that he had been given a mission to go to those far away, to go where others could not go. Did he think that he was better than others, able to do what others were unable to accomplish?

Without the Eucharist

Following his ordination, he left for Algeria in order to carry to others the Banquet of which he had become the servant. Who was even interested in what he had to share? Why did he come back to this country where he could not even celebrate the Eucharist? He had only been able to celebrate five times in the last six months, taking advantage of the two Christians who stopped to visit and were willing to assist at his Mass. Should he not have stayed in Beni Abbès where he could have celebrated every day? Wasn't that the most helpful thing that he could have done for the salvation of others? Even on Christmas, for the first time since his conversion, he was alone and without Mass.

Despite all of that, he had chosen to return and remain among people who were seemingly indifferent to his presence. Why? Was it his final error? Who had pushed him to make that decision and to justify his choice?

Shouldn't he have removed the Blessed Sacrament from the tabernacle before taking it to his bed? What would happen if he died? But did he have the courage to deprive himself of that one presence that he considered at the very source of his life? He firmly believed that the sacramental presence had a physical effect on the world around him. The tabernacle was just a few meters from his bed and that closeness was significant to him. He never believed that he had permission to receive communion alone. He did ask himself the question. He hoped to obtain permission to celebrate the Eucharist alone, even though no one had ever received such approval before. Jesus is the Master of the Impossible. This deprivation was at odds with everything he formerly believed that he didn't even dare speak of it to his family and friends.

Fortunately for him, he was unaware of the future: a few weeks later he learned that he did not even have permission to reserve the Blessed Sacrament in the tabernacle as long as he was alone. He removed the Blessed Sacrament, like a death in his soul. Over the next six years the tabernacle remained empty. He must have reconsidered his convictions and principles since he decided to stay on alone in the end.

I abandon myself to you

Charles de Foucauld did not have the "prayer of abandon" that his disciples later gleaned from his writings. But, under different forms, it was, at this hour, his only prayer.

He had so intensely desired the moment when he would meet his Beloved brother and Lord face to face, and yet now he was desperately clinging to the shred of life that he still had. His desire to live only grew stronger. He had never had as many reasons to want to live. He couldn't die like that with no one to continue his work. There was so much to do for these men and women.

The Tuareg were aware of their responsibility towards their guest and, with their limited means, did all that they could to save his life. Something happened that day, something difficult to measure but that had a real impact upon Charles de Foucauld and the people. "They searched among all the goats in a radius of four kms to find a little bit of milk amid this terrible drought."[185] "They were very good to me."[186] He was touched by their goodness but did not yet realize the critical change that was taking place in his relationship with the people, and of the real conversion that was happening within his own heart.

Too rich

I fact he had wanted to be poor in keeping with a monastic ideal and especially because of his own desire to imitate Jesus who, rich as he was, became poor. That was his reference point. In some ways he was living more poorly than some of his neighbors. But no one ever would have considered him poor; he ate poorly, dressed poorly, but that had nothing to do with poverty. His house was full of things to give away. He was there to give; it was his role as a Christian marabout. He was different from the local marabouts who collected gifts from people in exchange for their blessing or knowledge. He might not have been making large distributions as he had done in Beni Abbès; his almsgiving was personalized. He could keep accounts of what he gave away, whether in money or goods, and we can find in his Notebook the lists he made of the various poor people. But he remained the benefactor, ready to help and give to each one according to their need.

He gave away what was his own, his possession, asking his family to send it for the poor. He considered himself the Father who, according to St. Paul, must give and not receive (he wrote about this in 1903 while

---

[185] Letter to Bishop Guérin, January 24, 1908, in Charles de Foucauld, *Correspondances sahariennes,* Paris, Cerf, 1998, p. 591.

[186] *LMB,* March 8, 1908.

in Beni Abbès concerning the Arab Affairs Office). In 1904, in his account of how one should travel in the Sahara, he had written six pages giving detailed advice about what alms to give (money, fabric, food) according to the situations (during the marches or while staying someplace). He concluded, as a good missionary, "Don't accept anything, or if you have to accept something from them, accept only small things of little value."[187] He was afraid to feel obligated to anyone or to be bought. But how can one give without being ready to receive?

Too powerful, too knowledgeable

He wanted to be small and approachable. He could only see the distance that separated him from those with whom he wished to be close. He had come with a military escort, wondering if the day would come when the people would see the difference between priests and soldiers. Despite his religious garb and his almsgiving, he was still, even though he had no weapons, the representative of a feared foreign administration of which everyone was suspicious. In the eyes of the people, he represented power.

Didn't he come as a conqueror? Even if he refused to be called a missionary, this monk could only think about the conquest of souls. He borrowed the French military vocabulary of "appraisement," which means to grow accustomed to, to tame. He came to bring civilization and faith, sure of his knowledge and experience. He only wanted to serve and to promote the common good of the tribes. He had a clear plan for economic development and education. Had he ever thought that he would first have to discover who the people of this different

---

[187] Charles de Foucauld, *Carnet de Beni Abbès*, Paris, Nouvelle Cité, 1993, pp.116-117.

civilization were, with a faith and culture different from his own? As he questioned Ba Hammou, he began to enter into a real dialogue, but he was still preoccupied with the idea of sharing his knowledge and beliefs. His work set him on a path of attentive listening, the first condition of any true sharing. How could he ask others to listen to him if he was not willing to listen to them?

The situation is reversed

On that day, he had nothing left and was able to do nothing. And it was precisely at the moment when he was reduced to total powerlessness, with nothing left to say, entirely dependent upon his neighbors and totally vulnerable to their power, that they felt responsible for him and entered into his life. It took illness to reduce him to such a state of weakness in order for his hosts to approach him and offer him something on an equal footing. They shared their wealth with him: a bit of milk to save his life. They offered their knowledge and what they knew would be the best for him. They did what they were able to do within their limited means. They didn't think about it, didn't calculate the effect that it might have. They simply did what was normal to his save his life.

January ended on a note of resurrection, with Charles de Foucauld regaining some of his strength. On the 31st he received a message from Laperrine, announcing that he had received permission to celebrate the Eucharist alone. "Christmas, Christmas, Deo Gratias," he wrote in his Notebook. On February 1st he said his first Mass alone. He tried to go back to work but had to give up. Only by mid-February was he able to begin working on it in the afternoons with Ba Hammou. At the beginning of March two camels loaded with supplies arrived, four times more than he had requested.

He only began keeping track of visitors in his Notebook in 1913 but in his letters we see that beginning with this winter 1908, more people began to come to see him. He wrote to his brother-in-law on March 26, 1908:

> *"I am about three or four hundred meters from the huts of the village. I don't have any close neighbors and am quite alone. However, I see quite a few people. They come to see me. I don't go to see them."*

At the end of June Laperrine wrote the following to Bishop Guérin:

> *"He seems quite well, a picture of health and liveliness... On June 29th he galloped into my camp like a 2nd Lieutenant at the head of a group of Tuareg horsemen. He is more popular than ever with them and he appreciates them more and more."*[188]

His state of weakness and illness allowed him to develop a new relationship with these people who would become his friends. It was a real moment of conversion, a tremendous step forward in sharing. Maybe he had thought that he could make it without the reciprocity that defines real friendship, that precious pearl, "thing so rare in this world," which would help him to live from then on. He thought that he had given up everything, and he accepted to receive the hundred fold. The situation asked him to empty himself, to give up seeking religious perfection through his own willpower, to give up his calculated plans. He had to accept himself, stop wanting to be superhuman, become

---

[188] René Bazin, Charles de Foucauld, explorateur au Maroc, ermite au Sahara, Paris, Plon, 1921, p. 360.

more human beginning by sleeping and eating enough. He no doubt grew in that humility that impressed those who met him.

He also began to accept others as they were. He shared bread and milk with these men and women but also all of the other things that are a part of life: good news and bad news, plans, wishes and disputes. He became the go-between among them. He was no longer satisfied to write down his advice for Mousa. He noted the advice that he received from Ouksem and others and the information that he learned from Ba Hammou. He let himself be affected by them, he became attached to them, allowing the bonds of friendship to grow. He was the one who was being "approves," tamed. He shared the ideas of his day concerning Islam. He did not think that it could stand up historically or philosophically, as he wrote to a priest of Versailles on June 9th. But he also said, "The more I see, the less I think that we should expect to make conversions for the moment." That same year a Protestant Doctor by the name of Dautheville reported hearing him say:

> *"I am not here in order to convert the Tuareg people but to try to understand them[...] You are Protestant, Teissère has no religious faith at all, the Tuareg are Muslim. I am convinced that God will welcome all of us if we deserve it."*[189]

A parable of the reign of God

Charles de Foucauld did not measure the importance of this event nor its significance. Can we do so for him, and at the same time discover a parable of the Reign of God, a light for his life and ours? They did not speak about "reading the signs of the times" back then,

---

[189] Léon Lehuraux, *Au Sahara avec le P. Charles de Foucauld*, Paris, St. Paul, 1946, p. 115.

nor of discerning the signs of the Kingdom of God in order to recognize the Spirit at work in the heart of each person. And yet it seems that this man excelled in doing just that, even if he expressed it in a language that is not familiar to us. He was not preoccupied with it nor was it within his theology to make those observations. Bishop Guérin, however, wrote to Bishop Livinhac in November 1904 about Charles de Foucauld saying, "like all those who allow themselves to be led by the Spirit, he has a marvelous appreciation of circumstances." Was it not the charity of a Tuareg woman that led him to want to go to the Hoggar in the first place?

If he did not recognize the importance of what he was in the process of living, maybe it was because these realities of the Reign of God are not easily grasped. They are hidden, like the grain of wheat in the earth and the yeast in the dough. It is hard to say that it is here or there, when it is among us and within us. The littleness of these signs, their apparent insignificance, is characteristic: a little milk, a piece of bread. It makes us think of the poor widow who gave all that she had to live on. It wasn't much! We think of the child who gave a few loaves of bread to feed a hungry crowd. It was the insignificant gesture that made the miracle possible.

These signs are hard to grasp because they are so ordinary: a visit, a word, a gesture, a smile, tears. Is it not of their very nature to be done unconsciously? "May your left hand not know what the right hand is doing!" "When did we feed you?" It is like the lightning that flashes across the sky, as quick as a glance. But we have seen those glances that happen between people, leaving one thunder struck. They are real encounters with the other, like the way that Jesus glanced at people and changed their heart, making it burn within them.

Charles de Foucauld worried about "giving a good example." It does not seem that his calculated efforts had much effect. But everyone spoke about the effect that he had on them and to which he gave little thought: his extreme goodness, the happiness that shone from him, his humble gentleness. We don't always see this in his writings. But he did remember Father Huvelin saying that it was not what one did or said that was important, but who one was. What is the good of worrying when we think we see the hand of Satan interfering with the work of God? We risk pulling up the good plants along with the weeds. Whether we sleep or are awake, whether we think about it or not, the Reign of God grows. It is only on the day of harvest that we will separate one from the other. Mousa's plans were not all sinister. It didn't take long for him to see that his plans were failing because of the dishonesty of those to whom he had confided the collections.

Concerning this event in Brother Charles' life, we can see that the simple gesture of hospitality had an unforeseen impact. When he became the poor one, the sick one, the marabout was inviting those who came to his aide to hear one day, "Come and enter into the Kingdom; for I was hungry and you gave me to eat, sick and you visited me." It was no longer just a parable, it was the reality of the Reign of God. If he had thought of that, he might have found the comfort that he needed. He had anguished so much over how to bring salvation to them.

If he could not grasp the real significance of what he was living, he did understand what was most important. In his first letter to his cousin following this illness, on March 8, 1908, he spoke about the apparent uselessness of so many lives and of that which was also the life of Jesus at Nazareth and on Calvary:

> *"Jesus could have done so much good if he had evangelized people during the years of obscurity in Nazareth. But he thought that he was doing a greater good by remaining in his silence… And our father [Father Huvelin], his illness and crosses keep him from doing so much good! God must consider that he does more good by being on the Cross with Jesus… Two lines from St. John of the Cross shed light on this fact."*

He went on to quote St. John of the Cross, just as he would do in a letter that he wrote on the day he died:

> *"It is when we are reduced to nothing that we have the most powerful means of uniting ourselves to Jesus and of doing good for souls; It is what Saint John of the Cross repeats at nearly every line. When we are able to suffer and love, we are doing a great deal, the most that someone can do in this world."*[190]

We find the same message in something that he wrote in 1896 while with the Trappists. It was a difficult time for him, a time when he totally gave himself over in obedience. A month later he left the Trappists:

> *"It was at the moment when Jacob found himself on the road, poor and alone, sleeping on the bare ground in the desert to get some rest after a long journey on foot; it was at the moment when he found himself in that painful situation of an isolated traveler, in the midst of a long journey in a wild and foreign land with nowhere to lay his head; it was at the moment when he found himself in that sorry condition, that God filled him with incomparable favors."*[191]

We don't have any lack of difficult situations which lead us through a kind of death: when we lack the vital space that we need to live, when the

---

[190] *LMB*, December 1, 1916.

[191] Charles de Foucauld, *Qui peut résister à Dieu ?*, Paris, Nouvelle Cité, 1980, M.A.T. Genèse 28, p. 76.

situation seems without hope, when our competence, devotion or zeal become the very obstacles that block our way. In such situations it would be helpful and a source of hope to remember an counsel from Charles de Foucauld, one which he lived out himself. The prophets tell us that when a person is reduced to the point of not being able to do anything more, God intervenes. St. Paul repeats that he takes pride in his weakness because he has learned from the Lord that, "My power is at work in weakness" (or illness). We hear Charles de Foucauld echo this sentiment when he said, "The weakness of human means is a source of strength." He reaffirmed hope in the midst of our fragility and distress.

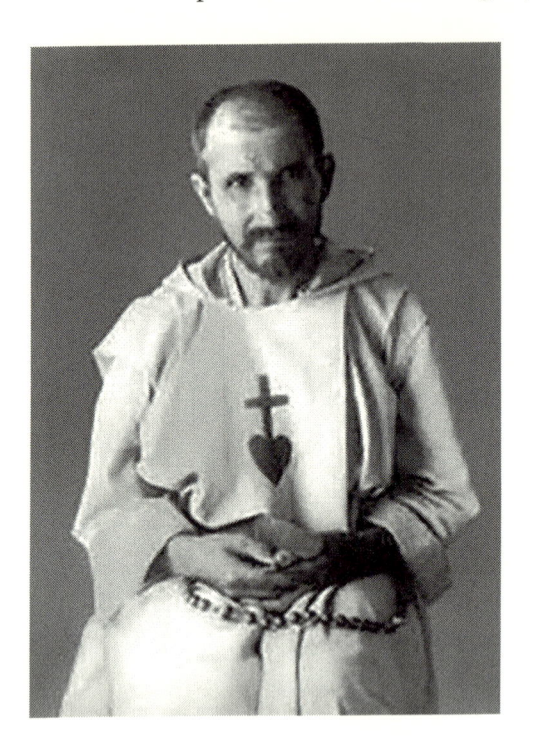

A NEW KIND OF MONK WITH A SPECIAL MISSION

If we refer ourselves to the root of Charles de Foucauld's vocation, a moment which, he says, was the same as the moment of his conversion, there is no doubt that he desired to live an entirely contemplative life. He wanted to imitate those who, in the past, had gone to live in caves or in the desert to live for God alone. He had no notion of wanting to live out this life amid the world. It was just the contrary. In a desire to "breathe himself out, to completely lose himself," this man of action who had sought to be so effective and productive, chose to live for God alone without any other goal. Given his temperament, there could be no half measure with him. For him, a life given to God had to be lived far from the world, from his world, in the most total separation, distancing himself forever, in silence and cloister. To not draw attention to himself he had no other choice, therefore, than to enter the monastic life as it was being lived in the Church of his day. With Father Huvelin's guidance, we can understand that he eliminated any form of religious life that undertook apostolic activity or works from his decision-making.

Leaving behind all that was source of his happiness, he separated himself from everyone and chose to deprive himself of every relationship of love, friendship or affection. He did so in order to begin a life that was geared to an exclusive relationship with God. It is important to underline the exclusivity of that relationship. He saw his place in the mission of the Church of the day, a Church that considered Contemplative Orders as having an exceptional role and invited them to make foundations in mission countries. With this in mind, he expressed his desire to go to live in a non-Christian country. He felt that in living out the absolutes of separation and distance from others he could accomplish both the commandment to love God and love one's neighbor. He would work for the salvation of others by no longer being distracted by them and in seeking only the glory of God. When he entered the Trappists he was trying to put into practice the call that he had heard, the ideal of which he had caught a glimpse in the streets of Nazareth during his pilgrimage of 1889. God had lived in this village of Nazareth for thirty years without being recognized. What a hidden life! Such obscurity! Such a humbling! The Trappist way of life seemed the most in keeping with his ideal because of the manual work. The Trappist monastery at Akbès fulfilled his desires for poverty, for going far away from everyone and for life in a Muslim country.

Having discovered the life of Jesus, he discovered what he thought his life should be: a life opposed to what it had been up until that day. His life had been one of wealth, of being notorious and then a celebrity, of self-glorification, and of success that brought with it being known and recognized wherever he went. His life had been filled with creative and useful projects. He undertook activities that he saw through to the very end, accomplishing them with perfection, precision and scientific rigor. If he wanted to change, he would have to do so by adopting positions at the other extreme of the spectrum. So, having given himself the image of Jesus of Nazareth as the model for his life, he could only imagine that it must be a total opposite of the life he had lived until then.

That insight was totally new for him and would be like the leaven in the dough that would take over his life. Like salt that gives flavor to food, it would give a special flavor to his daily bread. It would be the force that pushed him from within amid the most varied situations and places. That same inner urge pushed him to leave the Trappists who "wanted him to move up" and where he wasn't poor enough. He spent seven years faithfully living in a cloister that separated him from the world. It was a world where perpetual silence separated him from the other monks. It was a world where reading, meditation and prayer alone and in common made him live in another world. It was a world where manual work was both a pious endeavor and a means to earn their living. These years shaped a mentality that he was never able to undo. The Trappist life would always be the model and ideal of perfection and the elements that made up the monastic life would always serve as points of reference for him. He was never able to speak about his own life in other terms. He always used the vocabulary of monasticism to express what he was living, even though he was a man living alone, even though he lived out his solitary life in the world and engaged with the world. So when he described his life in Tamanrasset he wrote as a monk who fulfilled the multiple roles of Prior, sacristan, guest master, pharmacist, etc. In Beni Abbès he built a monastery. He even described the house of Jesus, Mary, and Joseph as if it were a monastery.

This life of Nazareth that he "uselessly sought among the Trappists" remained the ideal that guided him over the next years when he lived in the Poor Clare's garden in Nazareth itself. Once again, he transposed, idealized, and invented a model for himself according to what he was living, especially in terms of what he wanted to live with others. That makes it difficult to find in his writings from that period the seeds of newness and the originality of his emerging notion of

Nazareth. The Rule that he began writing in Nazareth, in which he thought he was laying aside all of the customs and practices of the Trappists, in fact would be an even more detailed series of regulations than those of the Trappists. In Beni Abbès he called himself a monk and believed that he was a monk because he had a cloister. When he was preparing to leave Beni Abbès he wrote:

> *"My vocation is for the cloister: I should only leave it for a serious reason. If you knew how much I feel like a fish out of water when I am outside of the cloister! ... I am not made to be outside of it."*[192]

The following year he also wrote, "When it comes to moving from one place to another or of going outside of the cloister for reasons of health, it is something that good monks never did and never will do."[193] But all of that did not keep him from undertaking one project after another, establishing pious associations, preaching, distributing alms or liberating slaves in classic missionary style.

In moving to Tamanrasset and a totally different situation, Brother Charles discovered something new about the life of Jesus of Nazareth and, therefore, in his own way of trying to imitate it. He could no longer dream about living like a monk in a cloister. He saw Jesus living without a religious habit, without a cloister, working eight hours a day, not having a lot to give away as alms, and always giving an important place to prayer.

So would his life now be that of a missionary? No. He refused that notion: neither a hermit nor a missionary. In 1906 he wrote to Father

---

[192] Charles de Foucauld, *Correspondances Sahariennes*, Paris, Cerf, 1998. Letter to Bishop Guérin November 24, 1903, p. 237.

[193] *LMB,* April 11, 1905.

Caron, "I am not a missionary: the Good Lord did not give me what it takes to be one. I am seeking to live the life of Nazareth here." The following year he wrote to Bishop Guérin, "I am a monk, not a missionary, made for silence and not for preaching."[194] In refusing the label of missionary he continued to define himself as a monk, a monk without companions, a monk in mission territory, but "not a missionary." The missionaries of the Sahara were the White Fathers. But he was different from them, and in order to highlight that difference and defend his identity he always presented himself as a "monk." We saw this in 1903 after the visit of Bishop Guérin. He said that he would not follow the Bishop's subtle tendency to push him into an apostolic life:

> *"He has a slight and subtle tendency to push me out of my life as a silent and hidden monk, my life of Nazareth, to that of a missionary. I will not follow this. To do so would be a lack of faithfulness to God who gave me this vocation of a hidden and silent life and not that of a man of words. Monks and missionaries are both apostles but in different ways. I won't change this. I will keep to this same way that I have been faithfully trying to follow"*[195]

On the way to Tamanrasset, amid the Tuareg camps where he is entirely overwhelmed by meeting so many people and with the work that he wanted to do, he expressed his concern to Father Huvelin writing, "If I am wrong to be doing this, if I should stop and do something else, tell me and I will obey."[196] When we see how he lived among the wounded and sick soldiers in Taghit for a month, we see the conflict between the ideal he had of his vocation and the reality of

---

[194] Charles de Foucauld, *Correspondances Sahariennes*, Paris, Cerf, 1998. Letter to BG November 24, 1903, p. 528.

[195] *LAH*, June 10, 1903.

[196] *LAH*, July 13, 1905.

that which he was called to live because of the situations. When we hear him talking about his horror of traveling, we are reminded of that 23-year-old man who rediscovered a meaning to life thanks to his travels and sense of adventure. Was he not denying his identity when he said that adventure threw him into anguish and that he had an "extreme horror" of traveling? Why? "Because they are not good for the soul and they cause one to be scattered." For him, solitude and the life of Nazareth are diametrically opposed to these travels through the desert that he considered a form of ministry of which he wanted no part.

When we read what he says it seems clear and yet it is difficult to be more complicated. So we have to sort through his different motivations. As we have already seen, some are part of one's nature, those that come from the heart and those that come from reason. He doesn't seem to have the tools to be able to reread his life nor to write out his feelings to understand them. Maybe that is why he felt so torn and why there seem to be such contradictions. In reality, his choices were much simpler because the duty that seemed at hand was not contrary to his own deepest desires and instincts. Wasn't it a sort of ideology that he called his vocation that came between his duty and his desire?

When he tried to explain his vocation, he could not dissociate his vocation to the life of Nazareth from the vocabulary of the monastic ideal in which he had wrapped it up. This monastic reference point only got in the way and complicated everything. But it did not keep him from living and doing what he felt called to do. It is what he often said in his letters, "My feelings, my clear opinion is that I must…" do this or that. Consequently, his fifteen years in the Sahara is hard to distinguish from the life of any other missionary. Comparing their lives to his, the

White Fathers of his day could have easily concluded that he did the same things that they did except for building schools and hospitals. But there is a difference on another level.

He contrasted himself with the White Fathers by not wanting to preach. But they found themselves in the same situation as Charles de Foucauld. Even if they had different methods and goals, they could not preach there. It was always clear for him that preaching was not his vocation, no matter where he found himself. He distinguished his vocation from the Franciscans and St. Francis whom he loved so much, in this way. "Do not preach with words, like St. Francis, but in silence."

So, an essential aspect to his personal vocation and charism clearly separated him from other vocations. It was his vocation to the "hidden life." He expressed it by the word "obscurity" which we find repeatedly in his writings and that of Father Huvelin. If he chose to enter the Trappists, it was to remain in the shadows, unknown, forgetting about his past life that seemed to be a quest for personal glorification. One of the reasons that he left Nazareth was because people knew who he was. We see that one of the temptations during his time in Jerusalem had to do with visibility. Even if he didn't use that word, that was the essence of it. "Back in the obscurity of Nazareth" he thanked his spiritual director for having saved him: "You are the one who defended me from these temptations to which I would have succumbed without you."[197] Of course he fell into the same trap the following year in the affair with the Mount of the Beatitudes." But some good came from it and he discovered the certitude that, even as a priest, God called him to a hidden life, one in the shadows and obscurity. Everything else in him

---

[197] *LAH*, February 8, 1900.

would have pulled him towards a life that sought productivity, effectiveness, immediate usefulness and visibility.

Today, his life would seem to us to be an extraordinary adventure, whether speaking of his youth, conversion, asceticism at Nazareth, or unusual life in Tamanrasset. The storybook side of his life might make people enthusiastic, but it can hide the reality of his daily life and keep one from seeing the message that was central to his life. His categorical refusal to accept that his name is used in the publication of his linguistic works is explained by his desire to remain in the shadows. But there were valid arguments against doing so from Laperrine, as well as from the scientific community in the person of René Basset, and also from Church authorities. It is not superfluous to pause on this significant aspect of his thinking. It helps to explain the label of "monk" which he used to define his path.

On May 31, 1907 he wrote to Bishop Guérin:

"I asked Laperrine to publish the Tuareg grammar and French-Tuareg dictionary which are finished under whatever name he wants, his own, or the name of the military Commander of the Oases. The same for the Tuareg-French dictionary that I am working on and the poems that I collected. The only condition that I imposed was that my name not be used and that I remain completely unknown and unidentified."

After reading that, Bishop Guérin reacted by consulting Father Voillard. He brought up the subject in a letter from September 1st that took eight months to reach Tamanrasset. He wrote a second and then a third which arrived at the beginning of January, before the first two. It was during the period of great solitude that began in July 1907, the period when he received no mail, which led up to his exhaustion and illness at the beginning of 1908.

A few letters arrived in Tamanrasset on January 15th. Brother Charles received the letter from Bishop Guérin dated October 18th in which he had written:

> *"Permit me to tell you how sorry I am to know that your work on Tamahaq that you have already sent to René Basset and those still to come would be published under someone else's name. As I was telling you, at the present time when religion is attacked so frequently, her children must not, through false modesty, hide what they have done in her honor."*

He added:

> *"It would still be possible and easy for you to write to the colonel who, as we, regrets your decision, and to simply sign your dictionaries and grammar studies: de Foucauld would not become vain, and the monk would offerto his mother, the Church, a loving and respectful homage."*

On January 15th, that most important anniversary, he renewed the offering of his sacrifice. His written response takes on even greater significance when we consider his state of exhaustion. It is a long letter but in the middle, he wrote:

> *"My beloved Father, my very dear Father, never, never, never will I permit that anything is published under my name in my lifetime, and I will formally forbid that it be done after my death… These are not the means that JESUS has given us for continuing the work of salvation in the world… The means that he used in the manger, in Nazareth and on the Cross are: poverty, abjection, humiliation, abandonment, persecution, suffering, the cross. These are our weapons, those of our divine Spouse who asks that we allow him to continue his life in us, he the only Lover the only Truth… We will not find a better one and he has not grown old… Let us follow this Only Model and we will be sure to accomplish much good since it will not be we who live, but he who lives in us;*

our actions are no longer our actions, human and wretched, but his, divinely effective."

And in the post-script he came back to it again:

"Beloved Father, that I am absolute and firm in saying that they ignore whatever part I may have had with the little dictionaries, etc., that are to be published under Motylinski's name. I will take a very dim view of it if, even after publishing it in his name alone, any mention is made of my work on it. Forgive me, dear, venerated and beloved Father, for coming back to this subject: monk, dead to the world, I insist on remaining so completely."

This is what is behind the word "monk" for him. It was not just the cloister, even if he speaks like that. [198] The original goal of the cloister for him, besides distance from others, was to put him into that state of obscurity, of being *incognito*, of not being visible in any way.

Being incognito, the absolute desire to remain completely unrecognized, was the new cloister for the learned monk.

The letter that he answered on January 15th was in answer to the last letter written by Bishop Guérin. The two previously written letters only arrived a month and a half later on February 29th with the rest of the mail took six to eight months to arrive. In Bishop Guérin's letter from September 1st he read:

"Coming back to the subject of your linguistic work, Father Voillard also sends his respectful reproach, or at least his regrets. He regrets – and even dares to reproach you – he regrets to see you allow your work to be published while you

---

[198] Letter to his brother-in-law, March 26, 1908: "They come to see me; I don't go to see anyone. I remain in my cloister."

efface entirely yourself. It seems to him that now – given all of the attacks under which the Church has come – that your humility should give way before love of and honor for the Church. He feels that you should not be afraid to sign your work as a priest and a religious. I see that you are pushing aside these considerations as being too human. I wonder, however, if it would note the wisest and most appropriate way to give honor to God. Think about it and fight this way of thinking within yourself. Write to Colonel Laperrine and Mr.

Basset and lift the prohibition that you imposed about using your name. Persuade yourself that you are not the only one involved in this decision. It is also a question of the honor of God and of the Church, which you love, which needs to be protected and spread.

He received another letter from Bishop Guérin dated September 21st in the same delivery:

"From every point of view, your work on the Tamahaq language is very important. I can only encourage you to continue working on everything involved in it. At the same time, let me again tell you once again that it seems to me that you should muffle your humility to allow the documents which you have sent to Algiers to be published under your name, Father de Foucauld; Not just de Foucauld but Father de Foucauld, unless you think it would be better to use your religious name, "Brother Charles of Jesus." The publication of this work under this name would be an occasion to procure an honor for the Holy Church that should not be missed. I say these things with even more assurance because I am transmitting to you the feelings of those who have more authority in these things than I."

These two letters called for a new response to the arguments set forth by BishopGuérin and Father Voillard. He wrote on March 6th:

"Regarding the question of signing my name to the linguistic work I have done: despite the authority of Father Voillard, for whom I have respectful confidence, and despite your own, I am not changing my mind… What you say would

probably be true for one of the White Fathers. But it is not so for me, vowed to the hidden life of JESUS at Nazareth, to his obscurity and silence."

We see some slight difference between this letter and the previous one, written January 15th. He did not make generalizations anymore. In the first he wrote, "These are not our ways, these are not our weapons." It was for everyone. In the second letter he refuted the arguments by simply highlighting that his situation was different: "What you say would probably be true for one of the White Fathers. But it is not so for me." So he saw it as a characteristic of his charism. We also notice that he is as self-assured as the bishop. There was not the least hesitation in what he thought was essential. He no longer generalized, but simply pointed to the differences. He knew what he needed to do. By so energetically resisting the advice of the authorities in this matter, he showed that he was aware of his particular place in the mission of the Church.

Is this not the uniqueness of his personal vocation? What did he hide under the label of monk? He was not a missionary like the others. His means of working for the honor of God were not the same. What was valid for others was not so for him because he was called to a hidden and obscure life, like Jesus at Nazareth. His response to that call was why he had closed himself up in a monastery and tried to live in Nazareth. Now, he still wanted to respond to that call, even though the activities that resembled missionaries', in the elaboration of his scientific work, and in the many relationships that developed with neighbors and friends. What better way to only seek to glorify God than by refusing to satisfy anything that would lead to personal glory. Even for the honor of the Church. We can say that he exaggerated, but he was always something of an extremist, whether in one direction or the other. It was part of his temperament not to be satisfied with the middle ground. He had to aim for that which was the most perfect. He could not do less than what he had done as a young man for his own pleasure and glory. So, he could not let himself be duped by the pride of authorship that he had enjoyed in his youth, a pride that his friend, Professor Gautier, considered as "the most venomous of all."

If he accepted to complete this work as perfectly as possible, it was because he was assured that it would be published under another's name. As remarkable as his work was, it could not give meaning to his life. He did not refuse to do the work. He only refused to be noticed in any way, even if it would bring honor to the Church. In his eyes, using his name was not the means for honoring God. He tapped into something that is central to the Gospel message: "May your left hand not know what your right hand is doing." This was at the heart of his personal vocation. He fulfilled his mission in the church by being faithful to that call. He brought to the Church something new, a message contained in what he called "the hidden life of Jesus at Nazareth." The Church is like a city built on a hill. It can only be seen. But the temptation of doing things to draw the attention of others, of becoming a spectacle, remains quite real.[199]

There is that aspect of mystery, secrecy, non-visibility and rejection of the spectacular in Jesus' life that cannot be ignored. Throughout his entire life, even until his death, he remained Jesus of Nazareth. Brother Charles brought out that aspect of Jesus' life, insisting on the obscurity, the *incognito* of the Word made flesh, who for thirty years seemed in the eyes of those around him to be just like everyone else. The hidden element in his life was his unique relationship with the Father, his divinity, in other

---

[199] *Cf.*, Mt. 6:1-5.

words, his essence. Despite the appearances, Charles de Foucauld remained faithful to his initial intuition until his death, no matter where he lived, what he did, his proximity or distance from others.

Wouldn't it be like putting the lamp that had been entrusted to him under a basket if he went along with the opinions of others, even these people who had a certain authority? He did not have the right to put his light, his particular mission, his vocation, under a basket. This thinking helped him to resist the pressures to give in. He did not spend a lot of time thinking about the implications of his categorical refusal. He simply acted from deep within himself, guided by his instincts, by an inner urge that flowed from source that could not be contained.

One could object that, later on and in a different situation, he did not refuse to refer to himself as a missionary. But this cannot be understood without taking into account all that we have just said. Did he come up with a new label in calling himself a "monk-missionary?"

We find it in a letter addressed to Fr. Antonin Juillet[200] on May 13, 1911. This text has often been cited and it differs considerably from the Rule written in 1899. He wrote it after returning from his second trip to France. While in France he had tried to launch an organization that would be grafted onto a religious order, "a sort of third order," he called it. But that religious order was inexistent and the founder, who by this time had begun signing his name 'br. Ch. De Foucauld' instead of br.

---

[200] We also find it in a letter that we have already referred to, written to his brother-in-law on March 28, 1908 concerning cloister and visits: "I remain a monk, a monk in mission territory, monk-missionary, but not a missionary."

Charles of Jesus, was beginning to realize that it only existed in the writings born from his dreams and his creative imagination.

The importance given to this text is legitimated by the fact that it was written to be read by others besides Fr. Antonin who was a Trappist monk of Our Lady of the Snows. He was one of a number of monks who desired to live a life somewhat more apostolic than life at the Trappist monastery. Charles de Foucauld's letter was written to attract companions. He tried to show them that the life in Tamanrasset was exactly what they were looking for. He was not describing what he was living at Tamanrasset but what could be lived, ideally, if they were two or three together.

In 1905, he wrote to invite Fr. Veyras, a secular priest from Nîmes.

He put noconditions on it:

*"I am not looking for a swarm of souls to enter into a rigid life-style or to lead a life where everything is regimented... No. What I am looking for at the moment is a good-hearted soul, who would agree to share my life, in poverty and obscurity, without any fixed rule of life, following his inclinations as I follow mine."*201

Now, writing to monks, and indirectly to secular priests, he proposed a monastic life. But as they wished to be missionaries, they would be monk-missionaries. What does that mean? Concretely, instead of manual work they would give themselves to apostolic work part-time, or even full-time if they wanted to. What became the most important was to do all one could for the conversion of the infidels. It

---

[201] Letter to Fr. Veyras, December 3, 1905.

was close to an idea that he had thought about in October 1898 of little groups (three or four or even one or two which would allow them to spread out and be more effective). Monastic life would take a back seat. But in 1899 he opted for the idea of monasteries with larger numbers that would allow for perpetual adoration of the Blessed Sacrament. To attract candidates, he was proposing a rule that was different from the Trappist model, something more flexible and less fastidious than their customs and practices. It would be a simple family life where everything would be done "at the proper hour and in strict obedience." It was a Rule that was even more detailed than that of the Trappist life. He was unable to free himself from a perfectionist temperament. He did not even struggle against it, as he was not aware of it. From day to day he adjusted to the events and the people around him with the freedom of the Spirit. But as soon as he tried to put his ideas on paper, he fell back into perfectionism. When he wrote to others, he sounded like a teacher. Nothing could be left to chance or doubt.

Let us also note that he wanted "only priests, excellent priests of mature age." This limitation corresponded to his immediate needs. His restrictions to "exceptionally virtuous subjects" if they were not priests, or "exemplary" people if they were, did little to encourage candidates. Who could imagine themselves as he described the profile?

It would be wrong to think that this letter accurately described the life of Charles de Foucauld at Tamanrasset. One has to take into consideration a literary style. It suffices to compare this letter with what he wrote about his schedule that same year. The monastic rhythm of 3 x 8 that he outlined to future members did not correspond at all with what he was living, and where the work, which was not manual, occupied ten hours and forty-five minutes of his day. We also know that he no longer shared his time among his "four establishments," as one might think from his writings. Even if he passed by Beni Abbès on his way back from France, he only spent three days there and never returned. We only find the expression "monk-missionary" in one other letter dated at the same time to Father Crozier.

Can we really find the last stage of Charles de Foucauld's thinking about his ideal in an isolated letter that was aimed at a very particular audience? Father Peyriguère thought so and used this text as a correction to what we call the Rule of 1899. Father Gorrée was the first to publish it, presenting himself as the first member of the "monk-missionaries of Father de Foucauld,"[202] after leaving the little brothers of Jesus in 1934 and then distancing himself from Father Peyriguère the following year. He thought that the notion of "monk-missionary" expressed very well the "double function that he (Charles de Foucauld) wished to confide to them." Would Charles de Foucauld have waited until 1911 to conceive of a life as a man of prayer and as an apostle "entering into direct contact with the indigenous people through the ministry of charity." [203]On the other hand, we can wonder if the formulation of his thinking would have stopped at that date when, until his death, he never ceased formulating and reformulating the texts that he considered the basis for his foundation.

We can also ask another question. Would he have accepted to sign his linguistic work had he lived longer? A few days before his death he wrote about it again. He had just finished copying the *Poésies touarègues* for the

---

[202] Georges Gorrée, *Sur les traces de Charles de Foucauld*, La plus grand France, Paris, Lyon, 1936, pp.321-328.

[203] *Op. cit.* p.119.

printer. He dated the introduction, written last and therefore in 1916, as if written in 1906, so that people would think Motylinski, who died in 1907, had done it. Is this proof that his decision to remain anonymous had not changed? This project had consumed all of his time and he did it with perfection. He did not want this monumental work make people forget that the only true work of his life remained hidden from their eyes. He summarized his life's work in notes written June 18th and 19th 1916: "Love our neighbor, that is all people, as ourselves." He also wrote, "The only thing we have to do here below, our only occupation the glory of God the salvation of souls."[204]

---

[204] Charles de Foucauld, *Voyageur dans la nuit*, Paris, Nouvelle Cité, 1979, pp.207-208.

THE MORE WE EMBRACE THE CROSS THE MORE WE BECOME ONE WITH JESUS

BR. CHARLES OF JESUS

The attractiveness of an exceptional personality

It is interesting to look at this new type of monk through the eyes of one of his contemporaries who was both clear-sighted and humorous.

Professor Gautier (1864-1940), who referred to himself as an infidel, was one of those who seemed to have best understood Charles de Foucauld's personality. The professor taught at the University of Algiers, was a geographer who made numerous expeditions through the Sahara and published ten books about North Africa. He had met Charles de Foucauld in Beni Abbès but really got to know him when they traveled together from June 8 to September 4, 1905. He wrote, "I ate with him twice a day for two months; almost all of my recollections come from those encounters." He would have been among those who would help the marabout build his house in Tamanrasset. Charles de Foucauld described him as, "a good heart and charming spirit whom I really like."[205]

He are a few extracts from a book[206] that Gautier wrote in 1920:

---

[205] Letter to Louis Massignon, May 5, 1915, Jean François Six, *L'aventure de l'amour de Dieu*, Paris, Seuil, 1993, p. 184.

[206] E.-F. Gautier, *L'Algérie et la métropole*, Paris, Payot, 1920.

> "One recognizes an officer who is out of uniform. But Charles de Foucauld had lost every trace of the former soldier; it was completely gone. He was a monk from head to foot, all humility and self-effacement."

And further on:

> "There was a time when the author of this book (Reconnaissance au Maroc) did not even want to remember that he had written it. I met Fr. de Foucauld in Beni Abbès in 1903. It had the discomfort of a first meeting and the ceremonial overtones of being presented to one another. What else could I have spoken about but his book that I had read and consulted, a book that is a tool for people in my profession? But instead of meeting the explorer, I met the monk who pushed the subject aside in such a way as to cut off any possibility of discussing it. He said something like, 'When one is completely taken by the idea of the absolute, that which is relative no longer counts.' He kept that optic for many years but not at the very end of his life, far from it."

He continued:

> *In 1906, Mr. Motylinski, professor of Arabic and Berber languages, undertook an expedition to the Hoggar I saw some of his notes and they seemed totally useless to me. But Fr. de Foucauld didn't think so. He undertook to publish the results of Motylinski's trip. In fact, the dean of the University of Algiers officially oversaw Motylinski's posthumous publication in every detail. He also wrote a preface in which he thanked this one and that, as is the custom. He thanked Mr. X…and Mr. Y… Mr. So and so who… And Mr. Whatever his name was… The list is long. And then there was a mysterious sentence, 'I also thank Misters X…, Y…, Z…, among those who I am permitted to name.'[3] This implies that there was someone that he was not permitted to name. Everyone who has lived in the Sahara knows that this person was Fr. de Foucauld[4] and they also know that he was the real author of the publications that appeared posthumously under the name of Motylinski. It was a little deception that the deceased could not protest and of which his*

friends and colleagues were complicit since it was the condition sine qua non imposed by Fr. de Foucauld."

He went on to list the books published by Motylinski and added the clarification, even though he grossly underestimated the numbers, that "it deals with a Berber dialect spoken by a few hundred individuals." He then added:

"There was a man who lived in the Hoggar for ten years, who made it his nearly exclusive occupation to listen to this language, to note the vocabulary and its various forms, and to write down the folklore stories that were told to him. It can only be a significant work. Legally it is all the work of Motylinski. It's quite curious though. It's a huge work that supposes that the author, the real author, burned with that sacred fire without which nothing is accomplished, that sacred fire of the intellectual layman, the passion for understanding. What were these feelings doing in a monk? It is true that when one got close to this monk one saw that he was very refined, cultured and curious. One could very well see that the intellectual in him was not dead, so it was natural that it finally came out. The appearance of these old instincts certainly frightened the Christian. Fear of the snares of the Evil one, if you wish; fear of that pride that can come with authorship is notoriously one of the most venomous. He surely also felt the triviality; the nothingness of the things of this world was deeply embedded in him; He had a smile, and the satisfaction that a nice little conversation, as well as these mundane feelings, could take a religious turn. I imagine that he was deeply grateful to this deceased professor under whose name he could do his thinking without risk of sin, or at least grateful to God who had put him on his path at a particular time.

Will this pseudonym endure? It was well thought out and could remain untouchable.

It is certainly what de Foucauld wanted. And besides, it doesn't matter. Whether or not these books have his name on them, or whether they continue to appear under the name of Motylinski, they are his and they make a beautiful sequel to the work he did in his youth. It is very solid work. It will have the kind of immortality conferred by technical bibliographies. It will not be possible to look at North Africa scientifically without reading de Foucauld. That is what will be said, or what will be written on his tomb, and to which the lay world is most sensitive. He certainly gave no importance to his published work. And I must admit that, despite my professional bent, I was much less impressed by the explorer and philologist, than by the monk.

I have a great deal of respect for explorers and philologists. I have met a great many. Had he only been that, one would not have felt the attraction of an exceptional personality when in his presence. His deepest instincts were that of a monk, or rather, a hermit. He was born that way. It just took him a little time to find his way. The deepest instincts of the monk are already visible in the explorer. De Foucauld traveled, unknown, throughout Morocco disguised as a Jew, and we know the abjection endured by the Moroccan Jews who were confined to ghettos. De Foucauld placed himself under the protection of public scorn. It was ingenious and produced remarkable results.

This disguise never tempted anyone else. De Foucauld was the only one who ever adopted it in Morocco and maybe throughout the Muslim world. In order to have chosen it he already had to have, from the time he emerged from adolescence, a taste for humility, some inner feelings that foreshadowed the monk: a resignation to live in filth, and ability to live in solitude, hidden behind a mask. He spent long months living as a Jew or Muslim, in intimate contact with these Oriental religions which involve the whole person, which remained very potent in their ability to infect others. De Foucauld came out of this experience thoroughly filled with Islamic sentiments. They say that he had gone so far as to consider converting to Islam for a time. This would not have been an isolated case. When one lives in the Muslim world one is quite aware of the attraction of Islam. In our fearful and hyper-civilized lives, when we glance at the infinite tranquility of Islam, I imagine that we all feel a bit of nostalgia.

These feelings nearly brought the young explorer to adopt the turban. At least that is what I have been told, and I believe it. They mention the name of the priest who kept de Foucauld in the Christian fold. He was not unknown, even if I should forgot now. Let us recall Littre, whose religious funeral was considered a scandal. The body of this free thinker was carried into the church with Father Huvelin's approval. This priest had graduated from the public school system in 1858, something of a history buff. He intervened in the case of Littré, not as a confessor in the strict sense of the word, but as an old and personal friend for whom the idea that Littré was damned was both intolerable and as well as absurd. It was this Father Huvelin who turned de Foucauld around, from Muslim catechumen to monk 'in five seconds.' The friend who told me this story considered Father Huvelin an impressive person; he very well might have had a strong personality. From his hermitage, Fr. de Foucauld considered him a very dear friend. I went to visit Father Huvelin on his behalf at the rue Nollet in Batignolles. I do not confirm the precise hesitations of the catechumen between these two religions from either one. But the fact that there were hesitations was confirmed from a reliable source and is quite probable. Seeing him, it was not all that clear that he was a monk rather than a marabout. His cotton robe could have passed for a gandoura; he wore something like a fez on his head. Even the indigenous people were mistaken at times. They say that Mouça-Ag-Amastane, the chief of the Tuareg in the Hoggar ,told him, 'How is that, marabout? Are you a Christian? But your austerities will serve for nothing in the other world!' De Foucauld never tried to clear up the question. In the fifteen years that he spent in the Sahara he never made one conversion.

After all, we, his infidel companions, also experienced Fr. de Foucauld's discretion. Throughout the long weeks of traveling with our little military detachment, Fr. de Foucauld surely said Mass every day, alone with no other witness than Paul Throughout all those weeks of eating together, the conversation never became churchy nor did he ever make the least effort to convert us. That is all very much in keeping with the personality of a hermit.

One doesn't retreat to the desert to preach."

Gautier summarized Charles de Foucauld's life including details that he could only have gleaned from personal conversations in private. He did not fail to point out the irregularity of this new type of monk from the point of view of his status in the church.

> *"For several months he remained a lay brother in this monastery (Akbès), completely anonymous, never opening his mouth; he cut wood and carried water. 'It was delicious,' he said, remembering it many years later. It is not a question of whether we are scandalized or amused by this. What strikes me is that, behind this lay brother who cut wood, we find the explorer who disguised himself as a Jew and the hermit of the Sahara. It was de Foucauld's deepest instincts, which he tried to satisfy throughout his whole life."*
>
> *"He called himself a monk and he wore the costume, but it was a bit of a usurpation. He was simply a priest: he was ordained by the Bishop of Viviers quite late in life; He never had any normal ecclesial status other than as a priest of the diocese of Viviers. It's absurd and has no relationship with the Sahara, but that is how it is. But he wasn't a Trappist. If it has to be said that he was a monk, it will have to be of an order that he would have founded, a kind of quasi-Trappist order of his own invention. This is no joke. He wore a red emblem that he invented on the front of his robe. It expressed his desire to belong to a new and distinct order. The only thing was that this order that he expanded to four monasteries,[207] only ever had one monk: Fr. de Foucauld. If we were*

---

[207] Gautier spoke about the places that kept souvenirs of Charles de Foucauld.

1) the house of Beni Abbès that he called the fraternity. 2) There is no trace of his ever having been at In Salah, the house that he bought in 1907 in Ksar el Arab has completely been covered with sand. 3) The little house that he built in Tamanrasset in 1905, enlarged in 1907 and 1910, which they called the *Frigate*, is the most moving of the places where Charles de Foucauld lived. No other place in the world is rivaled for the privilege of sheltering this man for as long as he lived there: eleven years. The *Bordj*, the fort that he built for the people of the village who were threatened by raiding parties and where he moved for the last five months of his life. It is now in the center of the town and is maintained as an historic monument. 4) The Asekrem has become the most famous of the places where he lived (even though he only spent five months there) because of its incredible site and magnificent view perched atop a volcanic plateau.

to imagine an interdiction of that order it would have been an inextricable juridical affair!"

"I remember the first conversation that I had the honor to have with him. We were marching at night. I was dozing off and on, sitting on my camel. Fr. de Foucauld walked nearby alongside of his camel, out of mortification I think. I was awakened by his voice, saying, "How beautiful!" That was it. We were crossing the old volcano of In-Ziza under a brilliant moon and it appeared absurdly jagged."

It is interesting to note, in passing, his comment of admiration. It shows that he had a sense of the beauty of nature because apart from the Asekrem and, exceptionally atBeni Abbès, he never spoke much about it. Gautier arrived at a stunning conclusion about the life of Charles de Foucauld, following upon these experiences:

"He was very happy living this way. It was no small thing and was clear to all. He had pushed himself to his limit; he was completely fulfilled; he was an absurdly complete human being. Maybe that was the secret of his happiness. His eyes shone with calm and silent joy."

"I imagine that they will build a tomb for him in the local style—a Koubba. The tomb will perpetuate what that man did. The miracles will begin. Do they know what will crystallize around that Koubba? The saints are particularly dangerous after their death. There is no dynamometer to measure the moral impact of a person. In his lifetime there was not only respect for de Foucauld. It sometimes happened that they would say, 'He's crazy.' A young and brilliant colonel said it once. And yet this young colonel had run the same risks, went to the same trouble, made gestures, assumed attitudes, and made a whole slew of intense efforts very comparable to de Foucauld. The only difference was that he had a different goal, one easier to explain in a single sentence. He absolutely insisted on wearing a white feather in his hat that he found to be quite reasonable. And yet he was convinced that de Foucauld was not. Maybe he was correct. It is possible, after all. The only thing is that since August 2, 1914,

we have experienced things that have lessened our faith in pure rationalism. And we have learned how heavily blind abnegation and absurd self-sacrifice can weigh upon the life of people. We have learned to salute them as we pass by. Even when we don't understand very well."

In conclusion and to respond to the questions of Gautier we can quote Charles de Foucauld himself. The fire that burns within the heart of the monk is not of this world. It came into being the day that his eyes opened upon a new light, "other than the light of the senses." He wrote about it from Nazareth on November 9, 1897 at a period when his life seemed even crazier:

"The one who lives by faith has the soul full of new thoughts, new tastes, new judgments; new horizons open before him, and he necessarily begins a new life, opposed to the ways of the world, which may seem like folly the bright path upon which he walks is not visible to others. To others he seems to be walking in an abyss, like someone who has lost their mind."[208]

Something else that he wrote might help to explain how, at a particular stage of inner purification, someone who wished to be a "monk" could allow himself to be guided by his deepest instincts. On the paper where he had written his daily schedule after 1911 were the words, "To bring fire to the earth." On the backside of the article he wrote, "Each thing lives according to the quality of its being" and then the following comment from St. John of the Cross:

---

[208] Charles de Foucauld, *La dernière place*, Paris, Nouvelle Cité, 1974, p. 120.

"The person who has managed to transform his animal nature into a spiritual nature, with every affection, tendency, and action inspired by the same Spirit, is carried without resistance towards God. For that person, each thing takes on a special quality of sweetness, of strength, of purity, of chastity, of joy and love."

He can follow his "instincts" and also follow that "inner movement" as Father Huvelin wrote to him[209], adding, "Go were the Spirit pushes you." We understand that this was the fire that burned within his heart, the thing that pushed him, becoming irresistible, because of which he wrote so many pages[210], and which imposed itself upon him with such invincible power. It does not keep him from discerning that which is simply temptation. Bishop Guérin recognized that it was the work of the Spirit, writing of him in 1904, "Our dear Brother Charles, like all those who allow themselves to be led by the Spirit of God, has a marvelous appreciation of circumstances."[211] He is like a bullet that has been shot and which nothing and no one can stop. These are all the words of Father Huvelin and, with him, we must recognize that the faith of his disciple transformed religion into an act of love. Only such a passionate love can account for all of these moments of his life and bring together his deepest instincts.

---

[209] *LAH*, September 2, 1902 and July 5, 1903.

[210] *Cf.* letter of Father Huvelin from December 28, 1904: "I can not tell you how much your letter seems written under the inspiration of the Holy Spirit."

[211] Letter to Fr. Voillard, Charles de Foucauld, *Correspondances sahariennes*, Paris, Cerf, 1998, p. 1015.

A MESSAGE FOR EVERYONE

There have been multiple interpretations of the life and writings of Charles de Foucauld. Often his message has been perceived as a call to silence, a spirituality of the desert or a form of hermit life. Others have seen him as the convert who went from a life of pleasure to a life of heroic asceticism. He has even been used to defend traditional values and nationalistic ideologies or to maintain nostalgia for an idealized past. Others have taken the opposite stance: they see in him someone who questioned institutions and who lived on the fringes, as an innovator who was ahead of his time, as something of a genius who understood it all before anyone else, or as someone who was very avant-garde concerning the Church. His participation in the colonial process has been seen by some with admiration and, by others, with reproach. He has been used as a model for mission based on an idea of "burying" oneself silently among a people, or by others, as having taken the side for an urgent need for preaching. Surely, each of these contradictory positions can be backed up by things found in his writings. Rare are those who have known how to situate him within the context of his own time without recuperating or interpreting his message in function of more recent historical situations.

There is still much to discover about the details of Charles de Foucauld's life through his letters. It is important to do so to place him squarely in the concrete reality of his relationships with the men and women with whom he wanted to become close. The same can be said for his relationship with God. Most of the time people read his life, content with clichés or images that speak about poverty, friendship, apostolate or contemplation, without any analysis of his actions and the concrete circumstances of his life among the Tuareg people.

What stays with us about this man who wanted to imitate Jesus of Nazareth until the end of his life? If there is one word that can express his message that word is Nazareth with all that implies historical reality, theology and mystical ideals. It is a call to live with a passionate love for Jesus in the most ordinary situations that people live, as in the extraordinary ones, following the example of Jesus. Jesus did not escape the constraints imposed by relationships with others. He became a servant to live out his uniquely intimate relationship with his Father, as part of a human family, with a job, in a village or on the roads of Palestine. Charles de Foucauld also lived out the realism of the Incarnation in an exceptional manner through very personal relationships with the men and women around him. After believing that he was called to live at a distance from others, in the silence of a monastery and later in the solitude of a hermitage, he learned that he was called to live in an ever-closer relationship with others.

Was it not his mission to show that "this spirituality of Nazareth" could be lived in any situation: as a celibate or married person, in religious life or family life, as a priest or a layperson, alone or in the community? It expresses itself in a language of presence to God and others, sharing life, friendship, and solidarity. It is neither a spirituality of the desert nor that of a hermit. It is a spirituality of relationship, relationship with both the divine and the human. It is a relationship of love with God who became one with us in Jesus – and whose presence is sought specially in the Eucharistic presence – and a relationship of love with men and women whose lives we are called to share. It is a call to live with them following the example of the "servant, "to love as Jesus loved, without exclusion, and in solidarity with the poor. It is an imitation of the life of Jesus of Nazareth, Jesus at Nazareth living a unique relationship with his Father through the most ordinary human relationships.

There are two texts from Jacques Maritain which explain something about this new form of contemplative life which has inspired so many who live an ordinary life in the midst of this world's affairs. The first text was written in 1928:

> *"In all truthfulness, I do not think it is possible to live a completely contemplative life in the world. I do think it is possible to live, in the world, a life whose essence is contemplative. It would not even have to occupy itself with direct forms of apostolate, like the Dominicans or Carmelites. However, it can only justify itself by a desire to serve others and, in one way or another, to give itself over to others. For their sake, it courageously puts up with all of the troubles, sorrows and useless comings and goings that are inseparable from the business of daily life. The only aim of such a life is, through its very closeness with others, to give witness to the contemplation of God and to the love of God expressed in the Eucharist. If you must remain a part of the world, I believe that it must be with the desire to allow yourself to be devoured by others, preserving only that solitude that is necessary so that God make of you something which is usefully devourable. What else is there? That impression, that idea, that hope, that the Holy Spirit prepares something in the world: a work of love and of contemplation that calls for people who are entirely given over and immolated in the very midst of the world."*

The second text is from notes for a class that Maritain gave in 1950 on the Gospel of John 1:4,7-8:

> *"Love of neighbor is the same love as love for God. Consequently, love for others unites us to God and makes us more like God. When we try to love others as Jesus loved them, looking at them with Jesus' eyes, that love becomes, better than any other way, a path for uniting ourselves with God. It is both obscure and experiential, in all the fullness, without limit, of that love. It supposes an evangelical approach to others, an attitude of gratuitousness that expects nothing in return. We listen to them, are ready to be of service, become attentive to all that they are, to their infinite value as people loved by God. That is what a contemplative attitude toward others is. It calls for a dispossession of the self, a true detachment, in which we no longer belong to ourselves. Love for others is as demanding and unmerciful as is the love of God. It demands that we live with others, that we exist with them. It is truly contemplation but of a particular kind. It is contemplation on the roads by which Jesus leads us, following him, going with him towards the little ones, in order to make us discover with them the loving face of God."*

Who can pretend to follow in the footsteps of Charles de Foucauld who lived at a different time and in a different place? Many will be content to simply admire him and love him as did Father Huvelin. Others, who do not take into account the distance and difference of the situations, will continue to judge and even to condemn him. Now that he has been named "venerable" many will believe that he is a model to imitate. Will the preceding pages make them change their minds?

It remains true that we can recognize the Power that pushed him and led him to the desert, not to run away from the world but to become close to those whom the desert isolated from the world. It was the road that he had to walk without knowing where it would lead. By spending some time looking at some of the turns upon which his journey took him, we have followed him on the path that led him all the way to Tamanrasset despite the temptations and hesitations.

May reading his story help us to follow our own path, different from his, by allowing ourselves to be lead by that Power which urges each one on, until we find that place of fulfillment in the deserts of our world.

About the Letter Written to Henri Duveyrier

On February 21, 1892 Charles de Foucauld wrote his last letter to Henri Duveyrier. It was not kept in the Archives of the Geographical Society as those who gathered that material considered it to be too intimate. It was an answer to a letter that Duveyrier, unbeliever that he was, had written to Br. Marie Albéric expressing his total incomprehension over the vows that he has just professed.

It is interesting in several ways. First of all, it exposes this scholar who was his friend, to the Credo of the Catholic Church. He then responds to Duveyrier's comment, "I receive your friendly reproach that you don't know very much about my past life…,"by sharing his story.

This is the first time he shared about his conversion. During a retreat[212] in Nazareth in 1897 he wrote for himself, before God, the journey that led him to this point. We were already aware of that text.

---

[212] Charles de Foucauld, *La dernière place*, Paris, Nouvelle Cité, 1974, pp. 92-109.

There is a third retelling[213] that is dated August 14, 1901. This one is also in answer to a letter from a friend, Henry de Castries who, while remaining Catholic, had questions concerning Islam after having written a book about Islam several years earlier. So, we have three accounts of his conversion which complete one another very usefully.

Letter to Henri Duveyrier, Feb. 21, 1892

Dear and excellent friend,

Since you write to me as a brother, allow me to omit the "sir" from our correspondence so that the intimacy of heart expresses itself exteriorly, as well… How I thank you, how touched I am by your excellent letter of December 28! You do not approve of, you question, the religious vows and you express to me your concern with the most tender affection: this affection is very sweet, it moves me and fills me with thanksgiving, the disapproval does not surprise me: six years ago I was about as far away from the Catholic religion as is possible, I had no type of faith at all, if I had had a friend would wanted to become a Trappist I could not have better expressed my attachment to him than by writing as you have done to me… so I am in no way shocked in any ay by your objections! I only see in it your affection and my only feeling is that of gratitude and the emotion to see how good you are!… However, I cannot tell you that your letter has in any way modified my resolution: This life to which I am so attached, I have desired for the last 4 years, been resolved to embrace for the last 3 years, and have been living for the last two years: Has there ever been a decision that has been thought about longer or more seriously put to the test? Why did I choose a way which is so painful, so cruel, for me and for those who love me? Far from me to have done so out of self-centered desire to live in peace! I speak to you about that peace because, without seeking it, I found it. But it was far from being my goal. The thing that made me leave behind everything that is dear to me, that is, this very small number of close relatives and friends, who, just to see them and spend time with them was sweetness itself and an infinite goodness, and who remain more and more present and dear to my heart, - as you know, I umber you

---

[213] Charles de Foucauld, *Lettres à Henry de Castries*, Paris, Grasset, 1938. Letter from August 14, 1901, pp.92-101.

among these -, it doesn't seem possible to me that you completely understand that reason being as you are far from the catholic faith, I would not have understood that reason six years ago, however I am going to tell you, your brotherly affection calls for such a brotherly outpouring and you will understand the intimate nature of it. We Catholics believe in a God who is one and who is spirit, and whose unity encompasses three persons (an incomprehensible mystery; we believe that one of these three persons, without ceasing to be eternally united with the two other persons, took on a human body and soul in time, formed by God without human intervention, that he lived upon this earth, working, teaching the truth and the mysteries of God, proving his words through miracles, giving rules and the example of virtue. This God, perfectly united with man, is Jesus Christ, - That I owe him live and obedience is evident. His will for man is that he work to become perfect and to make others perfect: these are inner virtues and, as you said, we can even practice them upon a throne as St. Louis witnessed. But the love of our Lord Jesus Christ calls those who are able, upon whom family or societal situation does not impose a serious duty, to lead a life that resembles as much as possible that life that God led upon the earth – there is no love that does not desire to imitate… and, as you know this imitation becomes a need when the one whom we love is poor, miserable, suffering or looked down upon… who would dare say that they love when they consent to live joyfully and comfortably while the one they love suffers in soul and body?-yet the life of Jesus Christ in this world was that of a poor workman, a lowly, poor and toilsome life; The last three years of his life played themselves out in an apostolate that earned him mostly insults, thanklessness and persecution; finally he was put to death and left this life in unheard of tourment… - I too, along with many others, unworthy that I am, wanted to love God with all my heart and to imitate him to the feeble extent that my laziness allows, to please God more and more! Jesus was obedient upon his earth, and I entered a religious order in order to be obedient as he was: I chose to live poor, lowly, working to share the poverty, abjection and labor of Jesus. Since the life of Jesus was all sacrifice and pain, I wanted to sacrifice with him and for him all that made my life happy, the presence of those whom I loved. You see, it is the sacrifice that I went so far to find, not out of any impulse of its own but because of a common vocation shared by the best of souls…- That is the story of my vocation; as you wished, I have not defended myself from your feelings and I have opened my heart to you… I repeat once more that it seems to mea difficult thing that you understand, more difficult than you admit what I have shared with you. Six years ago, I would have treated all of that as nothing but illusions, dreams, and I would have deemed the one who had written the preceding page, what is te word, as a little crazy if not very crazy… How is it that I have changed so much? You reproach me in a friendly way, that you don't know much about my past life: it is simple and, in a few words, here it is. At the age of 5 and a half, in 1864, I lost both my father and my mother. I was then raised by my maternal grandfather and my grandmother; my mother was an only daughter; I have a sister who was raised with me by these excellent grandparents. My grandfather, Mr. De Morlet, was a retired military officer and had retired in Alsace where we stayed until the war: after 1870 we came to live in Nancy; I finished my studies there and was accepted at St. Cyr. While I was there I had the tremendous sadness of losing my grandfather whose quick mind I admired so much, his infinite tenderness enveloped my childhood and youth with such an atmosphere of love that I am still moved to just to remember the warmth; it was a great source of sadness to me and after 14 years (Feb. 3, 1878) it is still raw; several years earlier my dear grandmother had become quite ill and had to go to a nursing home where she passed away quietly. When my grandfather died my sister went to live with my aunt, Mrs.

Moitessier, my father's sister who lives in Paris; from that time, their home became our home, and they were infinitely good to us. You see, when I look back I see that I only received goodness and I can only be grateful. I did not take advantage of the goodness of family life in my aunt's home: from St. Cyr I went to Saumur, then attached to a regiment of Hussards and then with the Chasseurs of Africa: in one year I went from the garrisons of Bône, Sétif and Mascara and an expedition South of Oran: in 1881-82 I spent seven or eight months living in a tent in the Sahara south of Oran. It gave me a real taste for the traveling that had always attracted me. I handed in my resignation in 1882 in order to give free reign to my desire for adventure. I spent a year and a half in Algiers preparing myself for a trip through Morocco, I then made the trip, and then I spent another half year in Algeria writing up the report about it. At the beginning of 1886 I returned to Paris to publish the report about my trip with the thought of preparing for another trip. I had been raised Christian but by the age of 15 or 16 I had lost all faith, my avid reading had accomplished that; I didn't adhere to any particular philosophical doctrine as I didn't find any of them to be based solidly enough, I remained in complete doubt, especially distant from the catholic faith as I found several of its dogmas deeply shocking to all reason… at the same age I began to squander my life and it remained so for a long time, although it never interfered with my lively penchant for study; my behavior with the regiment was very unruly, I was far from my family, I hardly even saw my family between 1878 and 1886 and the little that they knew about my life, especially during the early part of this period, could only bring them pain... I returned to Paris in 1886 in this state of mind. My sister was no longer in Paris, having married and moved to Bourgogne. But I was welcomed at my aunt's home as if I had never left or caused so much worry to those who loved me. Within these walls that became my home, although I was actually living in another house, I found people who modeled every virtue, combined with great intelligence and deep religious conviction. I became infatuated by such virtue and chose my reading material in function of it, reading the ancient moralists, yet was far from any religion, it was only ancient virtue that attracted me... but I found less nourishment and insight than I expected from these ancient philosophers... And then, quite by accident, I came across a few pages of Bossuet and I found in them so much more depth than I had in any of the ancients... I continued to read this book and, little by little, I began to realize that the faith of such a keen mind – the same faith that I saw each day in the bright minds of my own family – was perhaps not as incompatible with common sense as I had thought. It was the end of 1886. I felt an overwhelming desire for silence and recollection. At the core of my being, I wondered if truth were really known to men... I made that strange prayer to a God in whom I did not even yet believe, to reveal himself to me if he existed... It seemed to me that, in the state of doubt and confusion in which I found myself, the wisest course of action for me would be to study the catholic faith of which I knew so little. I went to see a learned priest, Fr. Huvelin, whom I had met at my aunt's house. He was kind enough to answer all my questions and patient enough to receive me as often as I wished. I became convinced of the truth of the Catholic faith; since then, Fr. Huvelin became for me like a real father and I have led a Christian life.

Several months after this turnabout I thought about entering a religious order but Fr. Huvelin, as well as my family, encouraged me to marry... I let some time pass... it brought me here and I am grateful to God... Like so many others I came here with a desire for sacrifice, and, in the midst of very real sacrifice, I found a peace of soul (not just of mind) that I had not sought. Now, all of my relatives have sided with my being here because they believe that it is God's calling for me: stand with them, dear friend to whom I write such a brotherly letter – for my part, what has helped me in the face of such cruel sacrifice is the conviction that the good work which is part and parcel of this sacrifice will gain an increase of divines graces for all those whom I love and that, because of this, they will receive far more through my absence than they would receive through a presence in their loving affection.

There, I have laid it all out before you. See in this letter where, alas, I have not had the time to ask about you, to express my regret that you are worn out by rheumatism, even though I have only spoken about myself, see in this letter the best sign of my attachment to you, of my gratefulness for your affection, of my desire to pay it all back as a brother. I send my thanks also to Miss Rose for her remembrance; I am very touched, poor monk that I am and, as her brother in God will pray for her, may she pray a bit for me. – I am truly yours, you know it and you see it, and I do not hesitate in closing, as I am sure you will permit, to embrace you as a brother.

Br. Marie-Albéric

PRINCIPLE WEBSITES FOR THE USA AND CANADA

www.charlesdefoucauld.info/.................... USA website
www.companionsofjesusofnazareth.com/............ USA website
www.jesuscaritas.info/......................... United Kingdom
www.charlesdefoucauld.ca/home-english.html....... Canada
Further questions: blchdefoucauld@gmail.com

+LITTLE SISTERS OF JESUS

www.petitessoeursdejesus.net/en............. International website
www.littlesistersofjesus.org/...................... USA website
• Canada Petites Soeurs de Jesus –
1800 Rue Bercy MONTREAL, Que H2K 4K5
• USA – 400 N. Streeper St., Baltimore, MD 21224 |
lsj.can.usa@gmail.com
• Ireland – 18, Donard View, Bishopscourt,
DOWNPATRICK BT30 - co. Down |
littlesistersjesus@btinternet.com
• England – 148 Fellows Courts Weymouth Terrace,
London E2 8LW | lsj.hackney@virgin.net

+LAY FRATERNITIES

www.brothercharles.org/wordpress/................ USA
www.charlesdefoucauld.ca/home-english.html....... Canada
www.jesus.caritas.montreal@hotmail.com.......... USA and Canada
moira.ukcdf@gmail.com......................... United Kingdom

+LITTLE BROTHERS OF JESUS – USA AND CANADA

Bernard Audigier, Little Brothers of Jesus,
410 Ashdale #1, Toronto (Ont) M4L 272, Canada
bernardaudigier@gmail.com

+JESUS CARITAS FRATERNITY OF PRIESTS

www.iesuscaritas.org/en. International website
www.jesuscaritasusa.org/. . . . . USA website

+DEVOTIONAL ITEMS

Devotional items . . . .
https://www.etsy.com/shop/StCharlesdeFoucauld?ref=simple-shop-header-name&listing_id=1017482350

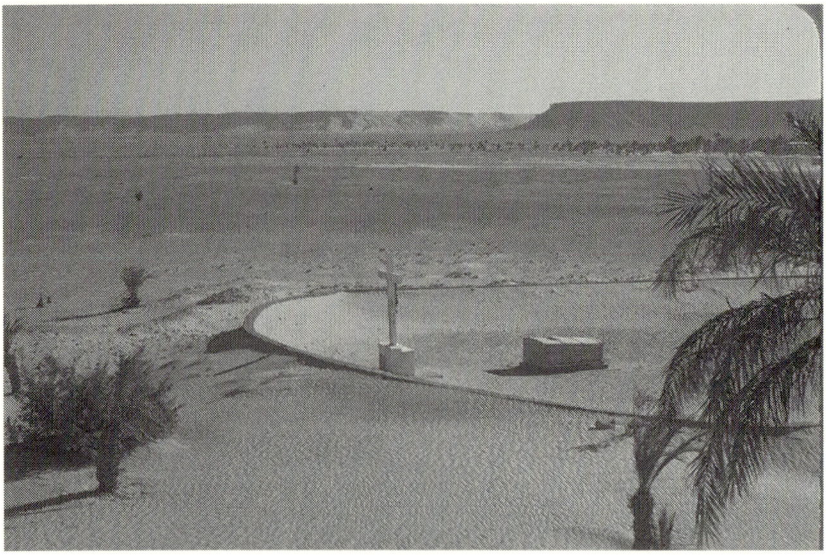

Made in United States
Orlando, FL
01 April 2023